High Seas to Home
Daily dispatches from a frigate at war

Allan Seabridge had a long career as a systems engineer in aerospace, retiring as Chief Flight Systems Engineer. He worked in engineering, project management and business development, which led to the production of a number of technical articles and co-authorship of five text books. He is producing new editions to two of these volumes, and as Editor of the Wiley Aerospace Series is encouraging authors to contribute to books on environmental and obsolescence issues in aviation. He is a Section Leader for two volumes of the Wiley Encyclopaedia of Aerospace Engineering and is involved in designing postgraduate courses for several universities and in delivering modules. He acts as academic supervisor to Masters and Doctorate students.

Allan lives in Lytham St Annes, Lancashire, and in the 1980s wrote a number of short children's stories, some of which were adapted by the BBC as scripts for Playschool, and by Thames Television for their programme Rainbow. They were also reproduced in albums and paperback books.

Shirley Morgan is a former daily newspaper journalist (for a short time following in Cliff Greenwood's footsteps as a sports reporter on the Blackpool Evening Gazette) but after a decade moved into the defence industry and for the past 12 years has worked as a freelance business journalist. She currently writes for clients across many industrial sectors, as well as for higher education, and recently co-authored a book with Allan Seabridge on air travel and health.

Married with two teenage boys and sharing the house with an ever-changing assortment of cats and giant house rabbits, she lives in Lytham St Annes, Lancashire.

David Chadwick is an award-winning journalist with a life-long interest in maritime history. He currently writes on economic and business issues for newspapers, magazines and online publications.

Formerly a political editor on a daily paper, he later worked as press officer for the Cabinet Office and as a public relations manager for a global accountancy firm. He is also a published author and has produced numerous novels and short stories. He enjoys sailing catamarans and lives in Bolton, Greater Manchester, with his wife, two teenage sons and two jack russell terriers.

HIGH SEAS TO HOME

DAILY DISPATCHES FROM A FRIGATE AT WAR

The previously unpublished letters of Royal Navy Coder Cliff Greenwood, newspaper journalist, written from 1943–45 from his training camps and from the frigate HMS *Byron*, which sailed on escort duties in the North Atlantic.

ALLAN SEABRIDGE, SHIRLEY MORGAN AND DAVID CHADWICK

First published in Great Britain in 2012 by The Derby Books Publishing Company Limited, 3 The Parker Centre, Derby, DE21 4SZ.

ISBN 978-1-78091-041-3

Printed and bound by Gomer.

CONTENTS

'The Battle of the Atlantic was the dominating factor all through the war. Never for one moment could we forget that everything happening elsewhere, on land, at sea, or in the air, depended ultimately on its outcome and, amid all other cares we viewed its changing fortunes day by day with hope or apprehension.'

Winston Churchill

INTRODUCTION

The conflict at sea between Allied merchant ships, their Royal Navy escorts and the German U-boats was christened the Battle of the Atlantic by Winston Churchill on 6 March 1941. It was a brutal and merciless fight for Britain's survival. Churchill said that the 'U-boat peril' was the only thing that ever really frightened him during World War Two, but 70 years on the men who sailed with the Atlantic convoys are among the forgotten heroes of the conflict. Figures underline the unrelenting danger – more than 2,500 ships were sunk by U-boat action during the Battle of the Atlantic. Britain's nadir came in 1942 when shipping losses were running at 650,000 tons per month – dangerously close to the 800,000 monthly target that the Germans believed would starve Britain to submission.

However, the U-boats did not have things all their own way. The U-boat arm deployed 863 operational vessels, of which 754 were lost; an appalling attrition rate of 87 per cent. The majority – 458 – were sunk in the Atlantic. When a U-boat went down, few survived. Some 39,000 men served in the *U-bootwaffe*, of whom 28,730 died in action.

But what was it really like?

The wartime career of Coder Cliff Greenwood started in 1940 when he joined the Lytham St Annes Local Defence Volunteers. Wartime had not brought many changes to the small town of Lytham St Annes. The biggest excitement was the night a German bomber mistook the River Ribble for the Mersey and dropped a bomb on an innocuous semi-detached in Church Road. The LDV (soon informally known as Look, Duck and Vanish) was re-invented as the Home Guard. In later years Cliff told stories of his time with them every bit as hilarious as any episode of *Dad's Army*, but the comedy ended in 1943 when he was called up at the age of 40. He chose to serve in the Royal Navy and was sent to Butlin's holiday camp in Skegness.

In the words of *The Standard*, 29 November 1939:

> In peacetime, summer holiday makers made merry behind the little lattice windows of a Viennese beer garden. Now the windows have been blacked out. The beer room is a camouflaged barrack room. In the gay little chalets bunks and hammocks are slung. Where Mademoiselle Azalea used to give consultations daily on the past, the present, and the future, dentists are looking after the teeth of the R N.

Stern petty officers, most of them pensioners, who have come back to the service, ride around HMS *Royal Arthur* on the yellow bicycles which only a few weeks ago were hired out to pretty holiday makers in slacks and shorts. Where once you sipped cocktails in the palm lounge, sailors with sensitive ears are learning Morse.

Cliff arrived at *Royal Arthur* after a long train journey from Preston and there he began the daily correspondence to his wife at home in Lytham St Annes that was to last for two years. The letters are a unique insight into life on a small warship protecting the Atlantic convoys, for in civilian life Clifford Garratt Greenwood was a seasoned journalist – 'Spectator' of the Blackpool *Evening Gazette*, who would go on to report on the legendary 'Matthews' Cup Final between Blackpool and Bolton Wanderers in 1953. His 20 years' experience as a newspaperman meant his letters were carefully crafted and detailed accounts, not the hurried notes dashed off by his younger shipmates.

Cliff's duties as a specialist Royal Navy coder meant he was involved in the encoding and decoding of encrypted signals transmitted in Morse Code by the wireless telegraphy signals team, a role that would have given him insights into the broader tactical picture, and which carried considerable responsibility. The letters show that Cliff certainly 'self censored' his correspondence, because in many cases events that HMS *Byron* was involved in are not directly mentioned; though Cliff might say that he 'had a busy night'.

To fill in the omitted details, this narrative contains first-hand accounts of these actions, recalled later in life by Cliff's shipmates onboard *Byron*. Events described by Cliff are also contextualised by articles on the broader picture, along with concise profiles of the escorts, U-boats, weapons and places mentioned. This additional material highlights the constant peril of a conflict in which the unpredictable element of the sea was an ever-present threat to both sides. When action was joined, no quarter was given or expected. In one account, we hear how 24 crewmen were killed, but only three bodies recovered, when an acoustic torpedo from U-1105 hit HMS *Redmill*, one of *Byron*'s escort group on 27 April 1945. Exactly one month earlier, *Redmill*, *Byron* and *Fitzroy* had sunk U-722. There had been no survivors from the U-boat's crew of 46.

As well as being a rare first-hand account of life on board a Royal Navy ship on escort duties in the North Atlantic, the letters represent a rich seam of social history. Cliff mentions the popular films of the time, the books he reads to pass the long hours, the places he visits on shore leave and even the itinerant 'pets' that join the ship. The letters also describe the poignant sunrise when U-boat after U-boat surrendered at a remote Scottish anchorage, and Cliff saw the face of his enemy for the first and last time after two years of bitter conflict.

Gentleman of the Press

Clifford Garratt Greenwood, living in Lancashire but with his roots over the border in Yorkshire, stood 6ft tall, earning him the wartime nickname of Lofty. He married Violet Hughes (Vi) in September 1925. No children were born to them, but in 1946 they adopted a baby girl, Susan Caroline.

Cliff was born in 1903 in Doncaster. He attended Doncaster Grammar School and shortly after the end of World War One, the family, including his older sister May, moved to Lytham St Annes. Cliff became a journalist by accident. He was on his way to an interview for a job in a bank when he saw a notice advertising a vacancy for a junior reporter on the local newspaper. By the end of the day he was a journalist and the bank he had intended to join had a lucky escape. He worked on the *Blackpool Gazette and Herald* and *Evening Gazette* at a time when Blackpool was the greatest holiday resort in Britain, if not the world. He met many of the great showbiz names, including Gracie Fields, Max Miller, Laurel and Hardy, Jack Warner (who later found fame as *Dixon of Dock Green*). All the glamour came to an end on 1 September 1939. In Cliff's own words:

> It was the day Germany marched into Poland. War for Britain was inescapable – and everybody knew it. That Friday night, a blackout was practised for the first time in Blackpool. I walked out of the darkness down the stone stairs I had so often trodden, to the Palace dressing rooms. In the room with the star on the door were two Americans. They could have booked their passages home the following day, when their Blackpool week ended, and escaped from a country soon to be at war.
>
> 'Going home?' they said, 'What do you take us for? We're staying with you. We'll be about somewhere or other, however long it lasts.'
>
> So said Bebe Daniels and Ben Lyon – and they have been with us, praise be, ever since.

After his years as a journalist, writing was as natural to Cliff as breathing, a need so deeply ingrained that it had to be satisfied under the most difficult circumstances. He shared his Navy experiences with Vi in the only way he could – in words.

Following his war service, Cliff returned to work on the Blackpool *Evening Gazette*. As sports editor he reported on Blackpool Football Club's most successful years, including three FA Cup Finals between 1948 and 1953. His war service had taken its toll on his health and he died in July 1965 aged 62. Obituaries in the *Gazette* called Cliff a 'Gentleman of the Press'. Jimmy Armfield, captain of Blackpool FC, wrote a tribute on behalf of the club, saying Cliff was a man everyone in the dressing room admired and respected. 'We can ill afford to lose people of his stature', he said, 'we will all miss him very much'.

After Vi died in 1969 their daughter Sue cleared the family home and in the attic she found a cardboard box. It was packed with letters, still in their original envelopes. They were dusty and it was difficult to make out the pencilled writing. Some were just a couple of pages, others thick wads of paper. It was clear that when Vi received each letter from Cliff she put it back in the envelope and stored it away.

Note on the editing of the letters

The selected letters are arranged chronologically. Though some have been reduced in length, we have tried to retain whatever is significant, either for Cliff personally or in terms of the events described. Writing every day inevitably meant that sometimes Cliff had 'nothing to report', and these letters have generally been omitted from this book. Our background research has shown that there are sometimes discrepancies between the letters and the actual actions described – this is probably only to be expected, Cliff was writing in an active theatre of war. Any obvious minor grammatical errors in the original text (there are very few) have been corrected silently, with 'dialect' words or phrases attributed to the writer's Yorkshire roots and Lancashire home left unchanged – exactly how Cliff would have wanted it.

ACKNOWLEDGEMENTS

The role of the coder called for a cramped and windowless cabin with close fitting earphones and lots of concentration on code books, message slips and the insistent bleeps of Morse Code in a small ship bouncing and rolling in high seas. There was not much opportunity to observe what was going on; in any event, the actions in poor weather or at night and in the vast ocean didn't provide much of a chance to see the whole picture. Luckily Cliff's skills with shorthand, typing and reporting got him onto the bridge where he was able to see some of the action first-hand and see the bridge officers in action. What he did see and hear, however, was likely to be classified and unlikely to find its way into the letters.

To fill in the blanks and to provide some background information, we needed some research, the help of people and organisations and access to their knowledge. First of all, acknowledgement must go to Cliff Greenwood who compiled the primary record while doing his job on board under difficult conditions, and also to Vi for keeping all the letters safe for many years to form a valuable primary source of information. To Sue Seabridge, Cliff's daughter, for painstakingly ordering, deciphering and transcribing all the letters into a suitable word processor format, and for providing access to her collection of mementoes and photographs.

As a result of her diligent research she met with Alan Hope (the radio mechanic), which enabled her to meet some crew members, including the captain, and to be included on the distribution list of correspondence and newsletters that Alan Hope generated. Many thanks are due to Alan and an old shipmate John Whithouse for talking to crew members and putting it all down in a booklet of recollections. They also formed the *Byron Association* and issued a series of newsletters to capture reminiscences, which has proved to be a valuable record of history and witty comment – worthy of a book in its own right. Alan Hope, long retired, still maintains a keen interest in history, and he has been extremely helpful. He has given his permission for his material to be included in this book. For many years he arranged an annual reunion of the ship's company at which he met many old friends, but sadly, he also notes the decline in numbers with each passing year.

Thanks are also due to museums and historical groups: Yvonne Oliver at the Imperial War Museum in London; George Malcolm and Alex Geary of the Royal Navy Submarine Museum in Gosport; the Museum of Lincolnshire Life; Jade Haywood at the Skegness Library; the Lancashire Records Office in Preston, Maggie at the *Lancashire Evening Post*; Diane McGill at the *News Letter* in Belfast. They all deserve our gratitude for searching dusty archives for photographs from the 1940s.

This book is for the crews of the 21st Escort Group and HMS *Byron*, mostly young men from all walks of life, who did a magnificent job under difficult conditions in a cold and violent theatre of war, and to those who looked after them and sustained them in port.

Allan Seabridge
Shirley Morgan
David Chadwick
Lytham St Annes, Lancashire

THE WAR IN THE NORTH ATLANTIC – 1943

By the end of 1943, the war in the North Atlantic had turned in the Allies' favour, largely due to the strengthening of the convoy system through more and better equipped escorts, combined with continuous air cover.

The spring and early summer of 1943 saw a dramatic reversal of fortune in the U-boat campaign, with 245,000 tons of shipping sunk in April, for the loss of only 15 U-boats. In July, shipping losses fell to 123,000 tons, with 37 U-boats sunk. The total number of U-boats destroyed that year rose from 85 to 241 – crippling losses for the U-boat arm. Meanwhile, shipping tonnage lost for the year had fallen from some 5,385,000 tons in 1942 – which had seriously threatened Britain's survival – to some 1,860,200 tons in the whole of 1943.

The threat of the German surface fleet was also diminished. On Boxing Day 1943, the powerful battlecruiser *Scharnhorst* was sunk off northern Norway by a British force led by the battleship *Duke of York*. Yet despite these encouraging developments, the U-boat continued to represent a formidable threat to Allied convoys.

HMS *BYRON*

While Cliff was completing his basic and specialist training, HMS *Byron* was being commissioned and sailed to the UK. The ship was formally commissioned on Saturday 30 October 1943 at the Bethlehem-Hingham shipyard in Boston, Massachusetts. A crew had been sent over on a variety of liners including *Queen Elizabeth*, *Queen Mary* and *Mariposa*. Many of these ships were also carrying German Prisoners of War.

The crews were welcomed by brass bands in New York before they made their way to Boston. After two weeks of acceptance trials and a familiarisation programme, they went to Bermuda for working up exercises. On 11 January 1944 *Byron* left Bermuda for Belfast by way of St Johns, Newfoundland. From there, she escorted convoy HX 275 from Halifax, arriving in Belfast on 27 January.

CITIZEN SAILORS

By the spring of 1942, men between the aged of 18 and 46, and women between 18 and 31, could be conscripted into the armed forces. Yet no one joined the Navy completely against their will. Everyone was allowed to volunteer for the Navy or the

RAF and anyone who did not, or failed the entry requirements, was liable to end up in the army. Many Hostilities Only (HO) volunteers were attracted to the Navy by its status as the Senior Service and the prospect of travelling to locations that would have been unthinkable in peacetime.

The Navy's major expansion period came in 1943–44 when its strength increased from 671,000 to 790,000 as the convoy escort building programme reached its height and preparations for D-Day got underway. This vast organisation was divided into branches comprising various trades. Not surprisingly, the seaman branch was the biggest, accounting for some 30 per cent of the Navy's total strength, while engine room stokers formed 20 per cent and Royal Marines 10 per cent. Signallers, including coders, were a specialist branch that worked closely with the seaman branch, and represented just three per cent of ratings.

Men were brought together from diverse social backgrounds and geographical areas and an array of HO training bases were established around the coast, often at converted holiday camps such as Butlin's at Skegness, which became HMS *Royal Arthur*. There, recruits completed their basic training over 10 or 12 weeks. A great deal of this involved foot drill, although early specialist training was also carried out in preparation for learning more advanced skills.

At the end of this period, men passed out as ordinary seaman, ordinary coders or the 'ordinary' equivalent of other branches. They were not yet the finished article, but they had acquired a sense of belonging and comradeship that would serve them well when they were locked together in a steel hull on the high seas.

THE CODER BRANCH

Communications had always been an important element of naval warfare, but the increasingly widespread use of electronics meant it had never been more crucial than in the Second World War.

Commanders needed efficient communications systems to direct fleets and convoys at a strategic level, as well as to order tactical manoeuvres when a convoy was attacked by a U-boat wolfpack, surface raiders, or Luftwaffe bombers.

Morse Code was at the heart of naval communications of this period and while visual signals (using flags and lamps) were still widely used, wireless telegraphy (W/T) was the key communication channel. A third means of communication, radio telephony (R/T), used voice, but this was not regarded as trustworthy in the early years of the war because records could not be kept.

A coder was a Royal Navy rating who worked in the signals branch, encoding, deciphering and encrypting codes and signals transmitted in Morse by wireless telegraphy. This was critically important specialist work that required intelligence, accuracy and the ability to process confidential information. It was not surprising, then, that these qualities were as apparent in Cliff Greenwood's work as a professional journalist as in his duties as a coder.

Coders worked closely with the wireless telegraphy team, and the specialist sleeve badge of the coder branch depicted two crossed flags over the letter C. Ted Taylor, who trained at HMS *Royal Arthur* and HMS *Caballa*, before serving on *Byron*, commented: 'The coders received and wrote messages to other vessels in the Group, other ships and aircraft. They read Morse and transcribed to message pads, and decoded routine messages. They also received message scripts from on-board sources that were coded and then sent in Morse. Secret and Top Secret messages were normally processed by the Signals Officer who kept the necessary code books and keys. The coder branch was said to be the best branch in the Navy, their work was regarded as highly confidential.'

6th October 1943, Wednesday. HMS *Royal Arthur*

I'm writing on my top bunk in the dormitory for 10 which has been allotted to us for the first night, and writing on the next top bunk is a buddy I've met already. He's a Scot from Aberdeen – Alec Milne his name. It was lonely on the train but we said a tentative 'How are yer?' when we met in the station entrance where about thirty others were waiting for a special bus – yes a special bus, as if we were civil servants! – out to the camp – which is a Squires Gate* on the grand scale but without the sand, avenues of chalets, cinemas, dance halls and the whole shooting box. Tomorrow we are to go into the chalets – three men to each – which will make it a little less of a congested area than this dormitory, even with the eight other lads out in the rain and the black-out.

Already we've fed twice. There was tea of bread and butter – and it WAS butter and plenty of it if you dived your knife in fast – and cake, and tea with enough sugar in it for three or four. Then three hours later, there was supper of fish and chips, bread and butter and another great mug of tea. You walk past stewards in a file and one pours you the tea into a mug you snatch from a tray and the other waits with the heaped plates. Not at all according to the Ritz, I know, but who's complaining about that? We've had a blanket issued to us for our own, to take wherever we go, and a towel and a cake of soap which resembles and smells a little like a week's ration of cheese about a month after issue.

Alec is listed provisionally as a coder, too, and so are one or two other nice guys we've met. The rest are babes in arms, or at least not a lot older and about as wild as bucking broncos. A booklet which has been issued to us contains the information that trainees remain here five weeks but we've heard that sometimes it's longer and sometimes it's shorter and anyway everybody seems to agree that you could be in a lot worse joints.

All the time bugles are blowing on the loudspeakers signifying various watches, but which watches we ignorant recruits don't yet know. And all the time too are announcements each prefaced with a refined 'Do you hear there? Do you hear there?' and until you get used to them you don't hear them at all, although there was one a minute ago which I did hear, proclaiming a gramophone recital of swing music. I only hope they don't broadcast that!

Now soon we'll all be in bed, informed in advance that we shall be called at 6.30am and that we must be in hall for breakfast at 7.00am. How ten men are to wash and shave at one small hand-basin in 30 minutes is one of those problems which seem insoluble, but maybe the morn will sort it out.

* Pontin's holiday camp just outside Blackpool, demolished in 2011.

7th October 1943, Thursday, 3.30pm. HMS *Royal Arthur*

Cor, stone the crows, what a day it's been. But I've loved every minute of it, except for yet another brief medical inspection in the nude, for here there's a sense of comradeship which may not be articulate, but is present all the time.

There was an address by the Commander which made you feel proud, after a sausage-and-mash breakfast at 7.00am and afterwards psychology tests were in progress all morning. What they determined we still don't know, or their purpose either. None of we older chaps may even be accepted as coders. None of us has yet a uniform or a number – so you still can't write.

Actual training apparently will not begin until tomorrow, but in the meantime rumours of our fate are thick in the air. There's the bugle blowing again and that, I have learnt already, means tea.

8th October 1943, Friday

I've done it, passed the test for acceptance as a coder and – wait for it – been appointed leader of the class. We've been issued with full kit today – it weighs nearly a ton – but have not yet worn it. It's bell-bottoms, sailor's cap and all the rest of it. I've seen myself in the glass in the clothing uniform store. It was not too great a shock. Expect we shall leave here a week today. The destination is unknown, but there are whispers that it is a few hundred miles from here. Sailors cannot be more explicit.

10th October 1943, Sunday

JX 617486, Greenwood C.G., 0/Coder, Class 44, FX Division, HMS *Royal Arthur*, Skegness, Lincolnshire.

There at last is the official service address – the address until next Friday night when we take the train for the distant North (or so we expect) and the number until I come home again. You know how I'm missing you. I know how you are missing me. Words alone cannot express it, cannot express the sense of loneliness and the separation which at times even in this packed land ship makes me want more than anything else in the world to see you again, to talk to you.

Yet dear, I'm not unhappy. I should not have time to be even if I had not met some of the nicest fellows I've ever met. For until this afternoon I've scarcely had a free minute since I arrived four days ago – is it only four days? Nor yet have we begun training. All this time we've been visiting doctors, dentists and equipment stores. Already our kit is colossal.

A test in the gas chamber – with masks off – and inoculations are some of the lesser ordeals awaiting us before we leave. Tomorrow too, we parade in uniform for the first time and that threatens to be an ordeal as last night the three of us in our chalet – a couple of 100 per cent guys, one 36 and the other 40 – dressed each other and took about an hour over the operation. And an operation it is – a major one to insert yourself into the jacket alone, while to extricate yourself from it nearly requires dynamite. They say that they become more pliant as the weeks pass. We only pray that it is true. There's two of everything – even white ducks, although we are told by our instructor that their inclusion does not necessarily imply that we shall eventually reach tropic parts – although he says you can never tell.

I'm standing up to it fine. It's pretty tough. Until I had a hot bath this morning, when all the uniformed personnel were at church parade and the bathrooms at last were empty, I neither washed or shaved in anything except water as cold as the Arctic, and that I can tell you is not so good at 6.15am, which is the hour when the bugles call us. The cold is the worst penance of all. All the food is good and there's a fair lot of it, but it's invariably cold too. And half the time you're waiting for something to happen – waiting in queues for this, that or something else – and that's cold too. Yet they tell us that to be kitted out in a week and sent away to another base is nearly a record.

We signed the allotment forms on Friday. According to the WREN behind the pay desk you will have 25/- a week from next Thursday and I shall be left with either 14/- or 17/6. Nobody seems quite certain what it will be. Actually my pay as a rating under training is 3/- or 3/6 (nobody yet knows which) a day, but the Government deduct 6d a day, which makes it 21/- a week at 3/6 a day. My allotment to you is 7/- a week which reduces the 21/- to 14/- but they seem to think that the Government contributes 3/6 of the 7/- and remit the remaining 3/6 to this bewildered Jack Tar, who was never too hot, in any case, on high finance. Still, whether they do or don't, I'll manage fine with all cigarettes at 1/6 for 20 instead of 2/4 and tobacco at correspondingly reduced prices, with an issue of half a pound of tobacco or 160 cigarettes completely free from duty at the beginning of every month. That brings the cost of living down with a bang, for there's nothing else to spend it on in *Royal Arthur* unless you count the cinema, where after church we're going tonight for the first time and that costs 3d. It's *Citizen Kane* at the top of the bill.

We class leaders have all sorts of obligations on us, not the least consoling the home-sick and there's four of them suffering from that complaint in the sick bay already. Perhaps I'm suffering from it too, but when I think of the home I've left and my dear wife that, I think, is only to be expected. But you've to hide all that and I'm making a credible job of it, I hope, but just to see you again my darling. Not that it will be too long. We shall not be allowed out of camp until we leave shortly before midnight on Friday and away wherever we're going. We're told it will be lessons and parades non-stop for 12 weeks. But at the end of six of those 12 long weeks we should have and probably will have 72 hours leave. Not long, I know, but one of the seven weeks dividing me from it since I left home has nearly gone – and that's something.

14th October 1943, Thursday. HMS *Royal Arthur*

You must be wondering where on earth I have gone to. You have sent me such grand letters. By every mail they have come since yesterday's first stand-easy watch which is between 10.15 and 10.30. Each time I have dived into a swarm surging near a great metal pail in York House, which is our mess, lowered my cup into about two feet of cocoa, retired to one of the remote corners of this great hall and read those letters and afterwards read them again and again until I think I know every word of them. Now, why haven't I written earlier? There are two reasons. The first is that I simply have not had the time. We're at it morning, noon and night from 6.15am to Last Post.

Consider this as a typical day. We're in a chalet for three in one of nearly 100 avenues. With me are Ted Taylor, a darned nice unassuming guy of exactly my age from Nottingham – an insurance agent in civilian life – and Ken King, another champion fellow from Bristol. In the next avenue is Alec Milne, the Scot from Aberdeen, who every night comes over for a last chat before lights out. There the four of us are, great buddies at the end of a week. There are 35 others in the class and not one of them who is not as nearly 100% as makes no difference. We're all pals. It's the friendship which counts in this new world we're in – it's all that matters. Well, take today. We're awake at 6am after tucking ourselves in our three blankets at 8.30 last night. We've slept in our blue jerseys not because it's cold, for every night when the sea mist has come in over the camp, they put the radiators in commission, but because we couldn't get out of them when we crawled into our bunks.

In the early afternoon we filed into one of the surgeries for inoculations and vaccinations. Arms bared, two doctors in sinister white smocks inserted needles into us at the rate of three or four a minute. There were immediate casualties. Alec nearly went out as soon as he reached the open air. Others went a variety of shades from off-white to emerald green. I was completely unaffected for a couple of hours, during which time we all marched up and down one of the barrack squares, casualties and all. Then came the dawn. We were waiting in one of those queues in which we seem to stand half the day, when we're not chasing our own tails all over the premises. Suddenly I came over all queer, but in to tea I marched, dipped my cup – it's always the same cup, even for shaving water and we're allowed no other – into the same old pail. This time tea came up out of the pail, the sort of tea they brew on Good Friday and serve on Whit Monday and rather unexpectedly nothing came up out of me, and I had a dinner and all after that.

But for the rest of the evening we were all pale shadows of our former selves and to bed we went early after suffering the torments of the damned extricating ourselves by brute force and sheer will power from our jumpers. The jerseys we simply could not manage. And all day today we've been skirmishing away from anybody who came near our left arms.

This morning we rose with the lark. 'You're a grand lot' said the instructor when there was a 100% roll call. I know nothing about that. But I do know that except for 15 of us, selected merely because their names happened to begin with the early letters of the alphabet, we were a miserable lot when we were told after another hour of squad drill that those 15 were on draft for Warrington and would leave at 6am on Friday. That was the news I had to keep secret in my other letters, dear. And now it's all gone up in smoke. Yet probably it's not gone altogether, for the instructor thinks that the rest of us may follow the other 15 next Friday week and that the reason we're not to go this week is merely because the Warrington station can't take us. We're still hoping, all except Alec, who would prefer Scotland, which, according to rumours thick in the air all the time, was to be our first destination. Well, after that little reverse we were given a lesson in the slinging and packing of a hammock and mine is already packed awaiting my departure – a minor miracle which could have been achieved only because I've a few good pals and because all these instructors, with a few exceptions, are considerate guys.

What else has happened since I wrote last? Lots and lots, if only I'd the time to tell you about it. We've been in the gas chamber with our masks off and darned nearly choked and we've had our photographs taken for our pay and identity books. We put in orders in advance for three postcard copies each. Today we've seen the originals which make us appear like candidates for inclusion in the next issue of the Police Gazette. Half the chaps intend to tear their postcards up but I'll send you one if you still have a little sal volatile in the house. We're not wearing our caps, which is a pity, for we consider, entirely without prejudice, that in our caps and all the rest of the gear too, once we've got into it, we don't look too hideous at all. You'll be able to judge for yourself, for once they let us out of here we intend to visit a decent photographer and ask him to make the best of us. Just the four of us. Yes, we feel like sailors even at the end of the week and look not unlike sailors either, so at least we think.

P.S. About the telephone calls. I think we'd better wait a little longer. We may – but only may – be given shore leave tomorrow night, but I understand that calls out of Skegness, which is packed every night with sailors, are invariably delayed and by the time we reach town the GPO will be closed and there are queues at all the call boxes. If we don't go to Warrington at the end of next week I'll take a chance but at the present time I daren't do it, for if you miss the station bus and are late back from leave they do everything but put you in irons.

17th October 1943, Sunday. HMS *Royal Arthur*

I hardly recognise myself these days. Our instructor has been put in charge of a new squad of recruits and since Thursday he has simply called at our chalet and given me the orders for the day. Fortunately Thursday afternoon, all Friday, and early Saturday morning were devoted to a series of lectures on Passive Defence, or to put it in other words, almost the identical course which LDV wardens take. I knew nearly all of it in advance. All it meant, therefore, was marching the class from one theatre to another, but when you have never before given a military order in your life, and when you have been given no instructions whatsoever, and when every avenue is packed with marching columns and you have to steer 30 men through the maze, all those 'Right Wheels', 'Left Turns', 'Halts', 'Mark Times' and 'Keep those arms swinging' are a bit of an embarrassment. Still nearly all the chaps co-operate. There are one or two exceptions. Three or four tough eggs who have failed a course as signallers have been drafted into our class for their sins, and they require a bit of the lash. The truth is I can't fire at them as they ought to have it – not yet! But I'll learn.

The climax came yesterday morning when I was left at the last minute to lead a practise march-past announced for today but cancelled because of the rain which as I write is pouring down, the first rain we've had since we came. Actually if a leading seaman in charge of a neighbouring squad had not come to the rescue I might have made a hash of it, for the ceremonial assembling of the class in columns of three, not one of us had ever seen. In the end we were in order and I had to approach some big shot in gold braid, give him a whacking great salute and retire to the head of the column where I marched past the flag, producing another salute over the prescribed distance, then barking over my shoulder an 'Eyes Right' when I estimated the first man had reached the flag and 'Eyes Front' when the last man had passed it.

What a blessed lessening of the tension when at last they gave us shore leave yesterday afternoon. But even that was one of those luxuries for which you have to pay, for before you are allowed to leave the premises you are inspected and shown no mercy at all if you are incorrectly dressed. Half a dozen near me were sent back to their chalets because their lanyards were not as white as the driven snow. Then there were the buses, or liberty boats, as they call them. If 1000 men are leaving camp they put only sufficient into commission for about 200 men. Then if you're not in the front ranks (and that's determined by the caprice of a few petty officers) you either wait for them to come back from Skegness or walk. On Thursday night we waited and by the time we'd left it was so nearly time to come back again that after we'd had one drink and a supper of fish and chips we'd to begin tramping the three-and-a-half miles back again. It's an unforgivable sin if you're late from shore leave.

Yet we shall go again tomorrow night. Those fish and chips, tea out of clean cups, and then bread and butter, are luxuries which we can't resist. The truth is that we are more or less hungry all the time, for the food at nearly all the meals is so often cold and in such a mess that, abundant as it may be in proteins and vitamins, we spend nearly every stand-easy queuing for fruit-cake – great slabs of it and good cake too at

2d a go. Or, to be exact, my buddies queue for my ration of it, for I seem to spend every stand-easy collecting and delivering mail, or in some other of the tasks which seem to fall the lot of a class leader whom, I can tell you, is a creature not to be envied.

Those Dead End Kids who have been cursed on us are a pest. One of them fell over his own feet and splashed half a pail of a boiling substance which the kitchen call coffee, scalded his eyes and had to be sent to the Sick Bay. Another fell asleep during one of those Passive Defence lectures – and honestly I didn't blame him for that – and was promptly banished from the hall, had his station card confiscated, which means the cancellation of all shore-leave, and was ordered to run ten times around York House, a distance of between two and three miles, to ensure that he should be completely awakened. And a Petty Officer was sent outside to see that he did it, too!

This doubling everywhere at the gallop is one of the major curses of the camp. Every morning at 9 o'clock we go on divisions and as a preliminary to the saluting of the flag we have to jog-trot in columns one-and-a-half times round the entire establishment. That's no joke in darned great boots. The first time it nearly put Ken out. Yesterday, when they graciously permitted us to walk but ordered us to wear gas masks the whole time, Ted had to ask permission to retire to the chalet for the rest of the morning. There was only me to ask and I gave permission, but what I want to know is when can a Class Leader give permission to himself to go and put his feet on his bunk and rest them?

Our instructor made one of his infrequent appearances at 7.00am breakfast today and whispered that definitely we were on draft again, that we should probably leave on Friday, and that our destination would probably be Warrington. But we're believing nothing now until we're on the train, and in fact our chief concern now is that some will go and some remain and that we shall be separated. That we don't want to happen at any price.

I only hope that when it happens it is Warrington, for at Warrington the laundry problem, and it is a problem, may solve itself for from there I should be able to send nearly all of it home again. I washed half a dozen handkerchiefs and one of my two service towels on Friday night in lukewarm water and Oxydol but there is no iron and nowhere to dry anything. The towel is still nearly as wet as when I rinsed it for the last time and the handkerchiefs although nearly dry, and clean too, look horribly crumpled and messy. Underclothes would be out of the question and what to do about pyjamas I don't know. The present pair will soon be standing up on their own.

18th October 1943, Monday. HMS *Royal Arthur*

We're going to Warrington. This time it's official orders, and except for a miracle we should leave on Friday, being called at 4.30am for the purpose. One of the draft who left last week sends news that Warrington is a Grade One base with everything which this establishment makes no pretensions to possessing, among them clean bathrooms, games rooms and rest rooms. We're all up in the clouds about it.

19th October 1943, Tuesday. HMS *Royal Arthur*

The news came this morning that we are to go to Warrington on Thursday instead of Friday. Are we glad? We agree that we cannot go too soon after all the reports drifting in by every post from the draft who left last week. We are not to be in dormitories but in chalets for three again. Each block of chalets has its own Games Room, the meals are served hot, and there are cups, knives, forks and spoons on the tables. You have not to wander from meal to meal clutching them and washing them when or if you can, which is the singular practise here. It will be a case of back to civilisation.

I'll write as soon as we reach the new base and tomorrow I'll pack my service vest and pants and send them home to be washed with a pair of socks. Don't be too revolted by their appearance. All sorts of dyes – not all of them blue – come out of these uniforms. Send the pyjamas back with them and then I'll post the present pair with the second set of vest and pants. So I suppose we shall have to go on for a time, unless the laundry facilities in Warrington are a lot different from those here. It's a nuisance, I know, but all the other chaps are being compelled to do it.

About the allowances. No, I don't understand them at all, but the fact that you cannot produce birth and marriage certificates does not invalidate your claim to them. Complete the form – every chap's wife has had one – and explain that you don't possess the certificates. They'll tell you what to do then. This Navy accountancy is a puzzle to everybody it seems. We were paid 10/- the second day after our arrival and have not had a penny since. Funds were falling a bit low until in yesterday's post a 10/- note came from Mother.

25th October 1943, Monday 10pm. HMS *Caballa*, Warrington

Now for the news. It's good and not so good. The good news is that the five of us are in one class. We shall be together now all through the course. What is not so good is that our instructor is a young PO, very ambitious and with a reputation which the entire establishment has warned us against. He's been snarling and roaring all the morning. And we're to have him until we leave. Our first assignment is to learn the whole Morse Code this week in our leisure time, whatever little we have. He said he learnt it in an hour – and no thunderbolt from on high smote him when he said it!

Still, we're together, which is all that matters, and we can take it. I've escaped at least one tribulation. We went for Dental Inspection today. Half the fellows have to have extractions or fillings. I was passed fit, he said the few teeth I had left were good and sound and when a Naval surgeon says that, they must be. He said that he could have extracted the lot and I should have had a complete set of dentures at the State's expense but when I told him my age he expressed the opinion that it would have been asking too much of a man in the middle of a course. And I think it would too!

27th October 1943, Wednesday. HMS *Caballa*

We're halfway through the first of the two weeks which everybody says are the worst of the lot. Actually it's not been too grim. I felt a bit wretched about it yesterday when the first physical training class was enrolled, I was so tired that I asked to be excused, and when I told the instructor that less than three months ago I had been under observation in hospital he said that I should be unwise to enter it and that in any case my age exempted me. Several of the others in the 35 to 40 groups are excused too. I feel a bit out of it but I'm actually profiting by it for these last two days I've devoted the 45 minutes which the class lasts to learning the Morse alphabet. Crikey, what a job it is. But we're progressing, 'dahing', which is short for long; and 'deeing', which is short for short, at each other at all hours in furtive whispers. Already I've reached 'T' and I know 'V'. There's a little of the milk of human kindness – a little but not a lot – in the new instructor who, however, broke the glad tidings today that's he's been summoned to a new assignment at the end of the week. We shall part without tears.

A new bloke who's failed his course for a commission is the new class leader – a sensible appointment, I think, but one a few of the lads were inclined to resent until I talked them out of it – we want nobody in irons – and told them that according to one of the other instructors my services at Skegness will be entered on the records. As a matter of fact I'm not too sorry to lose the job, for during the next 10 or 11 weeks we'll have to work like horses and I'll want all the time I can get for myself. Now for supper and soon after, bed. I'm too weary to dot and dash any more today.

31st October 1943, Sunday 11.45am. HMS *Caballa*

What time do you think I went aboard? Another 15 minutes and it would have been midnight. I waited and waited after your train had left, met a Fleet Air Arm mechanic en route from Blackburn and was introduced by him to a free buffet where you can eat your head off and drink tea by the gallon for nothing at all.* I had another cup of tea – yes, another – and when at last the train arrived all hope of making the connection at Wigan had gone. But this guy knew the ropes. There was, he said, a slow train to Lowton from the LMS Station at 11.10. So we wandered across Wigan, walked for half an hour the platform of the dreariest station I've ever seen and at last reached Lowton at 11.40pm.

Today it's raining and everything is about as dismal as it can be. Gosh, aren't I glad it was not like this last Sunday or yesterday. We were up at 6.15 for 7.00am breakfast and since that time we've cleaned the wash-basins in the laundry – a nice warm job – attended a captain's inspection and been to church. I should have gone to Communion afterwards but just as the service ended our watch was summoned to stack the chairs and collect the hymn books. So, I suppose, this long duty watch will continue, for every time the bugle blows we, as the duty watch for the day, have to gallop to it and do whatever has to be done.

* The Sailor's and Soldier's Free Refreshment Room on Preston Station was located in what is now the Waiting Room on Platforms 3 and 4. It was established in the First World War and a commemorative plaque is mounted on the wall in the waiting room, although there is nothing to mark the station's generosity during the Second World War when food and drinks were provided free to all members of the services in uniform.

2nd November 1943, Tuesday. Warrington

Yesterday afternoon we were given a test on the Morse buzzer for the first time. The transmission was only at the rate of a letter every five or six seconds, which is laboriously slow, I suppose, but I surprised myself by taking it about 80% correct. Today they gave it us at four or five words a minute – and we only require six as expert coders – and all of us were left miles down the field. That was asking too much of us. We're not shedding tears about that, for definitely we're progressing; and all by self-tuition too.

We still 'work ship', which is the Navy's polite phrase for all sorts of menial engagements. Yesterday we began the day emptying dustbins and today we washed up the breakfast crockery and cutlery in the petty officer's mess. That was just like home except that there was 50 or 60 of everything, but again we'd no complaints for when we finished the WREN cooks gave us a cup of tea – and good tea too – and a thick slab of bread and butter. Yesterday too we had rifle drill for the first time and on Thursday we go out to a range near Bolton for firing practise.

Alec and Ken are on fire-watch tonight. Ted and I won't be on until Thursday. Meanwhile it is raining again today as it's been raining since Saturday night. Not that it will make any great difference for rifle drill is on the orders again for this afternoon and afterwards we're on the Morse buzzer again. Tonight Ted, Jack and I will go to the pictures to see *White Cargo*, not a film any of us would choose, but it passes the time until we settle down after the leave to serious study.

6th November 1943, Saturday 2.00pm. Warrington

We've actually started on our course. Yesterday we were issued with notebooks and for an hour wrote from dictation about five pages on various codes relating to courses and bearings – latitude, longitude and all that. Some of the phrases I'd never read or seen since Geography classes at school, and that's a long time ago. These notes we commit more or less to memory. I've reserved an hour for that later in the afternoon. On Monday, Tuesday, Wednesday and until 4.00pm on Thursday this dictation continues. By Thursday we shall have written our text books for the entire course. Then the books will be taken from us until we return from leave and deposited in a locked room which is under perpetual custody. This method has to be adopted because the information is so secret that it is never printed. Penalties for losing a notebook are almost penal. The entire block is put out of bounds. Every inhabitant of the block has his shore leave, and every other kind of leave, cancelled. Yet we have to take these books out with us from classroom to classroom and our pockets are so small that they fall out of them on the least pretext and every day we have to lock them in our suitcases and pray to all the Gods that Mata Hari or somebody has not a duplicate key.

What with these notebooks and our pay and identity books we live in a state of perpetual jitters. One fellow lost his pay book the other day. They did everything except read the Riot Act. His four days leave, which should have begun on Thursday, was cancelled and he is confined to camp for 14 days and loses a fortnight's pay. Crikey, but you have to watch your step. An officer came on rounds the other day in the middle of the morning. Three classes had been at Physical Training immediately before and as they had not had time to clear away all their gear their cabins were in a bit of a litter. On the floor of one cabin cigarette ash was found. Smoking in cabins is strictly prohibited. We don't smoke but guys walk in and out of our cabins at all hours of the day and they're not so particular. Ash is scattered about and we've to sweep the floors half-a-dozen times a day, for circumstantial evidence alone is sufficient to convict you here, where you've no chance to offer a defence. This officer came, saw and reported.

The same evening 24 trainees were in the jug. Three-quarters of them spent two hours peeling onions in the galley. The rest shovelled coke. Yes, they know all about discipline in the Navy.

I'm coming along nicely in Morse. I think that at first we were inclined to slog at it too hard. You can do that. Now we're learning a bit of moderation it's not such hard labour and it's coming a little more fluently. We shall have to study a lot I know, and I'm going to, but I've found that an hour's quiet read in the Common Room leaves you fresher than if you swot away hour after hour. I'm keeping to that routine from now on.

8th November 1943, Monday 12.45pm. Warrington

Br-r-r-r! That means it's darned cold. All morning we've been sat writing pages in our precious notebooks in a classroom which is supposed to be heated and isn't. Still we should worry. We've been assured this morning that as coders we rank among the Navy's select force and certainly from the comparatively few notes we've taken it promises to be a dashed interesting job and not half as complex as a few folk make it out to be.

Tonight I'm on fire-watch. Or, to be exact, I've to sleep in all my uniform on a bed beneath the theatre stage and am to be called to stand the watch-tower on the theatre roof from 6.00 to 7.00am, the last watch of the series. Still, it's warm under the stage and if you arrive sufficiently early in the evening to stake your claim you're assured of a comfortable bed, and that's a lot.

25th November 1943, Thursday 12.45pm. Warrington

We were all a bit depressed on Tuesday. The course, which becomes more of a jigsaw puzzle every day, cast us deeper into melancholy. But now we've all sat up and are making the best of it again. Last night in absolute despair of ever sorting it all out and with our poor old brain pans fairly simmering, we gave studying a miss and went out to Leigh, where in the WRVS canteen for a total cost of 11d, I had four toasted crumpets, two cakes and two cups of tea as the prelude to a couple of games of snooker.

We've said 'To Hell' with regulations and we're all wearing gloves. My first pair has gone to Alec who says 'Thanks a Million' for them, and I'm wearing those you knitted, which I think are about the best and the warmest in the camp.

29th November 1943, Monday 5.45pm. Warrington

There seems to be a minor crime wave in the camp at the present time. In the cabin opposite ours some person or persons unknown piddled last night in one of the occupant's boots during the not-so-silent watches of the night. This morning there was no end of a hullaballoo. Petty officers and officers swarmed to the scene like a homicide squad and now one of my pals, the bloke from Newcastle who was in America not so long ago, has been accused of the offence and at the present time is up in front of a court of inquiry defending himself. He swears he's innocent and, knowing him, I'm sure he is, just as sure as that he knows the real offender – or at least suspects his identity – but could not be persuaded to disclose his name for all the tea in China.

Then tonight at evening quarters and in the presence of the entire establishment one of the coders was marched under guard in front of the Captain and sentenced to 14 days in the cells – the first three on bread and water and the lot presumably in solitary confinement – for swearing at an instructor, telling a lie to an officer and absenting himself from the camp yesterday for nine hours and 20 minutes. No, they didn't even forget the 20 minutes. That's discipline as they understand it in the Navy.

1st December 1943, Wednesday 6.10pm. Warrington

I'm showing a bit of wisdom, refusing to brood over my notes all day. It's coming off too. I clocked out 78% in the first Morse test and I was convinced I'd crashed from a great height. Yesterday, too, we had a trial examination as a sort of dress rehearsal for Friday's intermediate and I was one of only two to complete the paper inside the time limit. I don't suppose every answer was correct but I shall be surprised if tomorrow, when the instructor announces the results, I have not the 75% required for a pass in the intermediate. Again today we had an oral test and I gave correct answers to the few questions which reached me and could have answered three-quarters of the others.

5th December 1943, Sunday 9.15am. Warrington

Well, the course goes on and on. There are to be voluntary classes every night, or at least nearly every night, next week and already we've had our second Morse test at five words a minute. I made 78 this time in spite of feeling decidedly under the weather, but the big surprise was an 80 by Ken. That's just what he wanted. It's done him all the good in the world.

The captain chose this morning, the coldest Sunday morning we've had, to conduct a full-dress inspection, class by class, on the parade ground. It took nearly three quarters of an hour and by the end of it we were nearly perished. Dozens of men were reprimanded too for soiled lanyards, cut collars and those long tapes hanging a foot from the bow which have become a fashion all at once. Darned silly they look too. 'You can wear fancy dress if you want to' said the skipper, a decent old scout, 'but not on this parade ground.'

Which reminds me, that the black silk you sent back was folded a little too broad. It should be about half that width, the correct formula being apparently to fold it in half, then to fold the two sides until they meet and then to double the entire length over. Get me? We had to cut the stitches and, as the folds were then visible, it's being taken back by another of my pals to his home at Preston, where this afternoon his wife will iron it out again.

6th December 1943, Monday 7.40pm. Warrington

It's been a grim sort of day here. We all had to stand quivering and shuddering in the bitter wind tonight while another malefactor, who had absented himself from his patrol as a sentry while he smoked a cigarette in one of the boiler houses at 5.45 one morning last week, was sentenced to 10 days in the cells.

8th December 1943, Wednesday 8pm. Warrington

We're all tired after those days of voluntaries which increase our working hours to 6.30pm and often nearly 7 o'clock after beginning the day in pitch darkness at 6.00am. Yes, we're tired, but at last, I think, we're making progress. Ken sat up at last and began to discern a bit of the complex patterns today after being so down in the doldrums yesterday that he was actually talking about asking for an interview to be transferred to another course. We'd have dissuaded him from that little enterprise, but it'll show you the desperate sort of state he was in.

14th December 1943, Tuesday 8pm. Warrington

The trial examination lasted from 9.15 to 11.30 and as it was conducted in a lecture room entirely unheated and deprived us of our morning stand-easy and our cup of tea and cake, we were not only perished but in a state of extreme malnutrition by the time they called it a day. The one consolation this time was that I answered every question and as it was an exact duplicate of the first part of the final examination held yesterday there are still hopes apparently that I may yet be a qualified coder before Christmas. But aren't we suffering in the process. We were so cold this morning that we could scarcely grip our pencils and before the end you could nearly hear our teeth chattering. Still, we survived to endure a long afternoon during which the chief signals officer told us all we had done wrong in the first trial – and that was plenty – but there was another consolation in this session too, for as an officer was present the stove was a roaring furnace and in the unaccustomed heat everybody nearly fell asleep.

Whether I'll go to Warrington on Sunday I don't know. Probably I'll remain in camp to take Ken out somewhere. He'll need a bit of companionship. I had a letter from him yesterday. The funeral* has had to be delayed until tomorrow as there have been so many influenza deaths in Bristol that it could not take place earlier. As a result Ken's leave has been extended until Thursday and now when he returns he'll have to go into a new class and there may be a question of his transfer to another block. I only hope that doesn't happen. But I do think that without all his pals it will be nearly a miracle if he passes the course at all.

* Of his father

16th December 1943, Thursday 12.45pm. Warrington

It's been granted – the native-leave for Christmas. I appeared in front of one of the officers yesterday afternoon and without a murmur he gave permission for absence from camp until 7.00am on the days following Tuesday, Thursday, Saturday and Sunday. That means that I shall be able to walk out at 5.15pm on Tuesday and Thursday, at 1.00pm on Saturday (Christmas Day) and at 11.30am on Sunday (Boxing Day). And I'm out, too, the following day (Monday) on ordinary leave until 10.30pm.

It's still perishing cold, but at last the fog is lifting. How glad I am of those gloves you knitted for me. They make all the difference from the time we crawl out in the darkness for breakfast until we crawl back to the cabin still in darkness after the evening voluntary.

Now we're near the end of it all – and are we glad! All that's left now is revision and the finals on Monday after which, whether we pass or fail, we have a week on a routine called 'Clean Ship' which means that we're out of the classrooms altogether and given assignments ranging from serving in the mess-deck galley, preparing meals, setting tables, digging coke, scrubbing floors, acting as messengers and nearly everything else designed to make us forget all about this nightmare course. For a week that's in progress. Then, if we've failed, we've to take the last two weeks of the course and the finals again. If we've passed there follows a fortnight in the Distributing Signals Office, which is a sort of miniature ship's office or a Signals Office at a base, a week's draft routine and – eight days leave.

16th December 1943, Thursday 7.50pm. Warrington

Here I am in the cabin, squatting on my bunk, while Ted stitches the red crossed flags on our uniforms. We're both as proud as a couple of punches but we're not saying a lot, for there are no flags for Ken and I'm afraid the poor old lad feels a bit out of it.

Wasn't it grand that I should have finished level in third place with 84, the only old guy in the class to pass the 75 pass figure. Yet I'm taking it quietly, dear, for there are the finals yet and they're no picnic. Already we've had one voluntary class for an hour tonight and there's to be another tomorrow. It makes a long day of it – 6.00am to 6.30pm and at the end of it in another 15 minutes, Ted and I have to sweep out the block and clean the lavatories and bathrooms.

(**Later**) The little blue book – well I may take a glance at it for half-an-hour but no longer. We've done all we can, finished our instruction this morning and now, whatever happens, nobody can tell us that we didn't put everything we had into it. Monday will be a day and a half. The examination starts at 7.45 and continues, with an hour-and-a-half's break for dinner, until 4.00pm. The morning papers will be practical coding, the afternoon's theoretical.

One of us will go into this treat indifferent to his fate. This morning a telegram reached Jack Hammond, one of the four you met, the fellow who's given me an open invitation to his home when I go to Portsmouth, telling him his father had died of a stroke. He went for leave and it was refused because of the finals. They were polite about it, but firm. He can leave for the funeral as soon as the examination ends but not before.

THE WAR IN THE NORTH ATLANTIC – 1944

During 1944, technological advances in ASDIC (sonar) and radar increasingly gave Allied escorts the advantage over U-boats. The position of the Allies was further strengthened by the inexhaustible supply of merchant ships, in particular prefabricated American 'Liberty ships' which could be built, on average, in 42 days. There would be no return to the perilous period earlier in the war when the U-boats threatened to sink merchantmen faster than they could be replaced.

Greater availability of escorts also enabled the introduction of Convoy Support Groups. These comprised fast warships that pursued any U-boat that was detected, leaving the main escort group to maintain its defensive cover around the convoy.

What remained of the German surface threat was finally removed on 12 November 1944 when the 'super dreadnought' battleship *Tirpitz*, sister of the *Bismarck*, was bombed by RAF Lancasters and capsized off Tromso in Norway.

However, these events did nothing to diminish the tenacity and daring of U-boat commanders. Although the loss of merchant ships continued to fall in 1944, U-boat attacks on escorts proved increasingly lethal. Some 32 escorts were lost to U-boat actions in 1944, compared to 23 the previous year. When an escort was hit by a torpedo, loss of life could be appalling. The corvette HMS *Zinnia* sunk without trace in 15 to 20 seconds after being hit by a torpedo in 1941. On 6 December 1944, the Captain Class frigate HMS *Bullen* went down north of Scotland with 71 of her 156-strong company after being torpedoed by U-775. Although U-775 evaded the pursuing frigates and aircraft, they encountered U-297 and sank her with all hands.

In another episode involving great loss of life on both sides, U-486 sank the merchantman *Silverlaurel* off Plymouth on 18 December. Three days later, the U-boat dispatched the troop ship *Leopoldville* off Cherbourg. She had been carrying 2,200 soldiers and although many escaped, some 800 went down with the ship. Remaining in the vicinity, U-486 sank the Captain Class frigate HMS *Capel* on 26 December, killing her captain, eight officers and 67 ratings. Within a few minutes, the U-boat torpedoed another Captain Class ship, HMS *Affleck*. She did not sink, but was damaged beyond repair. U-486 returned to base, but had used up her luck. When she next put to sea she was spotted on the surface by a British submarine that fired a torpedo and sank her. There were no survivors.

HMS BYRON – 1944

In February Cliff joined the ship at Scapa Flow. After trials and readiness, *Byron* was considered fit for action and sailed for Arctic waters. From 22 February she formed part of a screening force for the aircraft carrier *Chaser* that had been ordered to join Convoy JW 57, en route to northern Russia. *Byron* remained with the convoy until 26 February.

After a spell in March escorting on North Atlantic convoys, *Byron* spent much of the spring escorting east coast convoys threatened by E-boat patrols in the North Sea. *Byron*'s main contribution to D-Day was in escorting tugs towing caissons for the Mulberry harbours and reels for PLUTO (the submerged Channel pipeline) from the Thames through the Dover Straits to Weymouth, mainly at night.

The ship was not directly involved in the D-Day landings, which was a cause for great disappointment in the crew. The group patrolled the mine-swept channels in support of flocks of landing craft as far across the North Sea as the Frisian Islands and keeping the channels free of E-boats. As the armies advanced into Europe their need for naval support declined and the escorts were re-equipped and re-formed to reinforce the North Atlantic Support and Escort Groups. *Byron* left Harwich on 2 August for Belfast to be fitted out for life in the North Atlantic – an operation that took two months. The re-fit included extra anti-aircraft weapons, relocating her Hedgehog magazine, and fitting a life-boat and shelter on the bridge. At the same time, the messing arrangements were changed and items such as ice-cream and Coca-Cola machines were removed.

In late October *Byron* and her sisters escorted convoy JW 61 from Loch Ewe to Kola Inlet in northern Russia. Vigorous action by the powerful escort group ensured JW 61 arrived without the loss of any merchant ships. However, when escorting the convoy RA 61 back from Murmansk to Loch Ewe in early November, one of *Byron*'s sisters, *Mounsey* was torpedoed by U-295 off Kola Inlet and was forced to return to port for repairs.

THE U-BOAT

More than any other weapon at Hitler's disposal, the U-boat came closest to defeating Britain. U-boats sank more than 3,000 Allied ships, amounting to almost 15 million tons. Their design comprised a pressure hull, tapered at the bow and stern, a steel outer skin and conning tower, from which the commander directed attacks. Although generally smaller than their Allied counterparts, U-boats were robustly constructed and capable of diving to greater depths.

Commanded by skilful and audacious captains, many of whom became 'aces', the U-boat was a powerful adversary for any escort. They typically carried 14 or 24 torpedoes, capable of immense destructive capacity and culminating in the acoustic torpedo that homed in on the sound of a ship's propellers. U-boats could also lay mines and often carried deck guns ranging from 20mm to 105mm calibre. The U-boat relied on batteries to drive it underwater and had to spend a great deal of time on the surface to recharge. U-boats were much slower when submerged – generally capable of around half their surface speed.

Various types of U-boats were deployed in the Battle of the Atlantic, notably the Type VII, the workhorse of the fleet; and the larger Type IX, designed for long-range patrols. The Type VII boat was approximately 67 metres long, with a beam of 6.2 metres. Displacing 759 tons surfaced and 860 tons submerged, the Type VII could make 17 knots surfaced, and 7.6 knots submerged. With a crew of 44, the Type VII had five torpedo tubes and carried 14 torpedoes, as well as mounting one 37mm deck gun and two twin 20mm guns.

The Type IX measured 76.8 metres from stem to stern with a 6.9 metre beam. Displacing 1,444 tones surfaced and 1,257 submerged, it had a top speed on the surface of 18.3 knots and 7.3 knots submerged. With a crew of 48, the Type IX carried 24 torpedoes that could be fired through six tubes, and mounted one 105mm deck gun, one 37mm and one 20mm gun.

31st January 1944, Monday 7.50pm. Petersfield*

At last we've found a bit of piece in all the turmoil. 'Ratings Quiet Room' it said over the door. David and I walked into a room furnished with easy chairs and writing tables, heated by a great open stove. On the tables are newspapers and magazines. All is so quiet as I write to you, my first letter from the camp. Talking is strictly prohibited. It's the little bit of heaven you find everywhere if you go seeking it.

The first news to greet us when we arrived back again was that all the coders with yellow cards (ours are green) had been given 21 days leave, subject to immediate recall. Bill Eaves and the fellow who came back from his honeymoon a week ago are among them. Two others have gone on draft. Frank was given 16 days as soon as he reached Newcastle on Friday. So if they can get it, why not us? That's what we're asking.

It was a faster train this time. I read and I slept, and I read and I slept all the way and I ate all the sandwiches too. And as I was in Waterloo an hour before the train left for Petersfield

I went and had my hair cut at the station. 1/6d they charged and I was given a very bleak look when I asked for 1/- change from half-a-crown. Still, I can stand bleak looks now.

* HMS Mercury *was a communications school at Leydene House, East Meon near Petersfield. Unofficially classified as a 'stone frigate', HMS* Mercury *was commissioned on 16 August 1941 under the command of Captain Gerald Warner. A signalling school had been established at Portsmouth in 1904 and the facility was transferred to Petersfield during the Second World War. The base went on to house both the Communications and Navigations faculties of the Royal Navy's School of Maritime Operations and trained generations of Royal Navy communications and navigational specialists until it was decommissioned in 1993.*

1st February 1944, Tuesday 9.20pm. Petersfield

I've lost David. After a long day out of camp, which is the best sort of day you can have at this camp, we arrived back at 7.30 tonight, our shore leave lost, to hear that David had been posted to a foreign shore base. He has to be available by the 15th. That means, if he has any leave at all, that he'll be given 14 days leave from tomorrow, will report back here and will then await a ship. He doesn't know whether to be sad or glad about it. He'll have a nice billet, with none of the discomforts of shipboard, but when he says 'Goodbye', to his wife and kiddie this time it may be for a year or two. He's the first of the old brigade to go (he's 39) and now the rest of us in the sere and yellow of the 35s and 40s are expecting a similar draft.

In the meantime I'm on what they call in the Navy a nice number. The job we're on promises to last the rest of the week. We went out by train and bus to a village only two miles from Guildford, packed portable dynamos on the trucks at a garage there and took them to another village four miles beyond Guildford.

We've all the freedom we cannot have in camp, smoking when we want, having, in fact, a gay old time. And when we opened our packs and found that the Navy had given us only unbuttered meat sandwiches we gave them to a column of poor old infantry on the march whose sandwiches had no meat in at all, and went to a sort of lorry drivers' pull-in where we had one whale of a blow-out for 1/7 each.

2nd February 1944, Wednesday 8.00pm. Petersfield

I feel a little lonely, not sad or depressed, but strangely on my own for name after name is called for draft on the loud-speakers and one by one the men I've known since the Skegness days go off and I'm left here. Not that I'm lamenting about it, for I've had another day out in Guildford and there's another to come tomorrow.

David was preparing to leave as I left at 7.15 this morning and by this time I should think he will be home. Don't be surprised if I come back as suddenly and unexpectedly, for it can't be a lot longer now, I'm sure, before something happens. In the meantime the present job near Guildford – the garage is almost in the shadow of the unfinished Cathedral on a great hill – promises to last another day or two, releasing us from fire-watching, floor-scrubbing and all the other watch duties.

Present today on the site was a big-shot from the Admiralty, who agreed with us that sandwiches were no sort of wittle for growing lads and allowed us two bob each for our lunches. And whacking great lunches we had, too! When we arrived back tonight in time for supper one of the staff at the Divisional Office which has detailed us for the commission had bought us 200 Navy cigarettes each for 2/- as he knew that otherwise we'd have missed the issue which was made while we were out of camp. There's nice guys about wherever you go, and I'm still amongst them.

9th February 1944, Wednesday. London

I'm writing this letter in the YMCA Refreshment Room at Euston en route with a draft of 30 or 40 others to Londonderry, Ireland. Three of us, a telegraphist, a steward and myself are posted to a ship whose name I'm not permitted to disclose, but none of us knows whether it's a frigate or a minesweeper. Opinions vary and in the end it may be neither. What will happen when we reach Londonderry, and when we shall reach Londonderry, is also beyond surmise. There may be leave but I'm afraid that it's a bit doubtful. We leave in half an hour for Stranraer and cross to Larne in the morning.

On Monday I returned from Guildford to be informed in Petersfield by half-a-dozen coders that during the day my name had been called for 14 days accommodation leave. I raced back to the Camp, went to the Divisional Office and was told that I had been misinformed. I still don't understand it at all. Back I went to Guildford yesterday and back I came at 6.30. There was no mistake this time. My name had been called – for the draft. I was given 45 minutes to leave the camp with hammock and kitbag and case and respirator, missed supper and, in fact, had nothing either to eat or drink between 4 o'clock yesterday afternoon and 7 o'clock this morning. The transport broke down four miles out of camp, I missed the train from Petersfield to Portsmouth, reached the barracks at 10 o'clock and after wandering hither and thither for an hour found a table to sleep on in one of the messes. And I was so tired that I slept until 6.30 too.

11th February 1944, Friday night. Londonderry*

I'm still on land – in Londonderry Barracks waiting every minute for a call to the ship which we've now been assured is one of the new corvettes or frigates. Now I'm standing at the side of my bunk in a great dormitory missing you as I never missed you before, still feeling strange in this strange land.

Talk about a week! After I'd written to you on Euston Station on Wednesday afternoon we left – about 30 of us, drafted to various ships in Londonderry and in Belfast – at 5.40pm and reached Stanraer at 4am on Thursday. At exactly 10.45pm we were at Preston and I was so close to you. We embarked at 4.30am on a ship so packed that there was not a square inch of space anywhere. They served us breakfast of the inevitable sausage and afterwards I'd a wash and shave to freshen myself up. It was not until 8am that we left the quayside and by that time you couldn't have swung a kitten on any deck anywhere.

I went out and watched the lovely coastline fade out as the sun rose, but there was such a wind blowing and such a sea raging that I soon retired below and finding one stairway with only about a dozen soldiers, sailors and airmen squatting on it I squatted too, for the next three hours while the ship pitched and lurched and at times seemed to spin in circles. I admit that I was half-asleep all the time. Others separated themselves from their sausages and the previous night's supper at such frequent intervals that the orderlies were racing about giving succour and a few kind words to three-quarters of the passengers. My time has probably yet to come but it didn't come in that little ordeal.

We berthed at 11am, boarded a train to Londonderry and discovered it such an outpost of Empire that even allowing for the strange antics of the train which stopped at every station and often where there was no station at all, we were not at base until after 4 o'clock. If I'm given leave from here I'll have to have about a week to spend a night at home.

Still, it's a grand camp. The discipline is strict, but shore-leave is liberal, lasts every other night until 7am, assuming you've anywhere to stay until 7am, which is improbable, and the food is the best in quality and quantity I've had since I entered the Navy. And they tell me that it's nothing to the food they produce – or, rather which you produce for yourself – on board.

Last night the telegraphist, the steward and I explored the city and discovered it took about a couple of minutes for it's the sort of Irish city all Irish cities are reputed to be, grim, desolate and a bit ashamed of itself. Until I sail I'm not permitted to mention the name of the ship and so for a long time, I suppose, I'll not have a letter from you. That I think is what I miss more than anything else.

* Apart from Campbeltown at the tip of the Kintyre peninsular in Scotland, Londonderry was the closest British port to the trackless killing grounds of the North Atlantic. Londonderry had important advantages over remote Campeltown. The industrial capacity of Belfast was close by, along with a large urban labour pool. This was especially accessible because, unlike mainland Britain, Northern Ireland was not subject to conscription. In early 1942 sections of the River Foyle were deepened; berths for escorts were built on the east side of the river; and a repair workshop established. By 1943–44, Londonderry had become the eastern base for 15 American, British and Canadian escort groups, with a staff of 1,455 under the authority of a commodore.

13th February 1944, Sunday 9.30pm. Londonderry

Another day has come and gone and we're still waiting. Now before I go to bed I'm writing to you as I lean against my bunk. I'd a night out in Londonderry last night with a young coder from Caballa who put me wise to a few of the little facts of life in the wireless operator's cabin as we wandered the dark, grim streets, calling en route for one supper of sausage and chips at the YMCA and another of greater refinement but a little less plebean in a cinema cafe where we met a gang of Yanks who walked all the way back with us. I think they were a little lonelier than we were ourselves. We seem a long way from home but they are further.

16th February 1944, Wednesday 7.30pm. Londonderry

As I walked into the reading and writing room of this old manor house which has been converted into a Sailor's Rest Home, the wireless announced the opening round in the commentary on the Mills-Gilroy fight.* Early this afternoon we were called to the drafting office and told to report again tomorrow morning at nine o'clock preparatory to crossing the water yet again to Scotland where presumably the ship is berthed or is shortly expected. What will happen then we don't know or even if anything will happen at all, for after last week's sudden summons and the sort of anticlimax which followed it I'm taking nothing for granted but merely living from day to day. But, of course, this may be the action signal at last.

In the meantime, this week in Ireland has not been completely futile, for at the Signal Centre I've learned to operate a machine which I'd never seen until yesterday morning, under the tuition of a WREN officer who was a martinet and a holy terror, every four-and-half feet of her.

And on Monday, too, I learned to be a Naval Patrol Guard, being drafted to a squad which was ordered to prowl round the outskirts of a big dance in a bigger hall and to dive into the scrum and restore order whenever the jitterbugs became a little too turbulent which, alas, they often did! Well, they all say that once on board ship all that sort of nonsense will end and that at least I'll be able to be a coder and they all say, too, that after the first unfamiliarity has gone I'll love every minute of it. Which is precisely what I intend to do.

* *Freddie Mills beat Bert Gilroy in the eighth round at the London Casino.*

18th February 1944, Friday 11am. Glasgow YMCA

We're off again, this time to the remote and distant outpost of Scapa Flow (Thurso to be precise) where according to all the authorities on this draft it is always about 40 below, where there is no human habitation for miles, one cinema for the marooned personnel and one canteen and not one darned thing else. There the ship should be waiting, but not until I see it and board it shall I believe that. Next week at this time I'll be writing to you from Plymouth I shouldn't wonder!

There are 10 of us in the draft this time – we grow and grow. We left Londonderry at 4pm yesterday, reached Belfast at 7pm and sailed to Glasgow huddled in heaps below decks, our lifebelts as pillows and our greatcoats for blankets until 8.00am when at last we docked. Now I've had breakfast, washed and shaved and feel a little less like a derelict hobo than I felt an hour ago.

And now we're marooned here until 6 o'clock tonight, equipped with tickets for dinner and tea wherever we decide to have it. They estimate that we should reach Thurso, after yet another sea crossing, before tomorrow night if we're lucky. Actually I'm told it's as far from Glasgow to Thurso as from Glasgow to London. Ain't life wonderful?

SETTING SAIL

At the beginning of March 1944 Cliff joined his ship – HMS *Byron* (K508), a lease-lend Captain Class frigate. These ships measured 93.3 metres from stem to stern, with a beam of 11.3 metres. Displacing 1,740 tons, they were built in American yards for the US Navy as Buckley Class destroyer escorts. Some 78 were built for the Royal Navy, where they were classed as frigates, in part because they were not fitted with torpedo tubes – a defining characteristic of a British destroyer.

The 'Captains' were named after naval captains of Nelson's era, and were designed using contemporary mass production techniques. They had a high freeboard (the distance between the sea and the main deck) and flared bows to weather the high seas of the North Atlantic weather. This made them relatively 'dry' ships, but they were inclined to roll in a heavy sea. Although many sailors suffered greatly from sea-sickness, Cliff coped with the conditions well.

Escort vessels – destroyers, frigates, sloops and corvettes – were comfortless in bad weather. Crews were often exhausted even without encountering the enemy. When Atlantic waves came crashing over the forecastle, water levels could quickly rise to two inches on the mess decks. This became even more unpleasant if it was contaminated by fuel oil. Space was also a problem. Most escorts had been designed for a crew of about 100 but often had to accommodate more than 150. One medical officer complained that there was only 81.5 cubic feet of air per man, compared to the recommended 200. Wet weather often meant there was insufficient space to dry sodden clothing. Sailors often slept under wet blankets that sometimes froze when temperatures dropped.

In heavy weather the ship would roll so far that she seemed in serious danger of capsizing. In these conditions, simple movements became extraordinarily difficult: drinks would spill, food would slide off the plate; cutlery would fall onto the deck. Heavy objects would roll away, then roll back and bang into people. Walking a short distance would be impossible without falling over as if drunk. Perhaps the most astonishing of all was that the crews not only managed to cope with these conditions, but did so in a way that enabled them to take on and ultimately defeat the U-boats.

Captain Class frigates had a top speed of 23.6 knots, enabling them to overhaul a surfaced U-boat, which could typically make 17 knots. Captains were armed with a forward-firing anti-submarine weapon called the 'Hedgehog'. This consisted of a steel base plate from which 24 spigot rods protruded, giving the appearance of a hedgehog. Mortar projectiles, each containing 35 pounds of explosive, were fitted to the spigot rods and fired 200 yards ahead of the ship to land in a circle about 100ft in diameter. The explosive charge would only detonate if the mortar scored a direct hit on a U-boat.

Captains were also armed with depth charges, launched from the stern of the ship. As their name suggests, these were set to detonate at a pre-determined depth. Although the explosion of a depth charge had a greater psychological impact (on both escort and U-boat crews), they were less effective than hedgehog projectiles. Captain Class frigates proved highly efficient in the use of both weapon types, destroying 35 U-boats from October 1943 to the end of the war.

Captains also had three 3-inch guns, which were too light for anti-submarine work, although the frigates' formidable anti-aircraft armament – nine 20mm guns and one twin 40mm gun – made them useful on convoy routes where air attack was expected.

THE CONVOYS

A convoy system for escorting merchant vessels was introduced immediately after the sinking of the *Athenia* on the first day of the war. Merchant ships were chartered by the Ministry of War Transport which designated cargoes and destinations, while the Naval Control of Shipping officer allocated ships to various convoys at the departure port.

At sea, convoys were organised in a box formation with a 'broad front', typically comprising seven to 12 columns of ships with three or four vessels in each column. A slow convoy could make seven knots, a 'fast' convoy 10 or 12 knots, which was still slower than a surfaced U-boat, with a top speed of 17 knots or more.

Merchant ships with the most valuable cargoes – such as petrol – would often be stationed in the relative safety of the centre of the convoy. In daytime, a standard escort group of seven warships would deploy two ships 4,000 yards directly ahead of each flank, two slightly ahead and further out on the beam at 3,000 yards, two right on the beam at 4,000 yards, and one directly astern.

At night, there would be one ship ahead of the convoy and two astern. This was because U-boats could mount a surface attack under cover of darkness, using their higher surface speed to close with the convoy. To launch a daylight attack, the U-boat needed to stay submerged and its slower underwater speed of about seven knots would make even the slowest convoy difficult to catch from astern.

3rd March 1944, 12.15am. HMS *Byron* – Escorting Convoy JW57 to Bear Island

At last I can write to you. I know you must have been wondering for days and days, wondering what on earth has happened, waiting for every post and waiting in vain. I've been where I still am, out on the high seas so high that even on this middle watch, midnight to 4 o'clock in the morning, when at last the calm has come and we're sailing for base again and expect to reach it in less than 24 hours, the little office in the W/T cabin where I'm tucked away is rising and falling, rising and falling and I can write at all only by pressing one foot at full length against one wall and leaning back in my chair against the other.

How the winds have raged and the gale has howled and the waters have tossed day after day for 12 days. Up and down this little frigate has pitched, stood on her head, sat on her tail, and at times seemed to spin in circles. Yet all the time, from the day we sailed from base, I've not once been sick or felt sick. I'm assured that it's nearly a record!

The inside has behaved itself. The outside is scarred and battered, every square inch of it, from being hurled about all over the ship. I've felt my age every now and again, for apart from the fact that most of the crew have their sea-legs already while I'm fresh from the cradle, I'm one of the oldest men aboard. One result has been that decent and considerate and companionable as everybody has been from the word go (even the ship's cat, 'Boston' by name, and black and white). I felt a bit out of it until two or three nights ago when a Petty Officer from one of the other messes, 33 himself and feeling a bit out of it too, wandered into our mess, sat himself down near my bunk and began to talk. Now we've found a lot in common even to a prejudice against touring the boozers every time the ship docks, if this ship ever docks.

This is our 12th day at sea and except for a little island whose cottages were buried deep in snow drifts where we berthed for a few hours the other day we've not seen dry land. Not that I'd have seen it anyway, for it's been impossible to go out on the upper deck, too cold and too wild. All the time I've been below-decks or in this cabin and the atmosphere in both you could cut with a butter knife.

It's a strange life. You're awake when you ought to be asleep and asleep when you should be awake. Every 24 hours is divided into watches: First, 8.00pm to midnight; Middle, midnight to 4.00am; Morning, 4.00am to 8.00am; Forenoon, 8.00am to noon; Afternoon, noon to 4.00pm; First Dog, 4.00pm to 6.00pm; Last Dog, 6.00pm to 8.00pm. Tomorrow I shall have only two watches: noon to 4.00pm and 6.00pm to 8.00pm. So, you see, there's plenty of time for sleeping, talking and reading.

How glad I am that I like books! Collect, if you can, as many of those Penguins, those pocket sized editions, as you can beg, borrow or steal. I'll take them back from my first leave. There's a library of sorts on board, but it's only open when we're in harbour. The lads will read anything but there's precious little for them to read.

The work itself? Well, it's a bit complex to begin with but I'm mastering it now. Sometimes you're up to the neck in it. Sometimes, as on this watch, you can go for hours with not a stroke to do. The cost of living is negligible and it's a good job it is, too, for my total resources at the moment are an Irish 6d, which the canteen won't accept, an English 6d and four pennies. But that will go a long way with cigarettes at 4d for 20 and it will go even further now that I've tired of the American cigarettes they sell on this ship and have begun to roll my own from a packet of our own tobacco which one of the lads gave me last night. They'll share anything, give you anything. You've only to ask and often not even to ask. They're a grand lot. And all of them are in my state of bankruptcy too, for some of them haven't been paid for six weeks and all of them are praying that the Admiralty will take pity on them and give them something, if it's only ten bob, for shore leave when we dock.

I know the first question you'll ask is 'Where have we been?' and 'When will you be home?' I'm not allowed to answer the first. All I can tell you is that it's been a long way, that it has had its excitements and that one day the newspapers may publish one little chapter from it. About leave – well it may not be far off. You know what rumours, or 'buzzes' as they call them in the Navy, are but there seems good reason for the latest buzz that it may be granted to each of the two watches when we land. I'm in the second watch and would have to wait until the first returned before I could go, which is fair enough considering that three-quarters of the crew have had no leave at all for seven months. Yet if this leave comes off I should be home within the next fortnight or three weeks, but if it doesn't we'll be off to sea again almost immediately for they keep these little ships at it hard these days.

5th March 1944, Sunday. Ashore at a YMCA Londonderry

I'm on dry land again. It seems incredible that the pavements and the roads are not tilting to port and starboard and that I can walk straight. The news is not so good. I sent a censored telegram from the Fleet Mail Office five minutes after I left the ship. In it I wrote 'No Leave'. I'm afraid there is to be none – not at least for my watch, but a short one for the other. That, at least, is the latest official rumour and there seems to be an authority for it this time, although no official announcement has been made yet. Still, it means that we shall be the first next time and next time may not be so far off for these little ships are seldom out long. By the time this letter arrives you will know, apart from the telegram, that I'm back from sea again, for yesterday I wrote a letter subject to censorship, posted it on board and was assured that it would leave by the first mail.

7th March 1944, Tuesday 5.30pm. HMS *Byron*

I met Ted and Denis and for hours we talked and talked – talked such a lot that by the time we'd had tea and talked a bit more there were long queues outside all the cinemas and we decided to give the films a miss and went instead to the YMCA where we began chattering all over again. It was grand meeting them again. John, the Petty Officer, was not a bit bored by all the chatter about Caballa and the old days. As I told you, neither Ted nor Denis has yet been to sea – Ted is quartered in a new ship which has not yet completed her trials, a similar ship to ours which one day may be in our group, and Denis has not yet left barracks, and so I was able to tell them all about it as an old salt.

Neither had a lot of news about the fellows from Caballa. The whereabouts of Ken was unknown to both of them, Old Scotty was taken seriously ill at Chatham and sent to hospital. Alec is somewhere at sea. A lot of the others have gone into a foreign pool, sent to overseas bases from which presumably they will sail for the duration, or to foreign shore bases where they will remain until the end of the war. I prefer my little ship, however skittish her behaviour may be, for at least I'll have leave some time or other and not too infrequently either.

10th March 1944, Friday 5.15pm. Salvation Army Hostel

I told you about Boston, the ship's black and white cat and everybody's pet. Well, ever since we docked other cats, all colours, shapes and sizes have been wandering aboard every hour of the day and night. Now Boston spends every minute when he's not curled up on somebody's bunk fast asleep, crouched in ambush glaring at these intruders and with a lot of spitting and snarling chasing them ashore.

I've come here from the Naval Outfitters. I had a chit signed by one of the officers for a pair of underpants, a vest and a towel, but when I reached the shop I examined the pants and vest, decided they were not thick enough and came out with a pair of towels at 1/6d each. I suppose I'll have to manage with two pairs of pants and vests, but I could do with another of each.

12th March 1944, Sunday morning 8.40am

You should have seen this ship last night. Mail which has been trailing all over the map for months was delivered at last. There were 33 bags of it. Some of the letters dated from last October. There were dozens of Christmas cards. I wasn't out of it either. There were eight for me. Three were letters you'd sent to Petersfield, a fourth which reached Londonderry after I'd left and before I sailed, a fifth was dated Wednesday of this week, or rather last week.

As I had all the wash basins to myself I decided to wash my smalls, purloined two basins to myself, filled one with hot and the other with cold water, produced a new pack of Rinso which I bought in the city without coupons, and washed two pairs of socks, a pair of underpants, a vest and the last half-dozen handkerchiefs I possess. Now they're hanging on a line close to a fan and a hot water pipe where I'm writing on the ledge beneath my bunk. It will probably be my last washing day for a time, except for handkerchiefs and socks, for as soon as the other watch return tomorrow the laundry will re-open. Well, as I washed, one of the wireless operators came down from the cabin, and thrust into my jumper the 8 letters. I waited deliberately until I had undressed and climbed into my bunk. Then I lit a cigarette and read the lot one after another. Some of the other lads, they tell me, were reading theirs until 1 or 2 o'clock in the morning. One chap had 55.

In the meantime, although I'm told that I'll never do it from here, a city off the main line, I intend to take a chance and telephone you tonight. I should have had a shot at it earlier, but so many of the chaps who've been here before said it was out of the question. I'm beginning to think that we've lost Ted, that his ship has sailed, for he was missing on Friday and we waited for him in vain yesterday at the place where we've always met.

12th March 1944, Sunday 8.45pm. Londonderry YMCA

To telephone you was not half as complex as I expected it to be. I went into one of the public boxes near the GPO at 6 o'clock, put in the call, was told that it would mature at 8.22 and after we'd had tea, left the 3d film show where I'd gone with John and Denis in time to walk into the box at 8.21. Inside five minutes I was talking to you. It was as easy as that. When I returned to the cinema the doors were closed and Full Up notices in position, and as no pass-outs are issued I couldn't get in again.

13th March 1944, Monday 2.30pm

In one of your letters you ask if I shave. You bet I do. Even at sea, when the ship was on its worst behaviour, I missed only one day. I had to choose my times. Sometimes it was morning, sometimes evenings and sometimes the afternoon and every time you could take a slash at the old whiskers only between the deck's upheavals and all the time you'd to clutch one of the washbasin taps with one hand while you operated with the other, and sometimes as you swayed, your face disappeared out of the mirror altogether. That was shaving on the high – the very high – seas. And washing, with one hand feverishly gripping one tap, was a similar hazardous experience. Once, but only once, I tumbled backwards head over heels out of the bathroom and into the gangway outside. Some of the lads think I'm a bit eccentric in my insistence on a shave a day. But I don't know, I can't endure walking about with whiskers thick on my map.

Who mans the laundry and who prepares the meals? Selected men in each case. We feed on the cafeteria system all in one mess and all the food on one tray which is separated into divisions. Actually it's a sort of British Restaurant in miniature for you file past various hot plates and each course is dished into one of the divisions on the tray. You ladle your own soup out into a tin mug – if you have one. After Mother's Bakelite mug went the way of all flesh, cracking in two as I cannoned off one of the bulkheads in mid-ocean, I'd either to borrow a mug or go without soup and sometimes without tea too, for you use the same mug for both. Now in town I've bought a mug of my own. I couldn't find an enamel one anywhere – it's plain unadorned tin – but it'll do.

16th March 1944, Thursday 12.20pm

My bunk is in a corner of the Mess, a bit out of the general congestion and whenever anybody wants a quiet chat they drift into it. They call it 'Coders' Corner'. Latest visitor, who has just ambled off for the 40 winks which are a tradition of the Navy every afternoon, has just learned that I was a sports journalist in Civvy-Street and has asked if he can nominate me for the Sports Committee as representative of the communications branch. I said yes. The committee is to cater for all games from darts to football, cricket, tennis, everything. It's just up my street.

18th March 1944, Friday 5.15pm. Londonderry

For once too I've been left in peace, for half the crew are ashore and the rest are either writing or sleeping. It's amazing how sailors can sleep at any time of the day or night. John's a thundering nice guy, lives in London and as an engine room Artificer, ranks as a Petty Officer. He's not in our mess at all but we'd only been a few days at sea when he wandered in, drifted to my corner, as they all drift sooner or later, said 'How are You?' sat down and began to talk. He made a habit of it for the truth seems to be that in his mess they are, I suspect, a hard-bitten, hard-drinking lot and as he neither smokes nor drinks he was searching for a bit of companionship when we met. Since then we've been nearly inseparable. He's 33 and a darned nice unassuming chap, unmarried and, I think, unlikely ever to be married for he's just not interested.

There's Harry too, who sleeps in the bunk above me. You'd like him, he's only a kid, 17 or 18, but he reads nearly all his letters to me and I've seen photographs of his father, his mother, his girl, and everybody else in the family to the third or fourth remove. Constantly he's confiding in me.

28th March 1944, Tuesday 8.30pm. At sea

Just think of it – I shall miss your birthday, the first I've missed since we met so long ago. There will not even be a card for you, and no present at all. All I can hope is that this letter will reach you before, or preferably on, Tuesday. That I know will be a little present at least. The rest will go to you as soon as I'm on dry land again.

I think I'm a sailor now. I can walk the gangways and the decks, even when the ship is rolling and heaving and shuddering – as she is inclined to shudder and quiver and quake, by way of a little variety now and again – without zig-zagging hither and thither and cannoning on and off the corridor walls every other yard. I'll have the roll of a Popeye by the time I come home and that may be soon, even if nowadays everybody is resigned to the fact that leave seems to have become an uncertain quantity. I admit that the first day out this time, when the ship was lifting up and down, up and down, hour after hour, I went a bit dizzy now and again, but nothing else happened and in the case of three-quarters of the crew a whole lot happened – and not always in privacy or in the buckets either!

Since then, however, it's been as different from the first time as it could be. Day after day the sea has been calm and placid and afternoon after afternoon, whenever I've been off watch, I've been out on the upper deck, sprawling in the sunshine, my back against the warm wall of one of the boiler rooms. Every time, whenever he has been off too, John has been with me and we've talked and read and yesterday afternoon, inevitably, I went to sleep. All that was missing were a few stewards, a deck-chair or two, and a pot of tea – yes, and something to eat too. For whether it is that we ate such a lot when we were ashore and cultivated the appetites of a pack of wolves or whether something has gone wrong with the works, it's a fact that although the food is as good as ever – we had a couple of boiled eggs each this morning for breakfast – there seems a lot less of it and this time, too, the bread supply has come so nearly to an end that for days we've been rationed to a slice – just one slice – each for breakfast and tea and there have been times when there's been no bread at all and we've had to chew and champ at ship's biscuits, a peculiar product which I'm sure young Judy* would never condescend even to sniff at.

* *Cliff's dog*

2nd April 1944, Sunday 4.00pm. Sheerness

Golly, what an afternoon! I was asleep in my bunk after the middle watch, the ship had docked and an hour later I was awakened. Young Harry had sent a messenger with the news that we might be allowed ashore and that six bags of mail had come aboard. I moved fast after that! For the first week this time out I wore overalls which the laundry had cleaned for me, but in the end I felt so darned untidy and dishevelled in them that for the second week I became respectable again in a jersey and my No. 3 trousers which by now are about No. 7 or 8 I'm afraid. Well, inside 15 minutes I was in all the glory of my No.1s waiting for an announcement on the broadcast and as I waited the mailbags were emptied, and one by one letters for me came down to the mess deck until I was the envy of every guy on the premises. Twelve of them there were when I made the last count and eight of them were from you.

3rd April 1944, Monday 1.30pm

Wasn't it wonderful to be talking to each other again? I'm still not allowed to tell you where we've docked but I can tell you that I made the call from a kiosk on a deserted promenade from which our ship was visible. These nine minutes went too fast. And they were worth every penny of the 5/- at 1/8 every three minutes which they will cost. As usual the ship is buzzing with rumours. We're going for a refit and there's to be 17 days leave for each watch. We're off to sea tonight and there'll be leave for nobody. We'll be here for days and nothing whatever will happen. I take everything with a whole cellar of salt now. Leave there will be some day but when and for how long I don't know – nor, if they're being truthful does anybody else.

P.S. The little black dog has disappeared. I think he's been given to another ship. At least it will be a home for him.

4th April 1944, Your Birthday 1.15pm. Sheerness

Many happy returns of the day. Did my telegram arrive? It seemed a pitiful little present but you know it was sent with all my love. All day I've been thinking of you. May you have as happy a day as either of us can have when we're away from each other. The celebration, in any case, may only be delayed, for today's news – and there is NO news this time – is that leave may not be as distant as all that.

I went out last night on the first Liberty Boat. I did not leave the ship until 6.00pm and the result was that nearly all the shops were closed and the few which had remained open either had no birthday cards at all or such an ungodly collection that there wasn't one among them I would have sent you. Even the Post Office was closing by the time I reached it, but I persuaded one of the girl clerks to accept the telegram (greetings telegrams are no longer being dispatched) and was assured by her that it would not be delivered until today.

P.S. The little black dog has reappeared. They'll be adopting him officially on this ship yet. I hope they do. He's still thin as a rake but his ears are almost cured and he's more affectionate than ever.

7th April 1944, Good Friday 12 noon. At sea off Southend-on-Sea

Yes, we're at sea again, that's why the letters ceased abruptly early in the week. But we shall not be away long this time for according to my information it's only on an exercise that we have gone and it should last only a day or two and, in fact, may end today. This is the strangest Good Friday I've ever known, there have been no hot cross buns, no Easter eggs, no nothing at all. But there have been oranges this week. Twice this week we've been given one each at dinner and my pal, the canteen manager, sold me a pound for 1/ld two days ago.

P.S. One of the stokers has adopted Blackie, the little stowaway dog. I felt the dickens of a weight on my feet early one morning and discovered the bad 'un curled up fast asleep at the foot of my bunk. Now whenever we meet he gives me a little flick of the tail and often he comes and sits near me in my corner. But now he's one master and one only and he seems to know it. He's even plaited a collar for him out of a bit of old rope. Tough guys, these stokers, but they've good hearts.

9th April 1944, Sunday 4.45pm. Sheerness

Tommy Handley's ITMA* is on the wireless as I write. He's the only man who can empty my little corner and make the entire mess-deck congregate in the other room where the speaker is installed. I can hear from here. That's sufficient for me, and while I'm alone I can write to you in peace and that's preferable even to ITMA (A little quote from ITMA: 'Are you Tommy Handley?' 'Well if I'm not I washed somebody else's face this morning.'). That made them hoot with glee. And I can tell you that is a bit of an achievement today, for everybody has had an attack of the miseries since the official announcement was made shortly before noon that prospects of immediate leave were so remote as to be almost out of the question.

* It's That Man Again

10th April 1944, Easter Monday, 1.45pm

John has come up with about a half dozen lengths of wood. We'd been talking only a few minutes earlier about packing all the chocolate I've accumulated for you and sending it off by registered post. There are between 25 and 30 bars and at present they're in a cardboard box in my locker. We decided that from somewhere or other we should have to unearth a wooden box to protect them in the post. Now John has scrounged the wood already and after taking measurements has gone off to the machine shop to make the box. And now I must go and join him I think, for although I'll be no great help, at least I'll seem willing.

13th April 1944, Thursday 6.30am. Harwich

It was a smashing day yesterday. Shortly after we'd anchored leave was announced from 4.30. Then a few minutes later, just as I was beginning the afternoon watch, the broadcast revised the time to 1.15. 'Off you go' said the Chief. And off I went with Tom Chatt, the young telegraphist. We were ashore for over 8 hours, went a lovely walk into the country in the afternoon – I never realised how beautiful trees can look until you go for two weeks without seeing one.

14th April 1944, Friday

Here I am again. I've just lifted my bunk on its chains so that I can sit on the ledge beneath it to write to you. For the last hour and a half, from 1.00pm to 2.30pm, after a dinner of roast pork and the usual etceteras I climbed into this bunk of mine, and was it good to climb in it too after those two midnight to 4 am and 8am to noon watches? Those two in sequence always leave you a bit limp. Now I'm off until 8 o'clock tonight and my only commission until that time, not counting tea and supper, has been assigned to me by seven of the lads who've asked me to repeat at the canteen the order which we gave last night for a 7/3d slab of fruit cake. They only sell it in these huge chunks and we have to cut it into seven great slices, each weighing about a pound. But it's such good cake that we don't mind.

16th April 1944, Sunday 2pm

Now what went wrong with Blackpool yesterday? Somebody made a muddle of the wireless and it was not until the lads came aboard this morning after all night leave that I read the result in the Sunday papers. And after Jock had scored in the first minute too. I'm afraid the odds will be against them next weekend at Manchester* for I see that Jock is to lead Scotland in the big international and Stanley Matthews is almost certain to be selected for England. And I was thinking only yesterday that if this rumoured leave should come off I might see the old team in the Final.

And now there's yet another dog and a cat too, on board. Where the cat, a grey Persian who has installed herself in the wardroom, came from nobody knows. The general theory is that she's been aboard for days and has come out into the open only when she decided that there was not sufficient food below decks. The dog, a little black and white puppy, with a bit of Pomeranian in him and a bit of terrier and a little bit of several other breeds was sold to one of the stewards for 10/- yesterday while he was on leave and while, I suspect, he was in a state of mind induced by strong liquor, which is indifferent to the value of money. I suppose sometime or other the skipper will come down like a load of bricks and order this menagerie to be reduced in size. In the meantime poor old Boston must be seriously contemplating suicide.

* *Jock Dodds scored both goals in 2–2 draw with Manchester City. They met in Manchester again the following week and despite Cliff's reservations won 2–1. Dodds played for Blackpool FC for six years and scored over 200 goals. He is included in the club's Hall of Fame at Bloomfield Road.*

17th April 1944, Monday 2.30pm

Just out of my bunk after nearly two hours in it. I needed them again, too, for the day began for me with the middle watch at midnight, continued until 4am and gave me yet another watch from 8am to noon. You feel like sleep after that little lot.

As I write young Harry, who while I slept went to the canteen for another 7lb slab of cake and, so he tells me, lifted my bunk while I still slept in it with the aid of another guy in order to deposit the cake in his locker – young Harry sits beside me now reading Philip Gibbs *The Street of Adventure* which I lent him in exchange for his library copy of *If Winter Comes* which I'm still enjoying, overwritten in parts and a little complex in its construction as it may be. Harry is one of those folk who once he begins a book has to be nearly forcibly prised away from it. He says he'll finish it before he goes on watch for the first dog at 4 o'clock. And he probably will.

He's promised himself a bath this afternoon and Harry's a lad for his baths. So am I. So I think is everybody else, for aboard you always seem to be a little grimy and gritty. Not that a bath itself is such a great joy because it isn't. You go into a narrow sort of alley which has three curtained cubicles on each side of it. In one hand you have a bucket and in the other your soap and towel. Each cubicle has a cold steel floor which is invariably under an inch or two of swirling water. You fill the bucket at a tap – there's at least plenty of hot water – and then, in a state of nature, while a little leak from one of the showers, which are out of commission while we're at sea, dribbles on your head, you scrub yourself with your flannel if you have one. And if you haven't, and in any case unless you have uncommonly long arms, you've always to invite your companion in the next berth to swab your back for you.

There's no other news of the ship's Noah's Ark. The little black and white pup which looks like nothing as much as a baby panda, is beginning to find his sea legs and to amble at his master's heels. And last night, if you please, young Blackie was actually waiting at my bunk when I came down from the watch and wanted to crawl into it with me. Earlier in the evening, while Parliament was sitting again in Coders' Corner, she'd crouched on my locker, curled herself into a ball and gone to sleep. But I simply couldn't have her in my bunk, for in spite of several baths and generous applications of disinfectant, she still smells a bit of the Irish port she came from – and that's not a nice smell at all.

18th April 1944, Tuesday 5pm

The canteen manager has decided that in future he will not limit the sale of this cake to gigantic 7/- slabs, but will sell it in 6d and 1/- slices. We've just shared – three of us, Harry, another signaller and myself – a 1/- slice. Very nice too. Now I'll be able to last through the two hours of the last dog until 8 o'clock dinner.

Not such good news today about young Blackie. The stoker who's adopted him told me this morning that he'd refused to eat yesterday and was definitely ill. I think he is a bit under the weather too. Yet when he ran me to earth in the cafeteria at dinner-time he seemed as glad as ever to say How d'ye do, and gobbled with considerable relish the slices of old horse I cut off my plate for him. I suppose he's certain to have his ups and downs. What he requires, I suppose, is expert treatment, but where or how he'll get it I don't know while this ship keeps on sailing and sailing.

19th April 1944, Wednesday 5pm

News is scarce again. It's inevitable, I suppose, when one day succeeds another in an unchanging procession. Out on the upper deck this afternoon, squatting in the sunshine, a couple of us – one of the new telegraphists and myself – couldn't decide whether today was Tuesday or Wednesday. You can tell from that how one day is a nearly exact duplicate of another.

27th April 1944, after leave, Thursday 10pm. Sheerness

It's just 24 hours ago, almost to the minute, that my train left St. Annes and from the window I saw our lovely home in the distance. It seems such a lot longer for I confess that until I reached Sheerness and met John outside the station – I must have missed him when he met the train at Chatham – I felt lonelier, I think, than I've ever felt since that day when I went on my own to Skegness.

The new cup went down to breakfast for the first time this morning and the first of the vitamin pills as soon as I'd finished breakfast and now at last I'm back in the old routine again. Dockies are all over the ship, hammering and drilling – two of them have just appeared to reinforce a cabinet whose foundations were nearly torn out on the Russian run – often, at that time, it swayed every minute out of the perpendicular and threatened every minute, too, to tumble on to our bunks. They've even taken possession of the heads. How long we'll be here I don't know but it won't be long. But while we are here we intend to make the best of every minute. We may be out tonight and if we are – well, I know where there's a telephone box.

I forgot to tell you that waiting for me with the letters was a parcel from the Parish Council Comforts Fund containing a pair of grey socks – I think I'll keep those for the day when I come home to stay home for they're really posh and nobody will ever see them while I'm wearing bell-bottoms and, in addition to the socks, a writing pad, shaving soap, toilet soap and toothpaste. Isn't it kind of them? I'll write to say Thank You today.

28th April 1944, Friday 11.15am. Sheerness

I've just finished the last of the book corrections required before we sail and half a dozen of us have ended the session with cups of coffee out of one of the bottles you packed for me. We had a grand evening yesterday. We left the ship, John, Alan, the young radio mechanic, and I; Harry had gone on special leave to Sevenoaks to meet his brother. We went ashore at 4.45 and after sandwiches and tea at the Navy canteen close to the docks and after booking beds for the night and immediately before I'd telephoned home and been told there was no reply, we took the train to Sittingbourne, a little market town about 10 miles from the coast. This gave us such an appetite that immediately we arrived we walked into an Odeon cafe and I had sardines on toast, a plate of bread and butter and a pot of tea. Afterwards in the hot sunshine we walked two or three miles out of the town down little rutted country tracks, past apple orchards whose trees were a mass of snow-white blossom and at the end of an hour sprawled down in the grass near one of these orchards and admired a view as lovely as any I've seen since our days in the Lakes. It's a flat countryside is Kent, but everywhere there are fruit orchards and the blossoming trees, patches of woodlands, windmills and oast houses, and everywhere too there is peace and silence. It was lovely.

3rd May 1944, Wednesday 12.15pm. Sheerness

You would have laughed if you could have seen me in the box last night. It was one of those automatic dials and the instructions were missing. I dialled 62, which is the customary number for calling the exchange with, and without 2d in the box. Nothing happened. Then in the flame of my lighter I noticed a panel which said 'Dial 0 but only in emergency'. I pondered, asked myself 'Shall I chance it or shan't I?' At last I decided that drastic measures were required if I wasn't to go to bed again without talking to you. So I dialled 0 – and expected any second either to hear the air-raid sirens to go or a fire brigade and a couple of ambulances dashing down the street. Instead the voice of the operator came on the line asking unconcernedly 'Number please?' and within less than three minutes you had answered.

P.S. Our chocolate ration has been reduced to three bars a week. I've scoffed only one since I came back from leave and had saved five for you. I'd like to let Harry have them to send to his kid brother who's only ten and has been taken seriously ill and sent to hospital for six month's treatment. I think it's a sort of epilepsy and is fairly serious.

6th May 1944, Saturday 2.30pm

I'm waiting for the broadcast of the Final at 4 o'clock and for tea at 3.30 assuming that I shall be able to eat any after 4d worth of biscuits. I seem to think I shall. Often I've been thinking this week of the day, exactly a year ago, when I went to the Final at Sheffield and Blackpool beat the Wednesday 2–1.

I'm cupless and mugless again. This morning after breakfast the ship lurched and I lurched with it and the cup fell to the deck – and it'll never be the same again. I'll buy another all the same next time I go ashore. Tea tastes such a lot nicer out of a cup than a mug.

Well I'm blowed. I've just seen a copy of the *Radio Times*. They're not broadcasting the Final after all. They've chosen England v Wales instead.

7th May 1944, Sunday 12.30pm

Poor old Blackpool.* Well somebody had to lose I suppose. But, at least, they made a great fight of it. I had to wait to hear the result until 7 o'clock. Then at 9.15 I heard a commentary – recorded extracts, by Tom Cragg who had such a bad cold that before he'd finished he had a raven's croak. So to bed I went, consoled by a cup of Camp coffee, was awakened at 2am to go to the W/T office to decode an important message, (Jock and I take turns for these emergency calls) crawled back into my bunk an hour afterwards and slept like a log until 7am And I was not a bit tired either.

Blackpool lost to Aston Villa in the Final of the League Cup Northern section over two legs, home on 29 April winning 2–1, away on 6 May losing 2–4.

8th May 1944, Monday 1.40pm. Sheerness

We'd a lovely night ashore. We intended to go to the pictures but as we walked to the cinema I decided to go to church instead. One of the new telegraphists who was with us said he'd prefer to go too. So we left Tom at the cinema, walked to the promenade, sat in the sunshine for nearly an hour and when the telegraphist confessed almost timidly that he couldn't go to the Church of England as he was a Methodist I said, 'That's all right with me. Find a Methodist Church and I'll come with you.' He found a little chapel, so small that even with a congregation of fewer than 20 it didn't seem too empty, although I admit that it was a little embarrassing when before the service opened a charming old joker walked the width of the building across to us and in a voice which sounded as deep and resonant as the last trumpet thundered 'Good evening, brother', and shook me by the hand. Well as he was about 80 I couldn't call him brother and certainly I couldn't call him 'Old Cock' now could I? So I said 'Good evening sir' and honestly, without any fooling, I've never been made more welcome anywhere, and the service itself, conducted by the local preacher, was so simple and so unashamedly sincere.

The latest craze, superseding the biscuits, which we consider too expensive, is tins of Chivers sweetened plums. They're 1/9 a tin and lovely. I've just had a half-mug of them – that's how we serve them – and are they good? I must bring a few tins home for you the next time I come on leave.

9th May 1944, Tuesday 3.10pm. Sheerness

Now the summer orders are out. From today we're no longer permitted to wear jerseys ashore. We have to go into our little white fronts. Won't we look cute?

13th May 1944, Saturday 2.30pm. Sheerness

Last night was, I think, the best evening I've ever had ashore. I went with Alan, the radio mechanic, on such a walk as you'd have loved. We were three hours on the road, down little narrow country lanes, skirting apple blossom orchards which were a mass of flowers and thatched cottages and hop gardens and, climbing gradually all the time, reached at last the top of a hill which commanded a great panoramic sweep of woods and fields, orchards and oast houses. It was so quiet, so lovely, the only noise a constant distant drone as planes passed over in packed formations to the coast of France and returned again, their formation a little broken and always with one or two trailing after the main group, all on their own. There were baby lambs in all the fields bucking and tumbling and butting at their shaggy and harassed mothers, and comic geese gabbling at each other on the borders of every pond and out of nearly every cottage a dog of some sort or another came excitedly out to meet us. One of them padded after us for a couple of miles until at the borders of the town we had to send him back. You should have seen the old chap slink dejectedly down the road, come to a halt every few yards and glance reproachfully back at us. One whisper and he'd have come galloping back after us. The sea and the ship seemed miles away, on another planet.

14th May 1944, Sunday 5pm. Sheerness

Those shirts you packed for me, and the golf jacket too are causing no end of comment. Why, when I went into the wardroom with a message for the Signals Officer early in the afternoon watch today the navigation officer sat up, and said 'That's a nice line in sport's shirts you're wearing, Greenwood'. 'Thank you, Sir' said I, suitably docile and polite. 'Yes it is' said the engineering officer. By this time the entire table was reviewing the ensemble. I nearly pretended to be a mannequin and said 'Thirty-theven-and-three' but it was probably wiser to be discreet and so I said nothing except to inform the assembly that there was a time in distant days when I played golf in the jacket and that the jacket was of infinitely superior quality to the golf. All of which reminded one of the other officers that I must certainly accept nomination on the ship's sports committee. The result is that now my name's on the nomination list and it seems to be taken for granted that I'll be the representative of the communications branch.

15th May 1944, Monday 11.15am. At sea to Weymouth

I'm just munching a slice of my birthday cake. There's only one slice left now. It's so quiet in my corner this morning for everybody's either on watch or asleep and I'll confess that after the morning watch and a fish-cake breakfast I climbed wearily into my bunk at 8.30 and remained in it until a few minutes ago. And at 5 o'clock I was so tired and there was so little to do that I crept silently out of the W/T office with a bucket and had a bath. That freshened me up a lot for the remainder of the watch and this time, too, I didn't fall down the stairs and make a thundering clatter even if the ship was rolling and heaving no end. Now we're nearly in port again and this afternoon or early this evening I expect to be at a football match, stokers versus seamen, searching for talent from which a ship's XI can be selected to challenge the other ships in port. Yes. I'm on the committee and last night at the first meeting in one of the officer's cabins I was deputed with two others to go ashore and watch these inter-mess matches whenever they were played and from them to find a representative team. Crikey, all I need now is a watch chain and a cigar and I'll be a football director. I never dreamed I'd sink so low.

17th May 1944, Wednesday, 3.00pm

I continue in my new incarnation as a Sports Director. Off we went last night – and wasn't it cold and bleak too – to play another ship. The motor boat was specially piped for the team and its one director. Nearly a mile we had to walk to a sports centre which contains tennis courts, a cricket field and two football pitches – and a hell of a lot of mud. It was not such a hot team that we were able to field. As I told you the stokers had played the seamen the previous night and had played with such ferocity that a couple of men have been left behind in hospital with torn ligaments. The rest of the seamen were so battered and scarred that few of them were fit last night and as the communications team is still an unknown quantity it was, by a process of elimination, nearly an all-stokers XI which had to be fielded.

Well, off they went like the charge of the Light Brigade, breathing flame and fury and they made quite a game of it, a good game too, but the other guys had the class, slowly wore them down and in the end won 4–1. Except for one officer and a couple of ratings from the winning ship I was the only spectator. Yet I served my purpose, for the referee arrived without a watch and as I was not lending him mine I arranged to signal to him when the end of each half approached, lifting three fingers when there were three minutes to go and two when there were a couple and so on. And all the time I was leaping in and out of a ditch, retrieving the ball when it went out of play, which was pretty often. How has the mighty Spectator fallen.*

* Spectator was Cliff's pen name at the Gazette.

19th May 1944, Friday 6.30pm

And do you know where I've been today and in the afternoon too? To a football match.* The old ship issued another challenge as soon as it reached a new port – some guys can take punishment. The challenge was accepted and this afternoon the team and its vast and loyal public – me and half a dozen others including Harry and John who were dragooned into it by this honorary director – were given 2 hours leave to go and settle the argument. We called at a Canteen en route and on the way back too, and arrived at a field which was lovely against a background of thick woods. In the grass – real green grass – we sprawled and the sun shone and everything was perfect. And it remained perfect too, for the ship scored three times in the first 15 minutes and led 4–0 at half time. It was in the bag. But then the sun disappeared, a wind rose, rain began to fall and, against the wind and rain – what a lulu of an alibi – the team split into its component parts and actually lost 7–4. Sensation!

Percy Noble recalls a level of gamesmanship that would be recognised in today's game: 'We played football against Conn with me in goal. We protested about Conn having a professional footballer in their team as we considered this unsporting. He was recognised by one of the three professionals we had on our side.'

21st May 1944, Sunday 6.30pm. Just before supper

We were paid shortly before we went ashore and as a letter from Mamie* which came with your two letters contained a 10/- note, I was able to have a real blow-out. And I needed one too, I can tell you for I left the ship without having had dinner. That minor catastrophe happened because a report of my accomplishments as a shorthand typist had apparently reached the wardroom where, summoned to the presence of the first lieutenant, I was asked to take a verbatim note of an inquiry which had been ordered into a bit of a scandal. 'Going ashore?' asked the first 'loot! 'Well sir' says I, 'I was, but if you require me…' Always polite this O/Coder. Why not? They treat me fairly enough. Well, to make a long story a bit shorter I arrayed myself in all my glory, equipped myself with a couple of pencils and waited, and waited. Then just as they were piping the liberty boat for shore a messenger came from the wardroom, dispatched from the first lieutenant, with the news that I could go on shore leave. That was nice of him for it had been only a minute or two earlier that the inquiry had been called off. The fact remained that I missed the boat and yet I was not on my own for both Harry and John had insisted that they wouldn't go until I was free and in the end I was ready and they weren't. Still, there was a second boat 15 minutes later and so off we went and within 15 minutes I was tucking into roast beef and jam roll. Then we wandered about the town, had a great pile of toast with jam, went to see Bob Hope and Bing Crosby in *The Road to Zanzibar*.

Cliff's sister

23rd May 1944, Tuesday 3.10pm

I've only just made my bed. And it's 3 o'clock in the afternoon. The truth is that for once this morning after being on the middle watch from midnight to 4am, I stayed in bed a few minutes longer than usual – actually until 7.15 – and as I was on watch again at 8 o'clock I hadn't half to race around to wash, shave and have my breakfast of bacon and egg all in three quarters of an hour. Then, after dinner I was still so weary that I simply climbed into my bunk again and have been in ever since. Now the blanket is precisely folded again, the green waterproof cover is neatly laid over it – the cover is a great sheet which passes under the blanket and has tapes on it to knot over the blanket and is presumably designed so that the occupant of a bunk can strap himself in and never in the roughest weather fall out on the deck – I've never fastened these knots yet but then I'm in the lowest berth and haven't far to fall.

P.S. That Nescafe is the goods. Tom, one of the telegraphists, and I have had a cup each out of the tin every night for nearly a fortnight and now and again Harry has come down for one from his cold vigil on the bridge. Yet there's still half the tin left.

31st May 1944, Wednesday 11.15pm

Here I am again, tucked away in the office after an exercise. I had a lovely evening ashore last night. This time John and I had our own way. Tom, the telegraphist, and Alan the radio mechanic, came with us. We found a new canteen – easy chairs, a help-yourself counter piled with home-made cakes and tarts and sandwiches, a big edition of the Church canteen at Lowton, and we shall certainly soon be there again and there, after a plate or two and a cup or two, we delivered our ultimatum. 'No pictures tonight' we said. 'We're going for a walk'. Tom went to the cinema. We headed straight for the open country – and lovely it was. We had a quarter of an hour in an old church built in the 14th century – it was so cool and quiet, and we walked probably a couple of miles until down a side-track we found a grass bank, faraway from everywhere and there we sprawled in the sunshine and talked and eventually for a few minutes slept. The scent of May blossom and honey-suckle was everywhere.

1st June 1944, Thursday 2.20pm

Just out of my bunk and after being on watch for 12 hours out of the last 18 – 4pm to 8pm yesterday and midnight to 4am, and 8am to midday today – I definitely needed the hour and a half I've had in it. All the others are still chasing the pigs home, some of them at least. The rest are out to the wide world. In the meantime watch succeeds watch again and I seem to spend every hour either in my bunk or in the office, although I'd a bit of a change this morning when the leading telegraphist asked me to type a few sheets of official memoranda for him and I went in the Ship's Office, and rattled away for half an hour in the intervals of chatting with the correspondence officer, the young fellow who was on the *Daily Herald* with Rodney Holt in Manchester. Of course we talked shop as newspaper men always talk it when they are together. I told him a few of my scoops and he told me about a few of his. Often he came to Blackpool in the old days and wrote his stories over a cup or two of coffee in the Savoy. As we talked we both agreed that those seemed good times in retrospect. We both said we'd go back to newspapers when this is all over but for myself, as I said to him, 'going back' to me means not primarily a reporter's room or a sub-editor's desk but to a lovely home and quiet days in the garden and a wee pup to take a walk.

In the meantime my appointment as secretary to the canteen committee has been confirmed and from now on it seems I'm free to go to the ship's office to hammer out all the agendas and minutes as often as I like. That'll suit me too. I still love to smack at the old keys and besides it's good to keep in practice.

3rd June 1944, Saturday 2.40pm. Harwich

Young George has just come up with a white front he washed an hour ago and asked if it's fit to wear. I'm the sort of father of the family. It's as dry as a board except on one shoulder. So I've sent him back to the drying room with it and told him to leave it in front of the fans for another hour. He's gone off meek as a lamb. They think that at 41 I know such a lot, and all I know is what you've taught me.

4th June 1944, Sunday 8.40pm. Harwich

I must tell you about the communion service in the wardroom. Only 10 of us were present and yet the wardroom is so small that nobody could kneel on the deck. The table was the altar. The wine was in the tiniest chalice, the bread on a silver plate, which was a plate in miniature, chased and inscribed. It was a beautiful service, so simple, about as unpretentious as I think the first communion must have been. Then the divisions in the mid-morning followed. This was all pomp and circumstance, impressive I suppose and yet not what I like. I remember it chiefly, I'm afraid, in spite of a thunderingly good five minute sermon by a young and manifestly sincere chaplain, for a little comedy which preceded it. From somewhere or other a harmonium was unearthed for the service. It was a peculiar dwarf of an instrument. It made noises, but that's about all. But the joke was that as nobody knew anybody on board who could play a harmonium it was decided to send out an SOS on the ship's broadcast. Unfortunately the quartermaster announced 'Will any rating who can play the HARMONICA report to the ship's office'. You should have seen the queue of mouth-organists filing to the office a few minutes later!

6th June 1944, Tuesday 12 noon. D Day*

I know you'll be asking yourself 'Where is he?' and 'What's happening?' All I can tell you is that I'm fine and that there is nothing whatever for you to worry about. All morning we've been listening to the loudspeakers. They've been recording history and making everybody mighty excited but that's all we know about it yet. I only wish this letter had wings and that it could reach you in a minute or two instead of a day or two and end your suspense. This letter is being posted for me by one of the lads, for we've all been given night leave, although this time I can't go ashore and shall probably spend an hour or two on the bridge with Harry.

The day's come – and we're not in it yet. We'd have been so proud if we had been – on this first day. Instead we've had to listen to the wireless, every bulletin since 8 o'clock this morning. It seems somehow such an anti-climax. We wanted to be there when it began at least and I can tell you that when we found today we'd been left behind, I don't think there was a man on board who wasn't a little bitter about it without being or pretending to be one little bit heroic. Still, there it is, and for your sake I'm not sorry although all of us realise now that for a day or two, until our letters arrive, you'll all have the suspense which you'd have had to endure if we actually had been there. Our one consolation was given us in the office this morning when our chief told us 'Somebody has to be in the second line some time or other. Now don't be such darned ninnies' – or words to that effect! I think that did us a bit of good.

Anyway, to cheer a few of them up, all night leave was given for one watch for the first time in a week or two. I wasn't in it but it's been nearly a holiday all the same for nearly all afternoon, muffled in a great duffle coat, I've been up on the bridge with Harry and now tonight I'm in the office, with a big supper and two cups of tea inside me, with the only other three men on the staff left aboard, plus John tinkering with one of the sets and enjoying himself no end. Soon, too, we'll be making some more tea and I'll take a cup up to the lonely and forsaken Harry – and then we'll listen to the King – and then, I suppose, 6th June 1944, the day which will be in all the history books, will be over.

* *The countryside around Harwich became quickly choked with troops and their equipment; the River Orwell was filled with landing craft; there were fighter and bomber sweeps overhead; leave was cancelled. On Sunday 4 June,* Byron *prepared for sea – and was stood down. The sense of disappointment was felt by many members of the ship's company, but expressed in contrasting tones. Dick Smith said: 'I was in the Plot with the skipper having a look at the echo sounder when the news came that the invasion had started – without us. He threw his cap on the deck and kicked it into a corner.'*

For Stan Briggs, an evening out turned flat: 'On the evening of D-Day I was having a pint in a pub in Harwich – which didn't seem right somehow.'

7th June 1944, Wednesday 2pm

There was to have been a service of intercession for the men in the Second Front adventure at 2 o'clock this afternoon but either there were too few volunteers – I gave my name to the coxswain – or for some other reason it must have been cancelled for no motor boat has been ordered out. We'll have to be content with our own little private prayers. Mine are not for the men of the Second Front alone but for those who wait, for you sweetheart, who must, I know, be in suspense every hour. Be brave, darling. It can't be long before we're able to send letters again.

In the meantime we're still out of it but now I at least have been able to find some sense of proportion, to realise that not everybody can be in it, that we're waiting if we're required, that even if we'd be proud to be called there's no sense to reproach ourselves if instead we have to wait. And we know all about it or, at least, we think we do for the lads who went ashore for the night returned today with all this morning's papers and I spent nearly a couple of hours devouring them. *The Express* – wasn't that a grand editorial in the opinion column – *The Mail, The Herald* and *The News Chronicle* – I read the lot. Gosh, wouldn't I have given something to have been one of their reporters.

14th June 1944, Wednesday 12.30pm

The days pass, one so like another that you've to consult a calendar to find out what day of the week it is. They've just piped 'Leave will be piped later'. That means that some time today we'll be on dry land again. Harry has just come scuttling down from the bridge. 'Coming out?' he's asked. You bet I am.

15th June 1944, Thursday 10.30am

Harry and John were waiting for me after I'd had my nap and gone out after them. And what do you think they'd been doing? They'd hired bicycles for the afternoon and been out into the country for a couple of hours. The charge is 6d from noon to 9pm for service personnel for each cycle, it's a hire system exclusively for us. Now, of course, they'll never be happy until I've gone out for a ride. Well, I'll require no persuasion. Off we'll go the next time we and the sun are out simultaneously in the afternoon. The country in these parts is at its loveliest now and there are few hills to toil up. We have it all planned – out to a little village which we'll find somewhere or other and tea in a little cottage which we'll also find somewhere or other. Last night we were content with one of the conventional sort of leaves and yet it was of the best I've had for a long time for apart from a grand supper of spam fritters – sliced fried spam in pancakes, served with fried potatoes and bread and butter – we found an obscure little cinema in a back street which was showing a re-issue of *Goodbye Mr. Chips* which I'd never seen. It was one of the best films I've ever seen, the best I've seen since I came into the Navy and by this time I've become a bit of a 'connoisseur'.

18th June 1944, Sunday 12.30pm

Another letter from you yesterday afternoon just before we went out again for yet another supper but this time I took pity on my old tum and refused to feed it liver and beans at 10 o'clock at night and instead was content with a few sandwiches and yet another visit to the pictures this time to see *In Old Oklahoma*, a western on the big scale. In the programme, too, was a grand long newsreel of the invasion, the Paramount version. Yet, do you know, I felt almost guilty as I watched it. I don't know why, I'm no hero and I've never pretended to be and all the time I never wanted to be given leave more frequently than ever before. All those grand guys are in the thick of it. I know that everybody can't be in it and I know, too, that we've to do what we're told and ask no questions and that we were not idle while they were preparing Act One – and yet, I don't know, it seems wrong somehow. Still, there it is.

25th June 1944, after leave Sunday 5pm

Everything went according to plan yesterday. After I'd written to you I munched my sandwiches and read my book and dozed and read and read and dozed. We reached London at 6.30 and, remembering my promise* I had only a couple of sandwiches and a cup of tea at the YMCA before diving underground and taking the tube to Victoria, where I'd only a short time before the train to the coast left.

There was a bit of excitement even during that short time but it amounted to nothing at all, and by 9.30 I was walking – and what a walk it was in the heat, a couple of miles and nearly all up-hill – to the docks. I was back on the old mess-deck again by 10.30 and until midnight, as he can't open his locker once I'm in my bunk and all his bedding was locked in it, I waited for Harry and as I waited I emptied my bag, and had a big slice of cake and put everything in my locker in order. By midnight I gave Harry up, went to bed and dreamed of visiting him in the cells as a deserter. Then at 2 o'clock I wakened, peered up into my bunk and saw him sleeping quietly and unconsciously beneath his overcoat. His train had been an hour late, the RTO had signed his pass confirming the fact and he'd come aboard at 1 o'clock and been immediately excused. Now what'll happen to the stokers who've only just calmly walked in I don't know, but it will probably be something a little grim. Harry had preferred to tuck himself under his overcoat than to wake me up, which is just like him, and there he spent the night.

Reference to a promise not to hang around in London during the V1 raids.

26th June 1944, Monday 3pm

This morning big fat leather cushions were issued to put on the steel lockers in each mess-deck. Our ration was 10 and for our corner, considering that nearly everybody comes and sits here at some time or other, Harry and I appropriated three. They're lovely and warm, I can tell you and soft too, after those cold hard lockers.

30th June 1944, Friday 2.45pm

I'm out on the upper deck, sitting on my cushion, leaning back against a big steel chest, gazing out across a wide estuary at a line of towering trees on the other bank. It's dull today but there's no wind, except from the ventilator shafts, and after a morning in the office correcting books and an hour in my bunk down below it's so cool and fresh out in the air. This is where I spent most of yesterday afternoon, after all the lads had gone, reading my book in the sunshine so hot that in the end, after tea, retired below and had my biggest wash-day since I joined the Navy.

Afterwards I read a bit more of the book and for nearly an hour had a chat with one or two of the young chaps who'd been left behind. Some of these fellows, 18, 19 and 20 and even younger, think a lot about the future after the war, are actually idealists, even if they don't know it and would never admit it. Their language is often punctuated with all sorts of curses and blasphemies and yet they want a better world and are prepared after this lot's over to fight and work for it. If the politicians betray them again – well there'll be a hullaboo this time.

2nd July 1944, Sunday 9am. Harwich

Five of us hired bicycles (6d for 9 hours, 12 – 9pm) and went a grand ride in the sunshine down to the sea front and then out into the country, where the lanes are so narrow and winding that they make you think of Devonshire. I was last man in the convoy all the time. 'You hare about if you want' I said 'but I'm making my own pace and it's not fast.' I'm learning a bit of sense with these young guys these days and they don't mind either.

We were back on board again at 8 o'clock this morning. And we came back too with a new member of the crew, a little black and white kitten called by the telegraphist, who took pity on it last night when he found it wandering the streets and smuggled it into his bed with him at the hostel, by the extraordinary name of Rita. It'll probably be a Richard, but at present it's a Rita, and hungry as a wolf cub it is and as sad as only a lost kitten can be.

I'd a lovely comfortable bed last night and I was in it for seven hours and yet I'm still all set for a nap. And so I can tell you is Harry, who left us last night to escort one of his WREN friends to a dance, reached the hostel at 1am to find all the doors locked, walked the streets for a couple of hours and spent the rest of the night in an air-raid shelter. That's been sufficient even to leave this young dynamo a trifle limp.

3rd July 1944, Monday. Harwich

This morning we were correcting books for a few hours and at noon I earned a little more of the 5/- a month I've not yet been paid, by taking the notes at a short meeting of the Canteen Committee which was concerned chiefly with a regatta on Wednesday in which we've entered one or two crews – can you beat the imperturbable Navy, holding regattas at the climax of a world war!

4th July 1944, Tuesday 12.45pm

This morning I packed 24 packets of chocolate nuts and six bars of Mars in the box and this time, after it had been censored, John made it so secure it will require a Raffles or a high-explosive charge to open it. I had intended to put 'So Little Time' in too and, in fact, had left it on top. Then the officer censoring the contents saw it, said he'd been searching for a copy for a month, and asked if he could borrow it. Well, what could I say? And I'd wanted you to have it so that you could change it for another long book and send it on some time.

5th July 1944, Wednesday 10.45am

Just down from the upper deck where I've been watching the regatta. It's an interminable and monotonous – and when the wind is blowing – a cold process. It's one of those events, this regatta, which like Tennyson's famous book, promises to go on forever. My only interest was in the first race in which a crew from the communications branch was entered. Harry was one of the six. They went down to the starting line at 9.30 and it was 10.15 before they were off and they were never off as fast as half the other entries. They never gave up but they were never in it and yet everybody seems to have been content when they finished fourth in a race of six, even if the fifth and sixth crews in their excessive zeal rowed clear off the course and were disqualified.

10th July 1944, Monday 9pm

I slept all morning until a pipe announced that the Canteen Committee was to meet at noon. Well, I have to earn my 5/- a month. So up I rose, equipped with my propelling pencil and a notebook, went to the first lieutenant's cabin and took a few notes. It was just a piece of cake when I think of those two and three columns in the Gazette which I used to write nearly every day. As soon as I'd finished dinner I went to the ship's office, drafted a report in shorthand and while Harry looked on with his mouth open, typed a report of three manuscript sheets in about half an hour. Then I delivered it red-hot to the first lieutenant, who was apparently not expecting it for a couple of days, and after he'd said 'Thanks a lot, that's fine' he ordered it to be posted on all the notice boards. And there it's on view tonight.

11th July 1944, Tuesday 11am. Harwich

Just written a letter to old Ted while everything's quiet on a mess-deck which is now so crowded since yet another two young telegraphists came aboard last night that every bunk is occupied, another tier has to be built in the fairway, and one guy has actually had to sling his hammock. Talk about a congested area! Tom's by my side and he's writing too, and backwards and forwards in front of us stalks young Rita, halting every now and again, crouching on her little hindquarters and every half minute pouncing on scraps of paper fluttering in the wind from the ventilator pipes. She's quite at home now is Rita. When I came down below after washing and shaving this morning she was perched at the head of my bunk looking as meek and innocent as a little black and white cherub – and as perky as a cock sparrow. 'She's a little love' I said and stroked her squat skull. Then down she leaped and on the inside of the green cover, which fortunately is waterproof, was a little pool. You'd never think that such a lot could come from a source so little.

12th July 1944, Wednesday 9.30pm

I had the loveliest day yesterday. We had to leave Harry behind, which upset Harry no end, but three of us, John, Jock and I, were out for nine hours, from 1–10 p.m. In that time, after the inevitable call for coffee and cakes, went shopping and then for the rest of the afternoon sat on the sands in the hot sunshine watching the sea – or the 'oggin as they call it in the Navy – as if we didn't see sufficient of it. It awakened a lot of memories.

13th July 1944, Thursday 9.30am

I changed into my comfy golf jacket and open-necked shirt and was preparing to go on watch when they piped another two hours leave from 8–10pm. Immediately Harry and young Tom Chatt, one of the telegraphists, dived back into their No. ls and demanded that I should go out with them again. 'Not ruddy likely' said I. And I spent the next hour spring-cleaning my locker and the next up in the office, where I made my first cup of coffee and cut my first slice of that lovely cake. Then down below I came again and was preparing for a nice long session with my book – when back came Harry and Tom. And where do you think they'd been as soon as they'd been left on their own and freed of my restraining influence? Into the boozer, where they'd begun with a pint of beer and followed it with a few whiskies. The result was inevitable. Neither was drunk but both were borderline cases. And between them they'd spent 24/- and, once the first excitement had faded, both were full of remorse. What a job I had waking them this morning. And what lovely heads they've got. Now they swear that never again will they go out without me. 'If you'd been with us it'd never have happened' they lament.

How I love all your letters, thank you for the cuttings too. I don't know who 'S' is – the initial at the foot of the review of the invasion newsreel – but whoever it is he or she can write. Yes, I have thought of writing an article if only we can find ourselves in some exciting incident or other, but the truth is that so far we've been the sort of Mrs Mopps of the show. That would make a good title too come to think of it. I'd seen the article about Nat Gubbins and the photograph of Sally in the *Radio Times* but I never heard the programme, never had a chance to hear it for these lads are all for American hotcha-cha-cha and will listen to nothing else. I had also seen the article, but not the report, of the pressman who died for his story. It makes you proud to have been a reporter when you read stories like that.

16th July 1945, Sunday

I've just smuggled a white front, a vest, a pair of pants and a towel into the laundry for a little private wash day. They've introduced a new system this month as a trial – you've to pay for every article instead of 1/- a month. Half the crew's boycotting the laundry. Those of us who have more sense, or don't spend three quarters of our pay on beer, prefer it, for everything's coming out cleaner and every now and then, as the laundrymen are not so busy, we have a few extras done out of official hours for a penny or two.

17th July 1944, Monday 11am. Harwich

I spent the afternoon on the bridge with Harry, reading the newspapers which Mother and Pop sent and had a bird's eye view of one little comedy-drama when two of the officers rigged a dinghy with a sail, after interminable preparations, climbed down into it, and, before they'd left the ship's side were pitched into the water as the boom shot over unexpectedly and capsized the whole box-of-tricks. Fortunately they could both swim and were soon hauled aboard. They took it grandly too, as a great joke, and didn't mind at all when one humble rating asked them as they squelched back to their cabins if they intended to apply for survivor's leave.

Now this morning after working in the office for a time, I've mended a little slit beneath the armpits in my No. 1 jumper and have made of it, I think, a little less amateur job than I made of my No. 3s, which by the way are now in such a deplorable state (at least the trousers are) that I've ordered a new pair of bags from the 'shops'. Nobody is very particular although they are forbidden the wearing of non-service gear while in harbour, which means that almost every other day for the last two weeks I've had to go into the old blue jersey again, nobody is too particular but I simply can't walk about like an old rag-bag indefinitely. So I've ordered the 'bags', which, if they match my No. 1 jumper may become part of my No. 1s, and I've ordered too another pair of underpants, another vest, and a towel and comb. This may make a bit of a hole in my wages but I've still £2 in the P.O. Bank.

P.S. Just been called with the rest of the crew to the upper deck where, with caps off, we heard sentence passed on one of the stokers who forgot to return from the last leave. He was 72 hours adrift and, being a habitual offender, I'm afraid, was sent to the cells for 21 days and had 18 days leave and 18 days pay stopped. Not such a bad sort of a guy either.

18th July 1944, Tuesday 4.30pm. Harwich

It's only an hour since I came off one of the busiest watches for days, four hours of it and not a minute of it idle. I've earned my 3/- today. And there's the last dog from 6pm to 8pm still to come and I'm down for the morning watch at 4am too.

20th July 1944, Thursday 7.30pm. Harwich

Now down below I've come again into a corner which I expected to be quiet, but which resembles a public meeting. Still I've turned myself away behind a rack of overcoats and gas-masks. In the far distance, audible even above the chatter and above the wireless programme, which nobody seems to be listening to – it's another of those blaring American dance bands – I can hear young Rita calling for her supper. Well, she can go and ask the Petty Officer stokers for it, for without any sort of apology and with no shame at all, she's deserted us on the lower deck to go and live in their private mess, where yet another cat has appeared from nowhere in particular and established himself. The two of them have been playing together all day, ambushing each other, pouncing on each other, and twirling about like little leaves blown by the wind. In the meantime Boston has retired into exile in a state of outraged dignity and, adopting the commissioned ranks, has been seen nowhere.

21st July 1944, Friday, 1.10pm

Thank you for that lovely parcel. It arrived an hour ago. For 10 minutes before dinner I prised at every nail, uncoiled the wire, but could make no further progress. Then afterwards the radio mechanic lent me a pair of pliers and although one side of the box collapsed, it was soon opened and, in the presence of an appreciative audience, all its contents were disclosed – all the magazines which will be such a nice change after the heavyweight stuff I've been reading, the two big segments of the cake I love such a lot, the large tin of Nescafe, the sardines, the tobacco from Mrs Davies, the pressed silk, and all those newspapers, now smoothed out and ready for reading. Meanwhile I'm accumulating a few 'rabbits' (as we call them) for you. I bought another tin of lemon cheese this morning and a comb too from the canteen. Then the 'shops' came aboard. The trousers were too short by inches, as I feared they might be, but now I've three changes of underwear, and there's a big thick towel and another comb.

22nd July 1944, Saturday 2.10pm

What a time I'm having with the papers which were in the parcel. I'm only half way through them. The first I opened, last week's Sunday Express, had the funniest article by Nat Gubbins about the misadventures as doodlebugs fell near the nest* and a story by CS Forester, author of *The Ship* about a group of submarine chasers in one of which Peter, one of the telegraphists served – I've cut it out for him for his scrapbook. Then at breakfast today, after I'd shelled my hard-boiled egg and buttered two thick slices of bread and butter, I took another at random from the pile – it was Tuesday's Daily Express and pretending it was old times again, read it as if it were today's – read all about the billeting prosecutions at Blackpool and William Hickey and William Barkeley and the leader.

I told you that my chief, Jerry the leading telegraphist, had become librarian. Well, I've always said that there would be plenty of books ashore for us if only we chose to collect them. This morning he put it to the test, sent one of the telegraphists to make a few enquiries. Within an hour he was back with a sack containing 40.

Now there's a lovely big letter from Mother, and in it a £1 note to help to pay for my new trousers. She doesn't want to think that I'm going about all shabby because I've not the money to buy new clothes. Shabby! Why, even in my old patched bags and even though I can now wear my posh shirts only when I'm at sea, I'm a positive Beau Brummel compared with 99% of the crew. Money, I admit, was a bit short and I'll never say no to a £1 note.

Of course, in the end I suppose, I'll have to invest in a new uniform altogether and that, made to measure, costs I think £3.2.6, so the £1 can go into the sinking fund for that purpose. In the meantime, however, Harry says 'I'd wait a bit' for he thinks as things are going at present and always assuming they don't want us against the Japs, who won't last long anyhow, we may not be sailors such a lot longer. Well you never know, the lads might be right this time.

* *Nat Gubbins wrote a column 'Sitting on the Fence' for the* Daily Express. *The nest refers to his home.*

27th July 1944, Thursday 12 noon

I went ashore yesterday from 4.30 until 10 o'clock. But this time we cut out the pictures for it was too hot, so hot that the wearing of uniform was a penance and getting into it like descending into Dante's inferno. I went with Arthur, the young coder, and Alan, the radio mechanic, who's no older, they're just a couple of lads. There are times when I miss fellows of the age of Ted and Ken and a few others of the Caballa gang. Still, these are nice lads and I seem to get on with them fine.

Eventually we reached the beach, cooled off in the breeze from the 'oggin, walked into town for a couple of cups of coffee, wandered out again, found a park and as we sprawled on the grass I told them all about the life of a newspaper reporter – both have routine jobs back in civvy-street – told them about the famous Tipperary Tim scoop,* the young man who wrote his own obituary notice, about the 6,000 miles a season watching football and about a few of the famous and notorious folk I'd met. Poor lads, they both wanted to be newspaper reporters by the time I'd finished and one of them, Alan, has just written a letter to his people, which he's shown me, telling them about it and describing me, if you please, as 'a fellow of 41 who seem a lot younger, who has a pronounced Northern accent, but is definitely too old to have been sent to sea – it's a darned shame.' Can you beat that? And he has the temerity to show it to me too. They've no respect for my grey hairs at all.

Tipperary Tim was the 100-1 winner of the 1928 Grand National, the only horse to complete all the fences. The 'scoop' is described in full in (Sir) Jimmy Armfield's autobiography. It seems that Jim had wanted to get into journalism and asked Cliff for advice. Cliff got him a column and taught him how to report and sub his own work, and when he had written an acceptable match report Cliff got it into the papers. In his autobiography, Armfield tells the Tim story when they were having lunch at a café in West Street, Blackpool. Cliff regarded this as his first big break. Here it is:

> Cliff took his dog for a walk every evening in Lytham, and a horse in a field befriended him because he brought it an apple each time. One morning the editor told him that somewhere in Lytham was a horse that was going to run in the Grand National the following Saturday. Nobody in the office recognised this horse so Cliff was told to find it and get all the background. It transpired that the horse was the very one that Cliff met every evening, he knew it as Tim. The owner had recently inherited the animal from her father, who had always dreamed of running a horse in the National. He had bought Tim, who was a decent jumper but no pedigree, and she had decided to run the horse in his memory. The editor was duly impressed and enquired about a jockey. When told there was none Cliff was told to go to Aintree, and if there was no jockey, to ride the horse himself. Cliff travelled to Aintree in the horsebox to report on his first ever race. The owner instructed the jockey to run around the outside and not risk the horse. The jockey reluctantly did that and the horse jumped well, much better than all the other horses; most coming to grief in a pile up at the Canal Turn. At 100-1 Tipperary Tim sauntered home a winner. For months afterwards crowds of visitors came to Lytham to see Tim in his field.

30th July 1944, Sunday 8.45am. Harwich

Weren't we lucky last night? I went out to the shops with a few of the gang at 4 o'clock, called in a canteen for a cup of coffee, weighed myself, and afterwards walked back to the docks with Alan, the radio mechanic, while the rest remained in town for the cinema and supper. On the way back we visited another canteen. Well, in the end I timed it so that I walked into the telephone booth at exactly 6.30 when I thought there was a reasonable chance of finding you in. The lines were booked, 'But' said the operator 'if you're back in the box at 6.55 I'll call you.' So I sent Alan off for an early supper to the canteen, sat on the seat in the sunshine, and it was lovely and fresh after all the rain, returned to the box as the bell rang and after the operator had said 'You'll be through in a few minutes', waited and waited and waited. I waited actually for between 20 and 25 minutes. Then at last I heard your voice saying 'Hello darling'. If they'd made the call even half a minute earlier there would have been no reply.

30th July 1944, Sunday 7.15pm. Harwich

No, I'm not a bit surprised that there was all that hullabaloo in the Channel the other night.* A ship sailing without lights or showing the wrong recognition signals can cause no end of a riot out at sea or anywhere else, I know – I've had some. Talk about panic when it happens. I don't wonder, once those guns began to fire that you wondered if action on the North-West coast had opened again.

Three of the crew and the skipper remained for Communion, a congregation of four, again it was a simple abbreviated service and again in it I seemed to come so close to you, my dear, as I prayed for you, and for our little family and for our lovely home. Now I'm writing in the cool of the evening in air so fresh after the afternoon's rain up the bridge with Harry. Earlier in the afternoon before I had my nap, I went up to the office on my own and made myself a cup of coffee out of a Nescafe tin which is still not empty. It's such a simple operation once you've persuaded the galley crew to disgorge a bit of sugar and a little milk. The water is so hot out of the taps, and as it's steam heated there's no pollution in it, that all you have to do is to fill a cup, pour in the milk and tip in the sugar, add the coffee and there's a nice 'cuppa' all hot and prepared in a couple of minutes.

There is no mention of this event in the local newspapers – it may have been the subject of censorship

31st July 1944, Monday 8pm

This morning we were up to the ears in book corrections which it will take us nearly all week, and at noon there was a meeting of the Canteen Committee which lasted until 1.30. I compressed it into three manuscript sheets of typescript and delivered four copies to the first lieutenant's cabin before 3.30 which again surprised him and seemed to impress him no end – he knows nothing of the times when I used to have a couple of columns in the old Green 'Un in an hour and a half – and already it's on the notice board.

1st August 1944, Tuesday 2.30. Harwich

Rumour has it that almost immediately we'll be leaving these parts for a certain port which is a lot closer to Gladys,* may even be closer to her than I've ever been before, within 18 or 20 miles. If it should be the latter I'll hunt up that underground dive where Jack ordered the mammoth mixed grill. If it's the former there's always the little cottage where they used to serve two eggs. Everybody's excited about it.

* Gladys was Vi's sister and lived in Newcastle near Belfast.

2nd August 1944, Wednesday. 5.30pm

We're off. We don't know where we're going until we're there – that's become our theme song – but I shouldn't be surprised if before the end of the week we're not within 18 or 21 miles of Gladys. If we are, and it's about 100 to 1 on that we shall be, and if we're there and given leave from the early afternoon I'll be at the railway or bus station in quick time.

3rd August 1944, Thursday 10.15am

There's sad news about Boston. Nobody can find him. We think he wandered off the other day before we left – he was so jealous of the two kittens – and has transferred his affections elsewhere. Several times he's walked over to another ship as if he were prospecting for new territory. Now he's gone and I suppose he's made himself at home where there are no acrobatic clowns to steal his limelight. We'll miss him, but still you never know, he might come back yet.

4th August 1944, Friday 3pm. Belfast

The lovely green fields and the distant hills are passing as I write, and every minute the channel is narrowing. What happens now nobody knows. Everybody has a definite bit of information but it's all speculation. Everything's buzzing like a hive of bees. We don't even know whether there'll be leave tonight, but if there should be I'll contact the Club* before anything else and at least if Jack's not there I can leave a message for him. And I've been thinking that even if I can't out to see them they might be able to see me. I'd prefer to go to Fairway to say 'Hiya' to the twins, but that may not be possible and the other alternative would be better than nothing – in fact, I'd get a whale of a kick out of seeing Jack and Gladys again for, come to think of it, I don't think I've ever even met them since that last lovely holiday we had with them before the war. Gosh, but aren't I excited – too excited to be tired although I've been on watch for 8 hours of the last 12 – and had an hour in my bunk this afternoon. Now I suppose I'll have to wait for days for your next letter.

This is Downpatrick Golf Club where Gladys's husband Jack was the resident professional. He eventually became the professional at Southport and Ainsdale.

6th August 1944, Sunday 11pm. Belfast

Just as we were assembling a Canteen Committee meeting was called and I'd to hare to the First Lieutenant's cabin with a notebook and pencil. But I'm not complaining for the meeting made it definite that there is to be leave, for its purpose was to sanction credit for bankrupt ratings to enable them to buy their cigarette and chocolate rations issued 'for the leave period' – the official phrase which made all rumours come true. Now everybody's in a flat spin. When will the leave start? How long will it be for? Nobody knows the answers to these questions yet. But they should within 24 hours.

8th August 1944, Tuesday 12 noon

Only a minute for we've to pack all our gear and transfer to a base ship. Now for the news – I am to go on leave from Thursday August 24th to Saturday September 9th – yes, it's our wedding anniversary and I'll have to travel on the 8th but we'll celebrate in advance.

9th August 1944, Wednesday 1.30pm

I've snatched a minute or two to write because no day seems complete unless I do, and because I do so want to make sure that yesterday's letter in a privilege envelope arrived with the news in it – the greatest news – that I'll be on leave from Thursday August 24th until September 9th – 14 days at home and two for travelling. It still seems all a dream. For the rest everything is a bit of a nightmare. Or it would be if those 16 days were not coming nearer and nearer every minute.

We've been transferred to another ship – a base ship – and it's not like our little old tub at all. We're all packed in one mess, so packed that no self respecting sardine would tolerate it. Yesterday we were half the day humping every bit of gear to these new quarters and when we eventually settled ourselves we found that we should have to sleep in hammocks in an atmosphere which made the Black Hole of Calcutta seem like a health resort, and that the space between each hammock was about one millimetre. I soon reached a definite conclusion about that. I hate hammocks anyway and in such a heat I'd never sleep.

10th August 1944, Thursday 1pm

Three of us went ashore last night and after seeing *Fanny by Gaslight*, a quaint title but a good film about mid-Victorian London for which we paid 1/9, a charge so insignificant apparently that we were conducted to the front row of the stalls, where I had to peer up at the screen from such an acute angle that when we came out my neck muscles seemed to be paralysed, and for an hour afterwards my head was tilted backwards and wouldn't go back again. Well, after that we had a supper of fish and chips and as the canteen was a converted hotel we booked beds there. And at 10 o'clock we found our room. And what a room. There were three beds in it, a wash basin with hot and cold, a dressing table for each of us and a whacking great wardrobe. And all for 1/-. We felt like kings and slept like logs. Among the mail yesterday was a long letter from Ted. He's had only four days leave since he left barracks and ever since the Big Show started he's been on convoys to the other side.

17th August 1944, Wednesday 1.45pm. Belfast

Last night with the old 'innards' still behaving most peculiar, I went in despair to a chemist. As soon as I told him of the symptoms he expressed the view that it was probably caused by a mild form of food poisoning, gave me a draught which looked and tasted as if it had been dredged from the bottom of a stagnant river, and he made me up a bottle of the foul brew. I'd another dose this morning and shall have another after tea. Already I'm lots better. I simply mustn't be ill when I come home and it was that I was beginning to fear.

18th August 1944 Thursday 1.10pm. Belfast

I'd a comic evening last night. I had intended to go out until 10 o'clock, which is permissible when you're on stand-by duty, but at the last minute I felt so tired and my tum was still at times so mutinous that I decided instead to spend the night at base. Harry, who could not go out in any case, was mighty glad about that and after a little supper at the canteen where, when I explained my forlorn state, they cut me four lovely thin slices of bread and butter and made me a special cup of tea (the women volunteers there are so kind) we heard a buzz that there was a free film show on. We boarded a ship, sat, about twenty of us, in one of their mess-decks, and saw *Stage Door Canteen* on a screen about the size of a table-cloth. I'd seen *Stage Door Canteen* before but I didn't recognise this version of it. Between every reel, as there was no double projector, there was an interval of about ten minutes. The first reel opened upside down, which caused no end of hilarity among the audience. In the third reel, until they faded it out and after another interval repaired the error, mouths opened and closed on the screen but no sound came out of them. In the fifth reel there was plenty of sound but nothing on the screen at all.

I was sprawled on a camp-bed among huge piles of litter and debris before 10.30 but I must admit I'd a restless sort of night and then morning. When my chief saw me I must apparently have borne such a close resemblance to Death Takes a Holiday that he ordered me to the sick bay and actually saw the sick bay attendant to ensure that I went. Gosh, wasn't I chokka about that. I could see somebody ordering me to bed and keeping me there and missing my leave. Oh, the prospect was grim. Still, as I'd had no breakfast and actually didn't want any and as I'd nothing except those four slices of bread and butter for 24 hours I decided that probably I'd better go. So off I went and laid myself down on a couch and had my considerably deflated tum prodded and punched by a surgeon who didn't seem too pleased but who never contradicted when I expressed the opinion that everything had been caused by one meal and one meal only at our new base, and that it was the sort of food which even the swine would not eat, and that at least a dozen other men had been affected. He said nothing to that, or at least nothing which in his rich Irish brogue I could interpret, but he must have come to the conclusion that nothing serious was wrong, for after prescribing a dose of castor oil he gave me a couple of lozenges to take at the end of the morning. I've taken them and it took me about half-an-hour to gobble them up and they made me nearly blow bubbles all the time, and I feel better than I've felt all week already.

19th August 1944, Friday 12 noon

You'll be wondering, I know, how the old tum is. Well, except that I nearly lost it last night when the castor oil suddenly took its toll it's quieter than it's been for several days and I don't think that this time it's a false alarm. I was left as limp as a lettuce after last night's upheaval but since then I've had a couple of sandwiches for supper and a slice of bacon for breakfast and there have been no dire consequences. I admit I felt so grim yesterday that I was almost certain they'd cart me off to the sick bay and once in there you never know when you're coming out again.

21st August 1944, Monday 9am. Belfast

I ought to be working I suppose, but if we work too hard there'll not be enough left until Wednesday night and that would never do, and so we're writing instead which, as you know, I infinitely prefer. First of all I'm HUNGRY. That's in capital letters and it deserves to be I can tell you. For a week, until yesterday, I managed to eat a sandwich now and again and a slice of bread and butter now and again, but nothing else at all. It was incredible – I actually couldn't eat. Then yesterday at lunchtime, after I'd been to the Nonconformist service for Jock's sake I ordered a lunch at the canteen. I'd a nice cup of soup, which tasted good, but a tongue and spam salad, nice as it undoubtedly was, would scarcely go down at all, and the sweet I had to cut. And at the end of it I felt as blown up as a Zeppelin and sick too. So I found a quiet corner and had a nap, and then Jock appeared and, although I was on stand-by duty and should have remained at base, such a prospect for the rest of the day seemed so appalling, that I required no persuasion to go out with him. So out we went and I left it all to him. We went to Bangor. Only 45 minutes on a fast train and 1/6 return on a Services ticket and I'd the loveliest day there. It was where Jock went for his honeymoon and he knows it inside out. It was a most beautiful day. We walked all round a big curving bay, sat ourselves down in the grass, called at a cafe for a pot of tea and bread and butter, and for once I didn't feel sick after it. Then we walked some more and in the fresh breeze I began to think that food wasn't so repulsive after all. So at about 7 o'clock we visited another cafe, ordered fish and chips and bread and butter and I scoffed the lot and every bit of it seemed good.

22nd August 1944, Tuesday 9.15am. Belfast

Another night between the sheets last night and this time Harry came out with me, he's come sadly to the conclusion after waiting several times for WRENS who've not turned up, that it would be preferable if women never entered his life again, and that there's a lot more fun for him in coming out with Old Grandpop. He'd only a couple of bob last night, and that was exactly the price of a seat in the Upper Circle. So I paid for his bed and for a sandwich or two before the show and then as I'd only half-a-crown left (with two days still to go, and 1/- required for a bed tomorrow night, and only 16/- left in the Post Office and I want to leave that in) we went to bed supperless. It's expensive when you're paying for nearly every meal you eat and practically, in self-preservation, living out. It can't be done on three bob a day.

16th September 1944, Saturday 2.50pm. Belfast

At Preston station I walked into one of our officers and one of the crew, talked to them about this and that until the train arrived late at 10.55 and in the stampede that followed wasn't a bit polite and commandeered a seat.

All the time until we arrived at 6.00am I dozed on and off but it wasn't until I went aboard for the crossing that I really made a night of it. Then I found a wooden bench, sprawled myself on it, rested my head on a lifebelt, and was asleep in a couple of shakes, and didn't waken until 9.15am, when I discovered everything in a bit of a turmoil, the ship tossing about like a young bronco, and a lot of unfortunates, sailors among them, soiling the decks. That, I was told, had been going on a long time but I, the man with the cast iron tum, had known nothing about it.

17th September 1944, Sunday 1.00pm. Belfast

The old gang is assembling, for as soon as he heard that I was back on the old pitch Harry worked a swap and will now be again in the bunk above mine. Poor old Harry, he's very sad just now, for during his leave his elder brother has been killed in France and his grandmother has died.

18th September 1944, Monday 10am. Belfast

We took a car out to Belle Vue (1d each for six miles!) and there we wandered in the grounds and had seven pennorth in the Zoo, where we saw wolves, monkeys, ostriches and all the bag of tricks. The animals seemed singularly unimpressed by the Navy, but we were not so thundering impressed by the animals except for one little orang-utan whose rear end resembled a rainbow and whose manners made us think immediately of our own mess-deck. We sat in the grounds afterwards until twilight. And then back we went to the city, which was so packed that we thought an armistice had been signed while we'd been away. Actually all that had happened was that half the population had come out to see the lamps lit for the first time in five years. Gosh, it didn't half seem to excite these Irish folk. Families were out en masse.

The traffic was nearly at a standstill. I saw dozens of wee kids perched on their father's shoulders gazing entranced at the lamps. Most of them had never seen streets lighted before.

23rd September 1944, Saturday 6.00pm. Belfast

I'd have given anything for you to have been with Jock and I this afternoon when, in a ground where the international was played a fortnight ago, we saw the country's two unbeaten football teams meet. There were about 25,000 there and the home team won 3–0 and it was a honey of a match and it cost us only 1/-, for when we decided to transfer to the stand the man at the turnstile said 'Och, would I be charging a couple of Jacks now' and passed us round the turnstile for nothing.

What will eventually happen about the interim demobilisation I don't know and I don't suppose anybody else does either, but according to the present formula I've reached the advanced age of 47, my own 41 plus a year for each two of my twelve months service and shall therefore at the end of another six months have made it 50, which is the limit. Wherever I am, however near or far away, and always assuming that in the meantime the Huns call it a day, I'll be sent home. That's how it should work. But I'm refusing to get excited about it, for theory and practice don't always agree and in any case I'm prepared to wait on events. It would mean leaving all the lads, even Jock has another 12 months to go, and chaps of Harry's age about 4 years.

29th September 1944, Friday 4.00pm. Belfast

I'm one of the three cooks for the first time. All morning I was scrubbing tables and floors, or 'decks' as we call them, and for every meal since dinner until dinner-time tomorrow I have to go to the galley for food, serve it out (an equal ration for 24 men and woe betide the cooks if one man has more than another!) and wash all the dishes and cups and assorted cutlery afterwards, wash them up in a bucket and dry them on any old scraps of rag which happen to be about. And after every meal you've to clean the tables and sweep the deck.

30th September 1944, Saturday 8.00pm

Today I've been on watch again from 8.00am to noon, hit the hay all afternoon, attended a meeting of the Canteen Committee and now back in the office I am again until midnight. Two stowaway kittens have again adopted me, and when one of the guys who hadn't made his bunk this morning made it this afternoon he found one of them curled up in his blanket as snug as any bug in a rug. You should see those two tumbling about on the deck. Where they come from nobody knows. They just come and go.

1st October 1944, Sunday 6.30pm. Belfast

Your husband is an old tar at last. Today, just before dinner, on the first day of the month I was issued with my 'tot', a cup of rum, one part rum to two parts water, for the first time. I'm giving it a trial on the recommendation of several sea dogs, and as it costs only 3d a day and, apart from everything else, can be bartered any and every day of the week for everything from the bed in the captain's state room to a rack of depth charges, it is I suppose cheap at the price. Today I drank about a quarter of it and gave the rest to a number of casual acquaintances who immediately became my blood-brothers protesting eternal friendship. But I'd have taken no more in any case for I was on watch all the afternoon and rum induces sleep and sleeping on watch is a practice strongly discouraged. Yes, I'll give it a trial. It can do you no harm and conceivably when you're out for long periods, if we're ever going to be, and the food inevitably becomes scarce and uninteresting, it's reputed to do you a lot of good.

5th October 1944, Thursday 2.30pm. Belfast

It is exactly an hour ago that I dried the last cup, the last knife and fork and put my own, wrapped in cloth, in my locker, wiped the table, swept the deck and climbed into my bunk. Now here I am in my corner writing to you again and waiting for 3.15 when I'll go off to the galley for the 6 loaves and the 2lbs of butter which are issued to our 24 men every day. Yes, today I'm a cook, this little assignment comes every sixth day and is no great hardship. Or at least it isn't for me, for as I offer to dry the pots after nearly every meal every day, I always have plenty of assistance. Everything was as neat and tidy as regulations demand half an hour after the last piece of plum duff had been served today.

Such a crisis as arose this morning when it was discovered that all the butter had vanished. It's suspected that somebody suffering from night starvation rose in the small hours, cut some bread and wolfed the lot and as the synthetic egg was distinctly revolting in appearance and worse when you took a tentative bite at it, we'd to breakfast off dry bread and syrup.

6th October 1944, Friday 12.45pm.

Now I'm ready for my bunk and I'll soon be in it too. What's it like, this famous bunk of mine? It's the lowest of three, and to insert myself into it between the mattress below and the blanket and green waterproof cover above I've to slide all in one piece off the table near it, twisting my neck en route to miss the chain which holds it in position. And once in you remain in. I pack nearly all my clothes under the pillow and leaning back against it I can half sit up and read, but even in that position my head brushes against the bottom of the bunk above. Yes, it's a bit of a congested area and when the mess is too hot it can be a bit airless. But I sleep fine, I've no complaints.

7th October 1944, Saturday 5.00pm

I've been standing with one ear cocked near the loudspeaker, which this afternoon is not all it might be, listening to Tom Cragg's commentary on the Blackpool–Preston* match. I didn't even know it was on until one of the lads came over and said 'This'll interest you, if you can hear it.' I heard it by nearly climbing into the amplifier, and good it was too, even if Blackpool didn't win both points.

* The result was 1–1.

9th October 1944, Monday 3.00pm

Yes, they're rum 'uns these young ones. Heaven help the girls who marry them – for they won't change. They eat like a pack of wolves – again all the butter went yesterday and I'd to have bread and pork dripping for breakfast, but as they'd to have bread and no dripping at all, for they didn't know there was a little hidden reserve in the galley, I'd no complaints. They fade away as soon they've eaten their fill and seldom make their bunks until nightfall and not always then. They're still a nice lot of lads but – crikey – what an awakening they're going to have some day when they have homes of their own.

22nd October 1944, Sunday 8.45pm

The wardroom, to a man, are growing beards. Strange, peculiar and revolting are some of the growths which are appearing. A few of the lower deck are at it now. As I shaved this morning, a razor in one hand, clutching a post with the other (we're in those sort of waters) I was asked repeatedly 'Why are you taking it off Lofty? Leave it alone.' Everybody's prepared to lay bets that I could give the wardroom the week's start they've had already and pass the lot in less than a fortnight. I probably could but I'm not playing. I like to feel clean and fresh in the mornings. To heck with those bits of fungus all over your pan. And besides once you've decided to grow one of these ornaments you've to grow it. There's no escape. You've to ask the captain's permission before you begin at all and afterwards you've to let Nature take its course and what a course she takes with some of them – for six months. Or else you're for it. No, I'm not interested. I don't want to come home looking like Moses or Isaac or Abraham or the old tar on the outside of the Players packet. I could if I wanted but I don't. Whereas those who do, can't.

I've a new lifebelt. Actually it's a thick padded jacket with a high rolled collar so thick that it's like a short overcoat and even warmer. So this morning I went out on deck for half an hour in a raging gale and smelt fresh air and a sea breeze and it was good. I was warm as toast too. The watches have been quieter. Now they've all gone into their bunks weary, worn and a bit sad. I'm left all on my own. I must go soon I suppose for a couple of hours before the middle. A still, small voice has just croaked from one of the bunks 'Britannia may rule the waves but I wish she'd rule them a little straighter.'

25th October 1944, Wednesday 5.30am

How do you write a word which sounds as if you're smacking your lips? Because that's the sort of noise I'm making. Young Tiny, the wee Tom Thumb telegraphist, there's only 5' 3" of him but it's all good, who lives at Little Hulton, Jimmy Hampson's village, has just been down to one of the boiler rooms for a can of hot water and the three of us (Tom is the other) have had a cup of Nescafe each.

She's as frisky as ever. The invalids are sitting up and taking notice by now though if I were callous I'd say that it was a pity for there's less to eat for us old tars. And now that Harry, the ingenious one, has manufactured a sort of Heath Robinson toaster out of a few bits of old wire and a broken packing case, we have toast. Admittedly you've to lay the bread on the wires, which means that every now and again it suddenly goes up in flames, but when you have for supper, as we had last night, tinned steak and kidney pudding which should never have come out of the tin and had no kidney and precious little steak in it, a slice of toast and dripping and another of toast and fresh butter are a bit of all right. Even if the toast is a bit charred.

Gosh, but we're a bit tired now. You can't sleep in a bunk which heels over 45 degrees to starboard one minute and lurches 45 degrees to port the next. If it would only stay 45 degrees one way or the other it wouldn't be as bad, but it won't!

26th October 1944, Thursday 12.15am

You soon learn to sleep in a bunk which seems to be affected with St Vitus' dance. I'm reported, by the way, to be the only man on board, officer or rating, who is shaving every day. They think they might give me a medal for that.

Oh, the trials and tribulations of a sailor in these raging seas. We were having tea when there was a great lurch. Everything tumbled off the table. Everybody tumbled to the deck. And into the middle of my bunk which I'd just left after a couple of hours sleep, tumbled half a cup of tea. It drenched everything except the blanket which was folded back. I ripped the mattress cover off, the pillow case, snatched up my pyjamas which I still wear every night, went straight to the laundry with them. My old pal there had not forgotten the tots I've doled out to him. 'I'll wash them, dry them and air them, Lofty', he said. They're in the process now. Meanwhile I'd a clean cover, pyjamas and pillow case. Everything's honky-tonk again. But crikey it would all get you down if you let it – but I don't.

28th October 1944, Saturday 7.50pm

There are times when you feel good in this little game. This morning at 6 o'clock was one of them. I stood alone on the upper deck and against a red and angry dawn over a new land watched a line of merchant ships steam into sanctuary. Not one had been lost. Heaven knows I'd little to do with it, except that I worked harder and for longer hours than I've ever worked since I came into the Navy and yet when I saw those ships I was proud, yes proud. It's meant again hours and hours on watch, I was on for about 18 of the last 24, and so dog tired that I was nearly asleep standing up, but when it's all over it seems worth it.

29th October 1944, Sunday

You've heard of the back of beyond, I've been beyond it this afternoon.* I can't tell you its name or the country which has apparently forgotten all about it. But it's Desolation with a capital D. We landed at two o'clock and except for half an hour in a free cinema where we saw a film which was presumably a comedy, although as none of the inhabitants chuckled at it, it can't have been a particularly good comedy and we didn't understand a word of it anyway. Except for that half hour we walked cobbled streets, past wooden shacks and a few tall gaunt sort of barracks and, having completed the promenade, walked back again. The people knew only two words of English. One was 'choklet' and the other 'cig-rette'. They offered (even tiny toddlers) bundles of worthless notes for them. And everywhere you saw ragged soldiers picking fag-ends out of the gutters. And all the time from the front of the few high buildings loudspeakers were blaring out the latest war news.

For nearly 5 hours we searched for food. There was not a bite in the whole show, not a cup of tea, nothing at all. So we walked and walked. We had to walk for we'd have been frozen in our tracks by a wind which had ice in it and blew clouds of grit in front of it. Gosh, were we hungry and cold and disillusioned. But, at least I've tried foreign soil at last and such a lot of it too, and now, even if there were only a couple of slices of bread and butter for us when we came back, I feel warm and fine and healthily tired and again we're to be in our bunks all night.

* *This was the naval base at Polyarnoe, 30 miles east of the front line on Finnish/Russian border, on the western shore of Kola Inlet, which led to the port of Murmansk. Normally the merchant ships of the convoy went to Murmansk and the escorts went alongside at Polyarnoe or Vaenga, a base on the eastern shore of the inlet. Tom Goff remembers going to a Red Army canteen and having a drink of what they thought was vodka. His lasting memory was of the spirit tasting like a mixture of old engine oil and fish oil. He remembers at night seeing the flashes of the guns on the Finnish/Russian border.*

The supply of war materials to the Soviet Union was crucial to the Allies' strategy of developing the war on two fronts. In practice, this meant sailing slow and vulnerable convoys across a vast expanse of Arctic waters, stalked by Luftwaffe bombers, U-boats and powerful surface ships such as the battlecruiser Scharnhorst.

In the summer months convoys went to Archangel, Russia's main northern port, but this was largely inaccessible in winter due to ice. Instead, the convoys headed for Kola Inlet, which was kept open by the Atlantic drift. Conditions were bleak. Only 30 miles from the front, these bases were subject to continual aerial attack. From 3 December to 19 January the sun does not rise above the horizon, creating three to five hours of twilight around midday.

Byron *was among escorts protecting convoy JW 61, which left Loch Ewe on 20 October 1944 and arrived at Kola Inlet on 28 October. Between then and 2 November, when she sailed back to Britain with Convoy RA 61,* Byron *was moored at Vaenga Bay. This comprised a large Russian air base and barracks, an oiling jetty, a single track railway to Murmansk, and little else. The pier at which the escorts were berthed had no power of any kind. Water was laid on, but was not drinkable.*

Leading seaman Dick Smith recalls: 'Hitherto we had regarded the Fleet Canteen at Scapa Flow as being the Worst Run Ashore in the Navy – we were wrong: the title belongs to Vaenga Bay. I remember spuds being frozen solid in the upper deck locker, the children who had never seen chocolate. Fleeting impressions are of Russian soldiers beating up a young lad who had accepted chocolate from us – or maybe they were just trying to get it off him. I also remember a wooden barracks with a large parade ground which had a gallows at one end.'

The Soviet and British authorities had good reason to want Convoy RA 61 out of the area. On 6 November – four days after Byron *cleared Kola Inlet – two fast ocean liners arrived at Murmansk to disembark 11,000 Russian nationals who had been captured fighting for the Germans during the Normandy landings in June. No British personnel – including senior officers – were allowed ashore on this occasion. The fate of these prisoners of war in the hands of the Red Army can be imagined. Britain's collusion in the affair is not uplifting.*

2nd November 1944, Thursday 1.15pm

Disaster yesterday, or at least I'd have called it a disaster a year ago. Now I've learned patience and resignation. It's part of the Navy's curriculum. A steam pipe near my bunk developed a leak. The experts said it was condensation but it wasn't. By the time they'd been persuaded that it wasn't and had made rough and ready repairs, it was discovered that water must have been escaping for hours, for when I opened my locker there was nearly an inch of it swirling beneath its duckboards. My tropical kit was soaked and my No. 2 jumper, which has seen its best days anyway.

But the bottom of my Gladstone bag was saturated and all the chocolate bars and sweets I'd been saving for you were damp. I'm afraid that the lot may be ruined. The sweets, liquorice allsorts, were in a horrible mush and I simply dished them out among the lads while they were fit to eat. Some of the chocolate too was past redemption and I'm eating it now before it curls up on its toes.

4th November 1944, Saturday 1.45pm

She's been bucking and rearing and shuddering and shaking every minute. Young Harry came to grief on the deck, fell in a heap and is now limping with a pulled leg muscle. The sick-bay was at it non-stop. I crashed half-way down another hatchway, gashed my arm and had to have it treated with antiseptic. It's your elbows which seem to take all the punishment. Mine are scraped and raw. Now a can of water has fallen over in the office and swamped the floor. Excuse me while I swab it up. That's done it. Gosh, what a life and all for three bob a day.

Today I've got a new job, I've been appointed shorthand writer to the stokers' football sweep. It's a pontoon, the first team to total 11 goals takes the kitty. Nobody can write out the results as fast as they come over the air. So I offered to write them in shorthand and Jock, who's OK again now by the way, copies them out afterwards at my dictation. They've given us two teams in recognition of our services. Mine is

Watford and Jock has the Wolves. I've started off today with three. In this sweep your team has to aggregate 11 goals exactly. If it passes 11 it begins all over again the following week at 0. The last sweep lasted weeks. In the end the first prize was £10. Now I could just do with that. But so, I suppose, could quite a number of stokers. We'll just hope. Watch Watford! And, by the way, what's the matter with Blackpool? Beaten 3–1 at home and by Oldham too.

8th November 1944, Tuesday 12.15am

A bit of a drama and nearly a wholesale tragedy last night. Early in the afternoon the captain was taken ill and the sick bay attendant diagnosed acute appendicitis. A few hours later, in pitch darkness and a high sea, a whaler was launched and sent across to another ship to bring a doctor aboard. Nothing happened until its return. Then the crew were called out to lift the whaler into position. Hail was lashing the open decks which were under an iced sheet of sleet. I was excused, the only one in the mess left below.

'You watch the pots don't all slide off the table' said the chief. I could have done nothing about it if they had. He knew that. Everybody else knew it too. But nobody complained. It was their decent way of saying 'This is no job for a guy of your age' and I suppose it wasn't. Actually they were out nearly an hour, soaked to the skin, frozen to the bone, and all the time they were tumbling over each other in the darkness and on the frozen steel of the deck.

For as soon as they began to lift the whaler the ropes tangled, the boat was capsized and half the crew were flung into the sea – a sea mountains high. Every man except the visiting doctor grabbed a life-line and was dragged aboard in a few minutes. For nearly half an hour he was in the ice-cold water at first under the boat, then clear of it, clutching at lines as they were thrown to him, gripping them for a few seconds and losing them again. Somehow or other, in the end, they slung a slinged rope over him and lifted him semi-conscious to the deck. He's not for Kingdom Come, but he was perilously near to it. Now he's sleeping in the captain's stateroom.

Meanwhile, as nobody can operate on the captain or can tell whether an immediate operation is necessary, we're racing back home, all on our own, as fast as the engines can take us, racing against time. Talk about the guts of these Royal Navy men. As soon as the skipper heard what was happening he left his bed and, dressed only in his pyjamas, trousers and a reefer jacket and doubled up like a jack-knife, climbed to the open bridge and directed the rescue operations from there. It makes you proud to serve under men like that.

Now it's all quiet again. Or as quiet as it can be with the old ship shuddering from stem to stern as we tear back all out to the nearest port which possesses a hospital. We should now be home a day or two earlier than we expected. It can't be too soon. We're all, I think, a bit punch-drunk. It's been one heck of a run. Nearly everything's happened to us – I'll tell you about it one day darling. And that day shouldn't be so far off. One watch may be given leave.*

No operation on the captain will be immediately necessary. We're simply racing for home where, I suppose, he'll go straight into a hospital. The doctor is almost fit again. That little chapter has ended happily.

* *Captain Southcombe had become seriously ill. The group's medical officer was on* Redmill *which was somewhere out in the screen.* Redmill *eventually closed with* Byron *and it was decided to transfer the doctor, Surgeon Lieutenant T.H. Hargreaves, from ship to ship. The whaler was deployed from* Byron *but capsized spilling all hands and the surgeon into the sea. The sailors managed to climb back on board, but not the surgeon. Visibility was poor because of snow, but nevertheless the surgeon was rescued, unconscious and suffering from hypothermia.*

A request for another doctor was turned down and the crew were told to 'use their own initiative'. They did this with the help of a manual on how to conduct emergency operations. The captain's temperature was monitored and a stiff dose of sulphonamide administered, on the premise that an operation by amateurs would certainly kill him, but an overdose of sulphonamide would not. The surgeon eventually came around, diagnosed himself as suffering from hypothermia and declared the captain not only out of danger, but very lucky. The surgeon declined to be put ashore and Byron *continued flat out to Belfast. The dogged determination and courage of everyone involved earned a certificate of recognition from The Royal Humane Society.*

The life-or-death drama of the situation is captured in the words of Eddie Chandler: 'We got to within a couple of hundred yards of Redmill *and then sent our whaler across to collect the doctor. We managed to get the whaler hooked on but as we were hauling her up something broke and the whaler overturned and those who could not grab a lifeline went into the oggin. We had a scrambling net over the side which all managed to grab and scramble back on board, except the poor doctor. Chaos then reigned; it's the only ship I was ever on with fifty captains, all shouting orders and advice whilst the poor victim kept swimming. It was bitterly cold and I can still see the doctor's red light on his lifejacket bobbing up and down in the sea. We kept trying and after I'd hit someone on the head with a grappling iron (Les Kingsley) a couple of people went over the side with ropes attached to themselves and after a mighty struggle we managed to haul the doctor on board.'*

Les Kingsley's head injury was mentioned in the certificate.

9th November 1944, Thursday 4.15am

Yesterday afternoon I left the office for a few minutes, went out on the upper deck and saw land. Faint in the distance, only a purply sort of shadow, I saw the mountains, snow on their crests. Soon, when dawn breaks, I'll be out on the deck again. Then I know I'll see a near and familiar coastline and it will be all over. Nobody will say anything and yet I suppose secretly we'll all be a bit proud that we've done it.

10th November 1944, Friday 10am. Belfast

Gosh, but you'd have laughed yesterday if you could have seen me in the No.1 bags which have been washed. They were as narrow, or seemed as narrow, as stove pipes and they came to an abrupt end at the top of my boots. Something had to be done about it. I consulted my finances. With the addition of Mother's 10/-, they totalled nearly £3. So I put on my No. 1 jumper, my new No. 3 trousers which, after the last few weeks don't look so new, hid all I could under my overcoat, passed the inspection and went off to the nearest Naval outfitters. There I bought an entire new rig off the peg. And good it is, too, the best Canadian serge, infinitely finer material than they're allowed to supply now for made-to-measure orders.

And is it tiddley? The bell bottoms are so wide that my boots are almost hidden. The tapes are so long that they nearly reach my knees. And the front is wide and cut with no end of a flare. I put it on and kept it on, bought a new cap too and a cap band and out I walked like a dog's dinner, the old clobber packed up and tucked under my arm. The bill for the lot was £2.14s.6d.

11th November 1944, Saturday 9.00pm. Belfast

I'd planned to go to see Jack and Gladys and the kiddies, had telephoned the club yesterday and, when Jack was out, left a message telling him that I'd probably be popping over. There was no chance of a week-end but 4 hours in that lovely home of theirs seemed mighty attractive. Alas it was not to be. The first lieutenant summoned me to the presence at 10 o'clock and asked if I'd take a short dictation from him and type 8 copies and prepare the manuscript for transmission. 'Only take a few minutes' he said. It took so few minutes that I was still typing at 1 o'clock and the train went at 1.45, and still awaiting his final approval of the draft at 2 o'clock. I'd missed the train.

So I decided to go instead to a football match. Jock and Arthur went on ahead and arranged to meet me on one of the stands. That was another vain dream. I was still hovering around on board a quarter of an hour before kick-off and the ground is about three miles away. So I gave that up too, went ashore on my own, called in the dock canteen for coffee and sandwiches for I'd missed dinner altogether.

Well after that, still on my own, I wandered to the Toc H, confirmed the booking of a bed for the night, had a bath, and a cup of tea and a couple of sausage rolls and went out afterwards to the cinema and there, waiting in the queue were Harry and his latest WREN friend. I walked past them to the end of the queue with a polite 'Good Evening' but off came Harry after me, insisted that I should go in with them and wouldn't take no for an answer. So there I was, odd man out, but the WREN appeared to have no objections and in any case Fate and a discreet usherette ordained that we should be separated when at last we passed the box office, for the building was packed and we didn't see each other again until it was all over.

12th November 1944, Sunday 2.00pm

Friday was quite a day. I was on duty aboard but in the afternoon the chief sent two of us out into the city for a case of new books for the library. My companion, the young telegraphist who had the appendicitis operation and is still not fit to be at sea even if they do send him, is one of the guys who goes into raptures over chamber concerts – yes, there are such folk in the Navy and nice folk some of them are too, Frank certainly is. Well you can imagine his joy when he learned that in the library depot was a music room where you could sit by the hour, select your own records and play them on a deluxe gramophone. So, for nearly an hour on Friday afternoon Old Philistine Greenwood sat at the feet of the masters and listened to Bach, Beethoven, Brahms and a few others of those old johnnies, and found myself liking it too. Aren't I becoming cultured?

13th November 1944, Monday 1.45pm. Belfast

I've some great news for you today. If it's possible you can come over and see Jack and Gladys and the twins. Yes, it's a fact. I heard a whisper yesterday that the wives of men based in this port are now permitted to visit the country if they supply an address at or near the base. The general impression seemed to be that it applied only to men based ashore but at the ship's office, they are making enquiries for me. Apparently all that will be required will be for each of us to fill in a formal application form. I'll let you know the rest as soon as I can.

No, the story on the front page of one of the papers had nothing to do with our last assignment although there were close similarities. You ask why I don't write a story and send it off to one of the Nationals. Often I've felt inclined but it's strictly forbidden without the permission of the authorities and that permission can be granted only after an application has been scrutinised by nearly everybody from the First Lord downwards. You've about 100–1 chance or less than that. Definitely it's not worth it.

The ironical part is that what I'd write, for few of us know sufficient about an actual operation to write anything else, would be purely personal, human, intimate sort of stuff, how men react to danger, how the lower deck is affected, all the never-told-by-the-communiques incidents, the sort of material which has made Godfrey Winn's *Home From Sea* a best seller. Yes, that's the ironical part of it, for such an article would not betray operational secrets at all and yet would be subject to the same strict censorship and would almost certainly be rejected. No I'll wait. There's the ingredients of a book in what's happening to me now. When I'm out it'll be different. While I'm in, 'shush' with a capital S is the word.

When shall I be out? What's happened today has made me begin to think again. A demobilisation chart was posted this morning. Everybody had to work out from it the number of his release group and to give it to the paymaster when we were given casual payment. I graded for 30/-, some sort of arrears I gather, some for less, some for more, and some for nothing at all – 'south-easters' they call those. Again I was reprieved from the bankruptcy court, but as I'd had to borrow 10/- from Jock – they never paid us at all on Friday, and I've still to pay for my slops, I'm still not in the lap of luxury even if I'm going out tonight on the strength of it and staying at the Toc H too, sleeping in a lovely comfortable bed while I can and for as long as I can. And in any case there's definitely to be a proper pay day this weekend so I'll manage and I'll have my new uniform and cap into the bargain, which I reckon is pretty good. My release group is 35, whatever that may mean, although it's certainly one of the earlier ones, for 90% of the other lads are in the 40s and 50s. Six months only it should mean if the European War ends in the meantime.

16th November 1944, Thursday 1.00pm. Belfast

I should have been on board tonight and, as there's still no heat I wasn't looking forward to it. Now I'll be ashore after all for only half an hour ago one of them offered to sub for me, and when I protested he said 'Go on, I can stand the cold better than you.' Yes, they're a decent lot of guys. They'd never let you down. Some of them have a new name for me now. They call me Stripey, a Stripey being a bloke with three stripes on his arm for 22 years service and as a result one of the old brigade. They all seem to think that at my age I'll soon be leaving them. Well, it'll be lovely to come home, but I'll miss the gang, yes, I'll miss them.

23rd November 1944, Thursday 5.00pm. Belfast

Harry has met THE GIRL, or at least he says he has this time. She's a WREN. Already she's written to inform a young Fleet Air Arm pilot that their romance is ended and that not even the melody can linger on. Barbara they call her. She's very nice too, and so she ought to be coming from Leeds which is in Yorkshire. Already I've been adopted by the two of them as a sort of official fairy godfather. They seem to think that if I can be so happy and contented after nearly 20 years of married life I must know something which is worth knowing. Already we're invited to the wedding. Harry's 19 and Barbara's 20. They make you smile and yet there's something so serious about them and so decent and trusting about them too that you don't smile for too long. Young Harry's just been in the office. 'But how on earth will we ever be able to get married?' he's asked, 'I haven't got a penny and can't save a penny in this game. Other fellows have jobs to go back to, but I haven't. When I volunteered I was only just beginning to learn a trade. Now I'll have to start all over again. Who's going to pay me a wage big enough to furnish a house and keep two of us?' What's the answer to that one? There'll be thousands like them when this war's finished and it won't be finished for fellows of Harry's age until it's all over in the Far East. He might be 22 or 23 then.

26th November 1944, Monday 1pm

It's only half an hour ago that the lower deck was cleared for the old skipper* to come and say goodbye to us. I almost wept for him. He nearly wept for himself. He perched himself straddle-legged on a form and called us all a lot of 'baskets' and I don't know what and he blasted and bloodied all over the place and yet he couldn't hide the fact that he was just about broken-hearted to leave the ship he'd commissioned. They pretend to be so tough – and they are tough – but they're very human too. Now he's gone, he's lost his ship because he was so imprudent as to contract appendicitis. Sentiment rates low in this game.

Lieutenant-Commander Southcombe had been commanding officer of Byron since her commissioning. After the operation on his appendicitis, command of the ship passed to Lieutenant John Burfield DSC, a courageous officer who had been captured and escaped twice.

30th November 1944, Friday 1.00pm. Belfast

Another beast of a day today, raining and blowing and with mud inches deep on the path to our berth. We've about half a mile to walk through the mud every time we go ashore and every time we come back again. I'm tired of cleaning my boots and brushing the bottoms of my bell-bottoms. And what do you think about this? I saw Barbara, Harry's beloved, when I called in the canteen at the docks this morning. Harry actually left the Bristol train at Leeds and called in Barbara's family. But, being a bashful sort of guy and requiring a little moral reinforcement (remember how he trailed me all the way out to Charlton to see her sister-in-law) he took in tow a young sub-lieutenant who's been on board a week or two and lives in Leeds. Latest news is that the sub-lieutenant is now taking out Barbara's sister and is apparently as smitten as Harry. Fast workers, these sailors.

6th December 1944, Wednesday 6pm, after leave

I've missed Ted again. His ship berthed next in the line to ours yesterday afternoon. I called for him on my way ashore. He'd been gone less than an hour on a visit to his brother who lives in the city. Even if he knew we were so close he'd never dream that we be leaving so soon. We seem fated to miss each other. There's little else to tell you except that I've a brand new knife, fork and spoon for my meals now – a little present from Jock's wife. It's so nice not to be hacking at everything with a bent and stained spoon. And these are not going to be cast into the deep either,* even if I have to wear them round my neck on a chain.

* Cutlery went missing regularly as it was inadvertently thrown into the waste bucket and chucked overboard!

8th December 1944, Friday 5pm

This has been – and still is – Upsy-Daisy day. Never has she rocked and bucked and lurched as she's rocking and lurching and bucking now. They're nearly all out as I write, flat out in their bunks. Even Harry has faded away for the first time since I've been aboard. It all began last night. When I came down from the middle watch at 4 o'clock in the morning the mess-deck was a shambles. Everything had fallen out of the bunks except the occupants and they were still in them only by the grace of providence. Clothes and boots were mixed up in heaps. The forms were overturned. Lifejackets were piled in a mass. And stalking through the chaos was young Sparks seeking somewhere to sleep. Water was swilling backwards and forwards on the deck above ours, all hatches were closed and cold air was gushing down the ventilator shafts. Now they're all sorry they don't wear pyjamas. I undressed between the rolls, snuggled into the blankets and, offending everybody's sense of the decencies fell asleep at once and slept until 7 o'clock – and I shaved too. And in those despised pyjamas of mine I'd been warm all night, or the little there was left of it. I'm sorry for these poor guys. And they say we'll be out for a week or two, and that all the time we'll be in these waters, which are reported to be the worst in the world.

9th December 1944, Saturday 8pm

As I write in my corner of the mess-deck everything's still going up and down including this table just beneath my bunk and nearly every guy in the mess is tucked between the blankets, except for half a dozen who, beginning at last to take an interest in this world, are disputing a noisy game of Ludo in the other corner and making one hell of a hullabaloo every time they shake a six with the dice. A comforts fund has sent them a Ludo board. It's a comfort to me. Now they won't be pestering me every few minutes to play whist. I prefer a book every time. Particularly on such a day as today when I'm so tired that I could nearly sleep standing up. I'm not sick – why, I've had five slices of toast and pork dripping since 4 o'clock – but golly, aren't I tired. And wouldn't anybody be when you can't walk a yard without exploring ahead for something to clutch and lurching forward and clutching it. And when the office books, racks, trays and everything moveable is cascading about your ears every minute or two. And when you've to work hour after hour wedged against one bulkhead and with one leg outstretched and wedged against another. And when you've to wash with one hand and grab the basin with the other and shave in a similar sort of contortion. And whenever you visit the heads, you've to balance on a narrow duckboard lifted a few inches above a swirling flood. And when, seeking rest at last, your bunk tilts backwards and forwards and you shouldn't be able to sleep at all, but sleep like a log as if you're being rocked in a cradle. It becomes pretty grim if it lasts longer than 24 hours. And this has gone on for a couple of days which can seem like a couple of weeks. Why, after this the Russian route seems like a Sunday afternoon in summer at Fairhaven Lake.*
* *Popular lake and recreational area between Lytham and St Annes.*

11th December 1944, Monday 2am

Golly, are we tired. Jock, who should have gone off at midnight, is still up – he's a grand guy, will never leave you until everything's about clear and now and again today it's been chaotic – has just gone on the hunt for cups of cocoa. We're so thirsty. Neither of us has had a drop to drink since yesterday tea-time. All the water is turned off during the night now to conserve supplies. Now he's back again with a big can. He descended into one of the boiler rooms and our pals, the stokers, took pity on us. At last it's a bit calmer. In fact, when I've finished this little note I'll wander out on the upper deck for a few minutes. It'll be the first fresh air I've smelt for three days.

13th December 1944, Tuesday 8.00pm. Plymouth

I've been at it in and out of watch now since 8 o'clock this morning. It's so lovely and peaceful now on the mess-deck, peaceful, at least, except for a Ludo school in the other corner and the wailing of a distant gramophone in the stoker's mess. On one side, as I write, is Sparks, still licking his lips after cleaning out yet another tin of sardines, the last this one, which I opened after I'd come down and found a mass of chopped meat and potatoes congealing on a tray, on the other is Harry writing to his Barbara. He managed 12 pages in his first little serial, and in the last four he inserted the word 'darling' four times after summoning up his courage for a couple of days and taking a sipper of my rum! He's so dashed serious. If we don't return to the old base he'll probably curl up and die.

14th December 1944, Wednesday 8.00pm

Saw my service record by chance last night. There were so many VGs on it that I almost blushed to read it. It reported too that I was 'efficient and conscientious' and that I had a good influence over younger men'. So now you know. Should I remain in the Service? I might become an admiral or something in about 50 years. No, somehow I don't think I will.

16th December 1944, Saturday 8.00pm

Great excitement during the night hours.* I can't tell you about it by letter but it resulted in the unofficial shorthand writer being called to the captain's cabin today while witnesses paraded in front of him. He's a grand chap this new skipper of ours, a gentleman every inch of him. This afternoon I missed my afternoon siesta because I'd to transcribe all my notes and type them and ever since I've been on watch.

Now, after supper, I've gone into my corner and left the rest to clear the table and wash up the few pots we have left – one cup now (not counting my little green mug from the Lakes which has definitely come into its own again) and a dozen plates, three spoons and about three forks and one knife for 21 men. And we'll lose a few more yet before we land in a day or two, for after a few quiet days she's beginning to buck about again. Yes, there they go. The buckets of washing-up water, thick with grease and all sorts of flotsam and jetsam, has just crashed off the form and the deck's swimming. I'll have to finish this little instalment tucked up on the locker above the flood.

The 'great excitement' Cliff refers to involved a collision at sea between Byron *and a Hunt Class destroyer, HMS* Tanatside. *The incident happened at 2.35am in the Bay of Biscay after* Tanatside's *captain mistook* Byron *for a surfaced U-boat and tried to ram her.* Byron *switched on her running lights and took evasive action, but hit* Tanatside's *stern killing one of her depth charge party.*

Although Byron's *bows had been damaged, she was able to resume her patrol. However,* Tanatside *needed major structural repairs and steamed for HM Dockyard Devonport where the work was carried out. Tom Goff recalls: 'Just before Christmas we had sailed from Belfast and picked up a convoy to escort through the Bay of Biscay. In the Bay we were in collision with a British destroyer, I think a Hunt Class. The bows of the ship were fairly well damaged and we had to return to Plymouth, arriving shortly before Christmas Day.'*

17th December 1944, Sunday 7.30pm*

We're so happy today. She's still pitching a lot, but early tomorrow we should be in port for our 48 hours rest. Half the men have headaches, the inevitable consequence it seems of a week or two in heavy seas. I've escaped that little malady, but I can tell you that there have been days this time when I've been about punch-drunk. I've just been talking to the sick-bay attendant who's in our mess and not a bad sort of guy once you get to know him. 'You know' he said, 'it's my opinion and a lot of MOs think so too, that no man over 30 should be drafted to ships like these.' 'That' said I, 'is as it may be, but I'll never find as happy a ship as this. I'll take the discomforts and there are plenty of them, just to remain with such a lot of guys as these.' And that's the truth. When the new skipper came aboard and cleared the lower decks to address the crew he said that everywhere in the Fleet we have the reputation of being one of the noisiest but one of the happiest ships in commission. No, I want no draft until they give me the last draft home.

Byron picked up a radar contact that closer investigation revealed was an abandoned LCM (Landing Craft Mechanised). Byron's *crew salvaged a coil of rope from its cargo well and the frigate tried to take the LCM in tow. When this proved impractical it was decided to sink the LCM with* Byron's *three inch guns because the abandoned vessel was considered a hazard to shipping.* Byron's *commander would have welcomed an opportunity for gunnery practice but Conn called* Byron *away before she could open fire and the LCM was allowed to drift on.*

19th December 1944, Tuesday 10.30. Plymouth

It would have been a bit of an anti-climax yesterday if there had not been those letters and your packet of newspapers too, and those six minutes. For where we are now, and how long we'll be here nobody seems to know, has been nearly blitzed to pieces, and is still such a desolation that after the base it seemed singularly depressing. We walked and walked, chiefly in circles, went in and out of all the shops (there was not a Christmas card of any sort at all left, tell the kiddies I'm so sorry I can do nothing about it) and as there wasn't a canteen open until 3.30 continued to walk and when one at last admitted us took refuge in the Odeon, where we saw Godfrey Tearle in *Medal for the General,* and the Ritz Brothers in *The Singing Musketeers*. It lasted three hours and that's all you could say for it.

23rd December 1944, Saturday 1.00pm

All I want is to move off. For we know that until we do move there can be no leave. If these orders had only come early in the week I'd definitely have been home for Christmas. That's a fact. Still, keep the decorations up. I'll see them yet!

And I'll not have such a bad time. Last night glee singers toured the harbour in a whaler and sang carols off all the ships. And every now and again you hear the old Christmas hymn on the wireless. They make you a bit sad when you hear them, make you think a little too much of home and all you've left and yet it wouldn't be Christmas without them, and somehow you'd hate losing it altogether.

5.30pm. They've come. The two cards and such a long letter too. Your card is beautiful dear. All our other cards – the cards, at least to the three in our little outfit – are on display in our office. Yours is too precious for that. Into my case it's to go with last year's and my birthday card in May. Always I'll treasure them. What a lovely letter too. I'll think of lighting the Christmas tree and in the afternoon while I'm on watch I'll think of you too, listening to the wireless in front of the fire and, I'm afraid, probably waiting for a telephone call which will never come. For we're not to spend Christmas in harbour after all, I can tell you now, for you'll not know until it's all over, that on Christmas Day we'll be at sea, that it will be just another day except for the turkey and the roast pork and the boiled ham.

24th December 1944, Christmas Eve, 7pm

So this is Christmas Eve. It's the strangest ever. I'm writing in my little corner. Holly is twined in all the pipes and festoons every bulkhead. Where it's come from I don't

Cliff and Vi on their wedding day in 1925. (Collection of Sue Seabridge)

Cliff in LDV uniform, during an official
inspection, and his original LDV
armband.
(Collection of Sue Seabridge)

Sailors at the Butlin's holiday camp at Skegness, designated HMS Royal Arthur. The sailors were billeted in the chalets and are seen here cleaning out their accommodation. (ML 15422, with permission of the Museum of Lincolnshire Life)

Original letters, written in pencil. (Collection of Sue Seabridge)

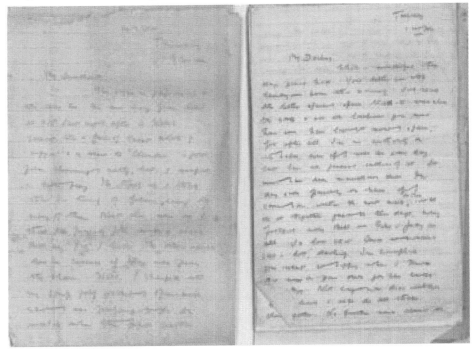

Coder C.G. Greenwood, taken at Hudson's Portraits, Lumley Road, Skegness in 1943. (Collection of Sue Seabridge)

HMS Cabbala was on this site which is now occupied by the Rose Centre, previously Lowton Civic Hall. The plaque is in the entrance hall. (A. Nixon)

Class of coders and their signatures. (Collection of Sue Seabridge)

Cliff and Vi's dog Judy.
(Collection of Sue
Seabridge)

Posing outside the house.

With Vi's sister Emily.

On leave in St Annes. (Collection of Sue Seabridge)

With Vi and evacuees.

Volunteers at the Pollock Dock canteen. (Courtesy of the Belfast News Letter)

A birthday card from Vi. (Collection of Sue Seabridge)

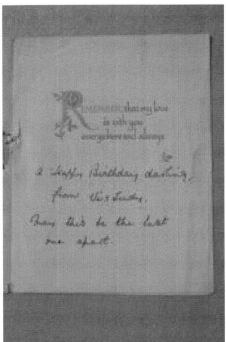

U-1009 and HMS *Byron* at Loch Eriboll. (Imperial War Museum A28521). U-1009 was a Type VIIC vessel – the workhorse of the U-bootwaffe. Her battle pennant is part of the collection at the Gosport Submarine Museum.

The commander of U-1009 Oberleutnant Klaus Hilgendorf surrenders to Admiral Max Horton, commander-in-chief, Western Approaches. (Imperial War Museum HU98325)

The battle ensign and pennant of U-1009 removed from the vessel by the boarding party from HMS *Byron*. (Trustees of the Royal Navy Submarine Museum)

Written on the pennant: 'From U Boat 1009, surrendered to HMS *Byron* at 0810 on 10th May 1945'.

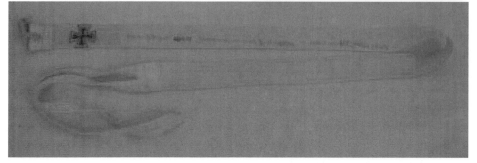

Men from all ships of the 21st Escort Group of Captain Class frigates with their Jolly Roger on board HMS *Conn*. They had returned from a patrol in which they sank four U-boats in less than two weeks. The group's total of five U-boat kills is shown top left. Crossed scalpels, bottom left, indicate two surgical operations performed at sea during patrols. (Imperial War Museum A29198)

Group lead ship HMS *Conn* flying the skull and cross bones. The identification number on her bow has been obscured by the censor. (Imperial War Museum A 28917)

Cliff's medals (from left): War Medal, 1939-45 Star and Atlantic Star ribbon. (Collection of Sue Seabridge)

Servicemen in 1940 being served by WVS ladies at the Sailors' and Soldiers' Free Refreshment Rooms at Preston railway station. Drinks and sandwiches were free to anyone in uniform. (*Lancashire Evening Post*)

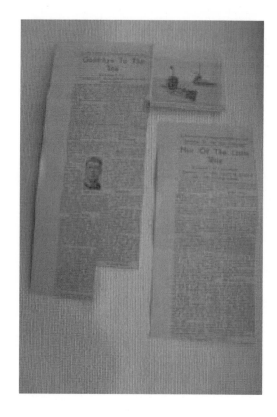

The original articles from the Blackpool *Gazette & Herald*. (Collection of Sue Seabridge)

know. It's all appeared since I went up on watch at 4 o'clock. There's even a spray of mistletoe, but as there are no WRENS on board it's purely decorative. Outside the lighted mess-decks the night is dark and starless and we're in a ship of war. Except for the holly and the mistletoe it's not a bit like Christmas at all. As soon as carols come on the air somebody switches them off. I suppose they make everybody a bit too sad if only they'd tell the truth.

Now it's nearly 9 o'clock and I've had the best supper I've ever had aboard and I'm listening with half an ear to a sort of Christmas Eve party on the wireless and wondering if you're listening to it too. Yes, it was a grand supper and it should have been cheese and pickles. It happened like this. We'd yet another contact this afternoon. Hedgehogs* were ordered and dropped. I refused to rise from my bunk until the hedgehogs nearly lifted me, for believe me, until you've heard a hedgehog explode a few feet below the surface and a few feet from your ship you ain't heard nothing yet. Then came the report that a submarine was surfacing. I rose then – quick sticks! I saw a silver-grey mass rising but it was not a U-Boat but a great shoal of fish killed by the hedgehog – hundreds of them, thousands of them. They forgot all about U-Boats after that. The scramble-nets were lowered. Down them some of the lads and one or two of the officers too, hurtled and with boat hooks spiked the fish by the dozen. There were sufficient fish floating in that little area to have stocked every shop in St. Annes for a month. Our mess took possession of two monsters, gutted them, cut them into 35 slices and the 21 of us had them for supper with bread and butter – about 1/2 lb each. And golly weren't they good and fresh. Some say it was cod, some say it wasn't. But whatever it was it was good. So you see it hasn't been such a bad Christmas Eve after all.

Cliff may have mistaken Hedgehog projectiles for depth charges because the former were designed to detonate only when they scored a direct hit on the hull of a U-boat. There was no doubt, though, about the enormous shoal of fish accidentally killed by the explosion – or the unexpected Christmas bonus that resulted. Tom Goff recalls: 'We were ordered to make our way to Glasgow where we went into a civilian dockyard in the centre of Glasgow near the Custom House. It was on our way from Plymouth to Glasgow we got the fish. We had so much fish we took it into Glasgow and it was sold to a dealer and all the crew had a little extra cash to go on leave.'

Christmas Day 1944, 3.10pm

I've just heard the King. As you were hearing him, I listened to him too. The band which ended his speech is still playing as I write.

No Christmas dinner, not a bit of it. Instead there was a sinister hotch-potch of hash and mashed potatoes and tinned turnips which young Sparks, expecting turkey, politely but firmly declined even to lick, retreating in disgust to the top of the heater, his tail erect and every inch of him registering outraged offence, after I'd chopped a few scraps up for him. What a cat! Still, we're promised the rest of yesterday's bag of fish for supper and during the evening, before I go on watch until midnight I'll lash myself up to one of my chocolate bars.

9.00pm here I am on watch. We'd a game of whist before supper, just four of us: Jock, Harry, Alan the radio mechanic, and myself and as we played I thought to myself 'Well, this is a bit like Christmas' remembering the times when we played with Mother and Pop. Which was about all the Christmas there was left for the supper was not the remainder of our fish, which we suspect some other mess has snaffled, but sausage (one per man) beans (about a dozen per man) and chips and there were so few chips that the chief of the mess – a killick as we call them – and my boss stalked back to the galley, one of the lads solemnly pacing behind him with the tray, and demanded an extra issue. In the end, as the result of this protest, we'd at least ten each. After that we'd had it, the strangest Christmas Day of all.

26th December 1944, Boxing Day 5.00pm

All the decorations have gone now except for the mistletoe and the holly and there was no egg and bacon for breakfast but salted herrings in tomato, which means that everybody contented himself with a couple of slices of bread and butter, and for dinner our old friend Flicka reappeared and I actually bent my fork stabbing into part of his anatomy. The bread too is not as fresh as it was. Still, it's getting towards the end now.

27th December 1944, Wednesday

Fresh air is good. We've been cooped below for hours since I wrote yesterday. There was such a lot happened last night that it was 2.30 in the morning before I crawled – dressed for once – into my bunk. I was up again at 4 o'clock and on until 8. Do you wonder that I slept nearly all morning and nearly all afternoon too? Yes, that fresh air was fine. I needed it. What a lot of clowns these lads are. As I write they're hurling all over the mess-deck the only three cushions we have left in a sort of mad-house rugby match. I know what it is. They're getting excited because this long assignment is nearly over and every day brings our leave nearer.

28th December 1944, Thursday 5.00pm

A new unofficial job today. After the usual two hours in my bunk, I stood in for the librarian who was too busy today to open the case with five packed shelves which, in a little room deep in the stern is our library. I was about half an hour on the job and in that time took 1/6, which is pretty good if not a record. The receipts average about £1 a week. And it all goes into the Canteen Fund, which now has a credit balance of about £140. It's used for all sorts of good purposes on behalf of the ship's company. The other day, after a rating had learned by telegram that his mother had been taken seriously ill and the captain gave him 48 hours compassionate leave, a special meeting of the Committee made a £5 grant to him. We've made other grants too, to men whose homes have been blitzed. Why we're in front of Beveridge!

30th December 1944, Saturday 8.30pm

Yesterday, the first day I think since I left you four months ago I didn't write to you. There were two reasons. One I was so tired. Second, I should never have had the time even if I hadn't been tired, for such a lot happened, such a lot that I can't write to you about. Yes, this is an assignment and a half. It's everything in it. Such a great deal that we'll all be glad when it's ended. We'll leave it at that.

31st December 1944, New Year's Eve 6.00pm

There's only 6 hours of the old year left. Every two or three minutes they seem to be singing Auld Lang Syne on the wireless. It would make you feel a little bit sad if it wasn't for the fact that it's probably the last time I'll have to see an old year out and a new year in without you, and if it wasn't for the other fact that we are coming home. Yes we're on the way. The signal came last night. Our relief arrived this morning. 'Thanks a lot,' he signalled, 'A good leave to you'.

No New Year celebrations for us. Except that we'll be the only mess not reduced to the old Sunday supper of cheese and pickles. In consideration of a tot of rum the cooks put another of the famous fish, slain a week ago, into the refrigerator for us and now, in consideration of another tot, have cooked it for us tonight. We're the envy of the ship and if it's half as nice as it was a week ago it'll be good. Afterwards I'll be on watch at 8 o'clock until midnight and because it's New Year's Eve Tom, one of the telegraphists a nice lad – insists on coming up to the office with me to ensure that I shan't be too lonely. They're a grand lot of guys – that's the one consolation of such a mission as we've been on – one which without them could have been nearly unendurable.

THE WAR IN THE NORTH ATLANTIC – 1945

As the war entered its final year, U-boat attacks became no less ferocious. In fact, from January to May 1945, 231,000 tons of shipping was sent to the bottom, compared to 313,700 for the whole of the previous year. Similarly, 15 escorts were lost in this three-month period, where a total of 32 had been sunk in the preceding 12 months.

As usual, frigates of the Captain Class were in the midst of the action. In the second half of January U-480 attacked convoy BTC 78 in the Western Approaches and sank the merchantman *Oriskany*. However, on 24 January two 'Captains', HMS *Duckworth* and *Rowley* engaged U-480 and sank her with all hands.

The tenacity and courage of U-boat crews was illustrated by a fierce engagement in March when U-546 sank the escort USS *Frederick C Davis* off Cape Farewell. Depth charged by another escort, USS *Flaherty*, U-546 was forced to the surface where she fired a torpedo at *Flaherty*, which missed. Even when the surfaced U-boat had been surrounded by eight escorts, she continued to fight, despite the inevitable conclusion.

For all their bravery and daring, the U-boats could do nothing to prevent Germany's defeat. They had come dangerously close to sinking their target of 800,000 tons of shipping per month, which Admiral Karl Dönitz believed would precipitate Britain's defeat. In the end, though, the U-boat campaign was thwarted by an almost limitless supply of merchant ships from US yards, combined with an increasingly lethal anti-submarine warfare capability, delivered in a large part by ships such as *Byron*.

HMS *Byron* – 1945

The year began with repairs to *Byron's* bows, and escorting convoys in thick fog, which earned *Byron* an official citation: 'Excellent work was done by both escorts in shepherding their charges, but particular credit must go to HMS *Byron* who almost certainly saved at least four ships from going ashore.'

This was followed by actions that resulted in the sinking of four U-boats in less than two weeks by *Byron* and her sisters of 21st Escort Group (27 March to 8 April). One of them, *Redmill*, was torpedoed on 27 April and towed to safety, but later declared a total loss. After VE Day, the group was despatched to Loch Eriboll and played an important role in the mass surrender of U-boats.

Byron was given the honour of escorting the first U-boat to surrender to British forces, U-1009 on 10 May. The captain made full use of Cliff's shorthand and typing skills to report the operation. This gave Cliff an opportunity to view at close hand an historic period at the end of the war, bringing him face to face with the enemy that had lurked menacingly below the surface, as well as in the consciousness of every Allied sailor.

The ship eventually returned to Belfast and then departed to Rosyth. There were two trips across the North Sea to return Norwegian sailors and to service Allied troops organising the withdrawal of German forces.

The repatriation of Norwegian sailors and the joy of their families at being reunited were scenes rarely seen from the deck of a warship and accompanied by fireworks, flares, bonfires and scenes of spontaneous jubilation. In addition, surrendered E-boats were collected and escorted to Bergen. After this, demobilisation was eagerly awaited, but did not come before several shore stations had been visited.

New Year's Day 1945, 12.30pm

We'd a few high jinks – but only a few. Tom sat in with me until a few minutes before midnight. Then, after we'd festooned the sets with a few uncomplimentary greetings for our reliefs, I went below to shake them, found them all, and everybody else in the mess-deck, wide awake, joined in the general chorus of 'Happy New Year' and 'The First Twelve Years Are The Worst' and until nearly 1 o'clock sat drinking coffee. We'd to toast each other in that for it's forbidden to reserve your rum for these little occasions, which was what we'd wanted to do and planned to do until the boss heard about it and insisted on our drinking our tots in his presence at midday.

2nd January 1945

Just a little epilogue today. We're back but no mail is waiting for us. It's been diverted, presumably in error, and there's no definite news of long leave, except that it is to be granted, but for how long or when nobody knows. Still there is to be leave – that's all that matters. But there'll be none for me today. It's not yet been piped but it's certain to be within the next half hour. And I can't go on it and give you a call for three of us have to remain aboard and when we made a draw for it last night I was one of the three to take a card with a cross on it out of the bag. It's just the luck of the draw, but still – never mind.

16th January 1945, Tuesday 1.00pm, after leave. Glasgow

I'm just finishing that bar of Cadbury's blended as I write, and good it is too, and a couple of minutes ago I put your lovely calendar in position. It will be such grand company for me. Now Harry's come up and is writing to Barbara, writing a few lines on a sheet of notepaper, tearing it up and beginning again. Not that I'm surprised at that for I've just read Barbara's last letter to him and, kind and considerate as it is, for she's a darned decent girl and couldn't be anything else, I'm afraid that it's curtains for Harry. There's no question, I fear, that she'll choose the Fleet Air Arm pilot after all. Poor Harry. He's very disconsolate. And what can I tell him to console him except that he's young and will probably soon forget, and he wouldn't believe a word of it.

17th January 1945, Wednesday 11.30pm. Glasgow

Our chief tribulation is that we're sort of living in the Polar regions without going there. The heat is switched off at 8.00pm every day but there's so little of it when it is on that you scarcely notice the difference. There was hot water to wash and shave in this morning but it's the first time that there had been since we went away. For the rest of the time you wash in cold water and shiver and when you visit the lavatories you've to walk about half a mile and once there begin to think after a few minutes that you'll require an ice axe to hack you off the porcelain seat. I squat on a few newspapers and hope for the best.

18th January 1945, Thursday 11pm

Br-r-r. That's me shivering. The heat's come on again for the day but with sleet and snow falling outside and half a gale whistling down every corridor, you'd never notice it. This morning at 7 o'clock I washed and shaved in water so cold that I'd nearly to hack ice off the old map as well as whiskers. But during the night, except for a polar region near the foot of my bunk, which I never explored, so that I'd to sleep curled up in a ball, I was as snug as you please in my thick pyjamas and under two blankets. And now, as I've been lent a blanket by Alan, the radio mechanic, while he's away on the long weekend, I'll at least be warm while I sleep.

They'll soon be off now. The mess-deck's in a turmoil as they pack their suitcases and hunt through lockers which look like the end of a jumble sale. With the few of us left we'll make it tolerable – and I've still a couple of my meat pies left. 'Never Mind' said my chief this morning, as we warmed our hands on our mugs of breakfast tea and gazed balefully at a tray of cold hard-boiled eggs which was our breakfast, 'it won't be long. They're beginning to weed out the old men'. One of the stokers, a man about my age, has already been given his transfer to barracks and expects to be out by April. His is probably an exceptional case, for he qualified for his pension years ago, but at least it shows the trend of events. And if only that Russian steam-roller will keep rolling along it can't last a lot longer. And gosh, isn't it rolling now. Here comes the rum. That's warming me up.

P.S. Sad news for John yesterday. A few minutes after he'd told me that he'd repaired my razor during the leave he had a telegram telling him that his father had died. He was sent off on compassionate leave in less than an hour. I'm so sorry for him. He was so devoted to his old Pop.

19th January 1945, Friday 12.30pm

Here I am writing to you in the little private caboose almost on top of a table radiator. You can hear the ice floes cracking and melting in my innards. It is cold. After a couple of hours in the office this morning I was so nearly encased in ice – or at least I felt as if I was – that my chief, principally I suspect for the benefit of the first lieutenant who'd just walked in out of the heated wardroom, said 'You must go below and get warm. Leave whatever you're doing and beat it'. I beat it. And after my rum and a plate of steaming hot soup I began to thaw out. Now slowly I can feel a lovely warmth creeping all through me.

21st January 1945, Sunday 11pm

Still no letter. I'd be a bit worried if I didn't know that you'd written and if so many of the other lads' letters had not gone adrift. There was not one letter for the mess yesterday and only three today, but as those three had come from long distances and were each dated the 17th it's probable that things are beginning to sort themselves out. I'll just have to wait and be patient, but if there's nothing tomorrow I'll give you a ring when I'm out in the evening. Just to talk to you for three minutes, my darling, would end this sense of loneliness for never have I missed you as I'm missing you now with no word from you after that wonderful leave.

I'd a grand half-day yesterday which was lovely and not too cold, with the sun shining and snow crisp and firm on the pavements. We set off – just two of us, Jim Morgan – one of the telegraphists – and myself – with a couple of cups of hot coffee at a cafe in the city, and afterwards saw the famous Rangers beat Hamilton Academicals 2–0 at Ibrox Park. Willie Buchan, Blackpool's £10,000 forward, played for Hamilton but before the end I was trying to hush up the fact that I knew him, for he was scarcely in the match at all.

23rd January 1945, Tuesday 9.00am

Latest news is that we'll be here until the end of the week or the beginning of next week. I'll not be ashore a lot for I've given one or two of my nights away to Jock, who lives nearby, and to Arthur, the other coder, whose sister or sister-in-law lives here too. I don't mind.

P.S. Now we're told that I can't let the others out as substitutes. So I'll be ashore tonight and on Thursday and Friday. Well, why should I complain? At least I offered. I wonder if you could telephone Jack Heyworth, the music shop fellow in Church Street, Blackpool, and ask him if he could send the Melody Maker to one of my oppos? This fellow, a grand guy, is interested in swing music (after all he can't help that!) and he used to buy this paper every week. I know Mr Heyworth could tell him where he could get it now, or supply it to him by post every week – he'd pay for it. His name is Telegraphist J. Morgan and his number is P/JX 580651. He'll be your friend for life if you can do that for him.

24th January 1945, Wednesday 2.00pm. Glasgow

They've come at last, the letters I've been waiting for. It was grand just to see your writing on the envelopes. And such lovely letters they were too. It's as cold as ever or very nearly. I'm writing this letter, for instance, on the mess-deck where I could scarcely have lived a week ago, writing here because since the other watch returned too many folk have discovered my little caboose and taken possession of it at all hours of the day. Thank goodness they'll nearly all be ashore tonight. As you see we're making the best of it. And I'm one of the few men on the mess-deck who've escaped a cold. Some of them are in a pretty grim state too. And now we've to walk out into the street and pay 1d at a public lavatory, for all ours are frozen. Talk about nature in the raw!

25th January 1945, Thursday 2.00pm. Glasgow

I was in my bunk shortly after 10 o'clock and remembered nothing more until I awakened at 6 o'clock and realised that I was nearly frozen to the sheets. The heat had gone off during the night, something had frozen up, and one result was that there was no water, neither hot nor cold, until after 9 o'clock, except for a thin trickle which lasted a quarter of an hour. I was there when it came and was washed and shaved before half the lads knew what had happened.

I'm afraid we'll sail without my pal. There's been not a sign of Sparks since we came back. He wandered ashore while we were on leave, they say he seemed to miss me, and has vanished. It's probable that he's found a home ashore and prefers it. I don't blame him either.

28th January 1945, Sunday 12.30pm

We're off at last. Where we're going we don't know yet. We may only be returning to base. But we're on the move. It's been a nice rest of three weeks and two days, including the leave. Already I've a new pal. It's another lost and orphaned cat, a tortoiseshell this time. They pick me out, I think. He (if it's a he) wandered into the mess-deck, presumably off the quay, this morning, climbed on my locker at dinner time, butted my arm and in the end gobbled half my pork – if it was pork – and that's not certain.

29th January 1945, Monday 1.00pm*

I'd three slices of bread and butter instead of the regulation two after my lone, lorn sausage at breakfast this morning. You know what that means. Yes, she's beginning to buck and roll again and they're losing their appetites and nearly everything else too. Why there was even bread from yesterday's ration left at dinner today. How these poor lads suffer. Everything's tumbling about. I'd not slept too well either, and wakened at last with such a headache that I'd to take a couple of Aspirins. They soon did the trick. Then I'd an orange, and didn't it taste luscious, and soon I was fine again, only tired. Talk about oranges. I'd another couple from the canteen yesterday and another two today with two apples as well. And now Harry, who doesn't like them, has sold me six. The old locker looks like a harvest festival.

January was an uneventful month for Byron *with much of the month spent freezing in dry dock at Govan. The latest ASDIC (Type 147) was fitted, together with equipment for trials of 'Nightshirt', an improved method of masking propeller noise as a protection against acoustic torpedoes. The Trial took place in Loch Long at the end of the month, after which the ship rejoined the rest of the group from the Clyde on 29th, just in time for the layover in Pollock Dock. The stay in Glasgow was marked by a visit to the ship by Miss Evelyn Lane, who was appearing in musical comedy in Glasgow. Miss Lane was a family friend of the 1st Lieutenant's, and his popularity rose as a result.*

1st February 1945, Thursday 1.00pm

Something has gone wrong with the works. It's seriously affected the fresh water supply, and probably as a result we'll be back at base (the old base too) within a day or two instead of a week or two. And already, they're preparing a leave list for the other watch, for the repairs may keep us in dock for a fortnight or so. Apparently they expect leave to be granted. If it is, our leave comes nearer than we ever dared to hope, within the next two months. It may yet be the beginning of April. How I hope it is, for I'd love to spend your birthday with you.

What a panic it caused when the news of the damage was first announced. This poor old girl is falling to bits. Last night when the fresh water tanks suddenly closed up, we were told that there'd be no further water for washing until we berthed. Everybody stampeded to the wash-basins and showers. There were such queues that I filled a bucket, retired into the privacy of our little caboose and swabbed myself all over (or nearly all over!) and shaved too. We went to our beds resigned to the fact that we'd not have another wash for two days, nor any of our cups or plates either, or even longer. It's not been as bad as that. But the water's on only for the briefest periods every five or six hours, and if you're not on the alert you miss the bus.

2nd February 1945, Friday 1.30pm

I've just been out on the upper deck. It was lovely in the fresh air and the sunshine. The sea had only a gentle swell on it and under the sun it glinted blue-green. Gulls, which have been following us for days, beating on ragged wings into the winds, rested on its surface. We're en route for home too. The water plant has been repaired, temporarily at least, and although the supply's been rationed, it's sufficient if you're up early in the morning, as I was again, washing and shaving in almost complete isolation and meeting, as I went below, a late stampede – too late, for by that time the taps were dry again.

They won't get up, these young ones. The result is that they've been wandering about begrimed and stained all morning and making an awful moan about it. They'll learn, they'll learn. Not that they're as worried as all that. Nobody is. For we're off back again. Do you think we're a selfish lazy lot? Sometimes I think we must be. We should have been out, I suppose, for about a fortnight. Now, at the end of less than a week, we're sailing fast for base and for leave for one watch, and you'd think, that we'd been away in the tropics for a couple of years, as some poor guys have been without a complaint. I feel a bit ashamed sometimes. Yet it's all in the luck of the draw. And this little ship has done its stuff in the last year.

They're all saying in the mess that Old Stripey will be out in a few months while they're acquiring diseased livers in the Far East. They will have their little joke. Still it might happen for all that.

7th February 1945, Wednesday 2.30pm. Belfast

This is a bit of a surprise for you isn't it?* I know you prefer letters which are not typewritten, even if my own writing is nearly illegible, but as I'm all on my own in the office and there's an Underwood in front of me, I decided that just for once I'd type a few lines to you and show you that I can still hammer the keys, that I'm still in practise. It's so quiet in this office. There's no sense of being confined in it. That is chiefly because being one of the exclusive regions it has a porthole. Immediately in front of me I can see framed in the glass a great range of hills, green as only the hills in this country are green, little white cottages scattered at the foot, hedges dividing the fields into perfect squares and rectangles. Now and again the masts of the harbour shipping pass and you hear the wail of the quartermaster's whistle saluting.

I'm definitely installed in the office for the rest of the leave. There's been no end of a commotion about it, for I'm in one of the closest trade unions on earth, and before it will release one of its men to another department there's inevitably a raging dispute.

The correspondence officer is a grand guy (he comes from Leeds so he could scarcely be anything else) and I'm only too glad to give him whatever assistance I can. Which is quite a lot, or it seems to him to be, as I'm the only man on the premises who is not a one finger merchant on the typewriter. Just an hour ago he left me with work which he said would probably keep me at it until it was time to go ashore at 4.30. Well, it's exactly 2.45 now and I'd finished a quarter of an hour ago. 'Why' said he, when I'd dashed him off a few letters yesterday, 'I can't understand why you've never gone in for a commission. They'd recommend you if only you'd ask. Why in heck don't you ask?' 'Sir' said I, 'Thank you very much and all that, but I don't particularly want a commission. In any case, by the time I'd qualified for it it'd be time for me to go home at the rate the war's going now'. 'Yes' said he, 'I suppose it would. And yet…' We left it at that.

Strange regiment this when, apparently, it's a reasonable qualification for a commission if you can hit a typewriter's keys with two or three fingers instead of one. Or is it my nice refined ways which impress them? I don't think it can be that either. For if I ever had any I'm afraid I've lost them now. Still, I should worry. I'm happy enough, happy enough just to wait until the day when they say 'You can go home now'. They won't have to tell me twice. It's just a year ago yesterday since I was given my draft, since they said 'Pack your hammock even if it's not marked Charlie 'Arty, and be off in 45 minutes.' I slept the night in barracks on a table in front of a stove fire, and the following day left for Londonderry, speculating on my fate, a little fearful of it, if

I'll be honest. Just a year ago! What a lot's happened since. It's a year ago almost to the minute that I was in the YMCA at Euston, writing to you, telling you that I didn't know when I'd be able to write to you again, saying the first of a long list of goodbyes. I'm only a year older, but I'm about an eternity wiser, and yet I don't think that in all those things that matter I'm such a lot different. I hope I'm not. You could soon grow sceptical and bitter at this game.

A rare typewritten letter – Cliff usually wrote in pencil.

8th February 1945, Thursday 1pm

Do you know what your husband's gone and done now? He's gone and taken a couple of young WRENS to the pictures. It's a fact. I was out on my own again last night, wondering which cinema I should visit, when I met Harry's beloved Barbara and one of her pals, Stella by name. Both were in a state of acute depression. Less than a couple of bob was the limit of their resources. It was, I suppose, a fortunate sort of meeting, for before he left on leave the love-lorn Harry had implored me to talk to Barbara as if I was her father confessor, not to persuade her to accept Harry but to dissuade her from accepting the Fleet Air Arm suitor merely because he'd been a family acquaintance for years and because it was expected of her. A delicate sort of mission. I promised I'd do what I could if the chance presented itself. Afterwards, we drifted to the canteen, where these two lasses are also numbered amongst Mrs Nield's clientele. And what did I tell Barbara? Precisely nothing at all.

She talked about Harry, admitted that she was fond of him, said – and I couldn't help smiling when she said it – 'But he's so young, you know, he takes everything so seriously,' and said it so seriously herself. She's so old, exactly 20. Still, I had the impression that she's lots of common sense – as these Yorkshire lasses have – and there was no indication whatever in anything she said that she intended saying yes to the Fleet Air Arm, if she says it at all, merely out of politeness and for courtesy's sake. So I left it at that. It would have been so thundering presumptuous and impertinent to do anything else. And, after all, I can't be matchmaker and a sort of matrimonial bureau to the whole mess.

9th February 1945, Friday 1.00pm. Belfast

A lovely letter from you yesterday and a packet of newspapers from Mother, including a copy of the Melody Maker. You should have seen Jim Morgan's face break into a big broad grin as soon as he saw it. He was still reading it in his bunk when I went to sleep at 10.30.

10th February 1945, Saturday 1.45pm. Newcastle, Co. Down

I've just tumbled into the train, clutching a couple of sandwiches and a bun, which I'm eating as I write. I'm off, just for four hours to see the family and to crash into a certain telephone call, if I'm given the chance. Less than an hour ago I was in the office, hammering like mad at the keys, racing against time. I'd been at it since nine o'clock. At 12.45 I tore below, changed into my No. 1s, was finished in time for inspection (nobody noticed that I'd not even washed) walked fast for a mile to the dockyard gates, took a taxi to the station, arrived five minutes before the train left, booked my ticket (it's only 2/6) bought my sandwiches and bun and fell into this packed, jolting compartment.

I'm writing now, because this may be the last letter to reach you, but not the last I'll write, for a time, even for a long time, for if the latest rumour is correct we're going somewhere definite and not just pottering about. I hope we are. The time passes such a lot more rapidly that way.

11th February 1945, Sunday 1.30pm

Wasn't it lovely to talk to each other again last night? It was, admittedly, a spasmodic sort of conversation, but at least we said hello and goodbye and I've told you all the news in my letters. You sounded so sad when I said we might be off today. We haven't gone after all and we might not go tomorrow either, and yet go we must someday soon. All I'm concerned about is that you shouldn't worry too much. Worry a bit you will, I know, that's inevitable, but not a lot for there's no reason to where we're probably going and in any case wherever it is it's not half as hot as it has been and you know that the winter seas don't affect me a little bit. I'll be fine, wherever I am. Always I'll have your love and your prayers to protect me. That knowledge alone makes all the difference. It always has and it always will.

12th February 1945, Monday 1.30pm

We're six hours out already. And already the old routine seems as familiar as ever. There are even the inevitable stowaway cats and, just as inevitably, they've wandered into our mess. Now I'm back in the old office. The calendar is above me as I write, the first 11 days of the month crossed off, the twilit Derbyshire scene making me forget all about the sea and think only of the happy days which are to come. It's restful in harbour, but everything's at a standstill there. Now we're out and every day, every hour, I'm coming nearer to you. Nothing else nothing in all the world matters.

13th February 1945, Tuesday 11pm

Everything's quiet. The only excitement we've had is when the wireless programme was interrupted last night to announce the decisions of the Big Three. Nearly everybody leaped out of his bunk to hear it when the music suddenly faded at 9.30. Then came the anti-climax. For, before the announcer had said more than a dozen words, the quarter-master whistled 'Pipe Down' and in the wireless office, where the ship's broadcast is operated, and where they knew nothing of the special bulletin, they switched it off. We'd to wait until this morning before we knew what it was all about. They seem to mean business this time. Well, it's better to finish it once and for all. This mustn't happen again. Here comes the rum. Down the hatch with it.

14th February 1945, Wednesday 1.30pm

That's all the plates and cups stacked away and the deck swept – I'm a cook today. We suffered a lot for a couple of hours last night when we sailed out of the calm into a tempest and out into the calm again. Chaos in those two hours! For the first time one towering wave crashed through an open door and cascaded spray down into the mess-deck. In one cupboard a pickle bottle broke and spilled its thick brown juice all over everything, soaked into the jam and poured over every shelf. Two buckets piled with all the gash from tea and a kettle full of cold tea skidded half the length of the deck and fell over scattering something which looked like the bottom of an ash pit. What a shambles.

15th February 1945, Thursday 2pm

Out on the upper deck the sun is shining. There's a cold wind blowing but the air's as fresh and fragrant as a hill top, after a storm which came out of the blue last night. This time there was an accident too, for in one of the seamen's messes a kettle of tea fell from a table over a man in his bunk and scalded his face so severely that the sick-bay attendant told me this morning that the poor guy – bandages covering every inch of his face except one eye – may be disfigured for life. Now I've just crossed 14 off my calendar. The days are passing, sweetheart. It's just a year ago today that I left Londonderry on draft to this ship.

16th February 1945, Friday 1.30pm

Just had another orange!* They issued three at the canteen yesterday – 15 in three days unless my arithmetic's all wrong – and half an hour ago I missed a lemon by about a couple of minutes – a lemon I'd intended for home, for I suppose it wouldn't have shrivelled up in the few weeks only which are left before I'm home now. Yes, only a few weeks. Isn't that wonderful?

* Oranges were a rare luxury in the Navy as well as at home. John Whithouse wrote in a letter to his family: 'We got an orange each today – a round, orange-coloured thing, about the size of a cricket ball.'

18th February 1945, Sunday 5.00pm

What a surprise we had today. The morning dawned with us near a port. We anchored for a short time. Sorted out the instalments of my serial, packed them in a privilege envelope, gobbled my Sunday breakfast and raced up to the ship's office with it a few minutes before the boat left. Then off we went again. I hope the letter has arrived. In the meantime don't we have fun and games? You'd never think there was a war on. It may be a sign of the times, a sign that it's nearly all over but already they're beginning to re-introduce the old peacetime routine. First intimation of the minor revolution was a notice posted yesterday that in future lanyards would have to be worn whenever we went ashore. Lanyards! All these old Jacks were outraged! They couldn't have been more nauseated if they'd been told to wear bibs and tuckers and nappies.

But that's not all. No ordinary rating under 20 is any longer to be allowed all night leave, and there are whispers that soon we're to be called every morning at 6.15 instead of 7.00, that all messes will have to be cleared out by 9.00 instead of any old time before noon, as is the casual way, and that there are to be divisions and evening quarters – as at Caballa – whenever we're in harbour, which will mean changing into No. 3s every day. Personally I don't give a hoot for all this – it'll do some of them no harm to smarten them up a bit, even if it all seems a lot of nonsense, but to one new regulation, which is in force already, I have strong objections. This is an order that now we're to sleep head to tail, that no longer is it permissible for you to sleep with you head practically on your neighbour's pillow which is not too hygienic, I agree, but with your feet near the head, which in certain cases might not be so darned hygienic either! What'll happen? I don't know. It should be interesting.

Just before 11 o'clock tonight will be the first anniversary of my coming aboard. I'll be on watch but I'll drink a little toast on my own in cocoa to a year which wouldn't have been bad at all if it hadn't meant a separation from you. Yes, I've made the grandest friends I've ever had – such grand friends – but I've missed you, how I've missed you.

19th February 1945, Monday 1.30pm

My, but wasn't I excited and surprised last night? I had just gone on watch just after 6 o'clock, when one of the lads raced into the office. 'Come out on the upper deck – there's something that'll interest you' he said. Out I went and far away in the distance was Blackpool Tower! It was exactly 12 ½ miles away. So near, and yet so very far. Where were you, I wonder dear? Resting after tea – if you ever rest now – and listening to the 6 o'clock news. If only you'd known I think we'd have been visible, far away on the horizon. I borrowed a pair of binoculars. I could see the tower of the White Church,* the white bulk of the Woolworth building to the right of the Tower, the Casino and below the line of the Promenade, the golden-brown plain of the Blackpool sands. It was all in view for half an hour. I stole that half-hour out of the watch and looked and looked and looked until everything faded out in the twilight. That was yesterday's high spot.

In Ansdell, North of Lytham.

20th February 1945, Tuesday 1.30pm

After yesterday's storm the sun is shining and the sea is calm. And somewhere, not visible as we pass this time, but not far away, is the Fylde coast. No I've not been such a long way away these last few days. And still nothing out of the ordinary has happened. One day is so like another that I've to think twice – or look at my calendar – to know the day of the week. We're busy on every watch, busier than we've ever been, but that only makes the time pass faster than ever. Now there's a chance that we may come in for a couple of days before continuing our present assignment. If we should I'll have one night ashore and definitely there'll be a telephone call included in the itinerary.

22nd February 1945, Thursday 5.30pm

We're back again. Only for two days, but it will be a rest, a lovely rest. Now, in an hour and a half I'll be ashore. You know where my first call will be. I'm only afraid that we've been delayed so long that all the lines will be booked and that, and I may not go out tomorrow – we've to share the two nights and I've unluckily drawn the first and shorter one – I may not be able to talk to you after all. Still, at least I'll try and definitely I'll be able to post this letter. But I would love you to know that for two days at least we'll be snug in harbour, sleeping all night and resting, for I've still a bit of a suspicion that you worry yourself about me and honestly this time there's been no need for you to do so.

All afternoon I've been at a canteen committee meeting. Now I've typed all the minutes and delivered them to the First Lieutenant who, I suspect, considers this speed almost indecent and almost incredible in this regiment. And now I'm on my last watch for at least a couple of days. Then I'll be off just to try and book a line.

23rd February 1945, Friday

As I feared I was too late last night. By the time I reached the telephone it was 8.15 – and all the way through nearly a mile of thick mud I had to walk and in drizzling rain, too – and as soon as I asked for the number the operator said 'All lines engaged for the night'. It was only a 100–1 chance at the best and it didn't come off. So I resigned myself to the inevitable – it's surprising how you accustom yourself to doing that – posted a little serial to you and the letters to Aucklands and Scarborough too. Called with the young radio mechanic, Alan, in a pub where, according to agreement, we had half a pint to celebrate his promotion to PO and, afterwards we wandered to the canteen where there was the usual joyous reunion with Mrs Nield. There was another consignment of eggs in the kitchen. So we ordered them poached on toast. The ration was one egg per customer. But when our plates came out of the kitchen there was an extra slice of bread and butter on the edge of each of our plates and beneath this slice an extra egg was hiding coyly. Afterwards we'd two lovely slices of bacon and bread and butter – and doesn't brown bread taste good when you haven't had it for ages? Having polished off that little lot, back we went aboard. It was early but both of us were impatient to be back in case the mail had been delivered. And it had. Near my bunk, on the table, was a pile of eight letters and two packets of newspapers – four letters from you and two each from Mother and Mamie. I've not even opened the newspaper packets yet but I read all the letters as soon as I'd peeled off my wet overcoat and then, once in my bunk, I cuddled up, lit a cigarette and read four again. What lovely letters they were too, and longer than ever. In them, in all your letters, is all the sort of news I love to read. You don't know what a difference they make.

P.S. Just seen my classification in the ship's list. I suppose I shouldn't have seen it at all and I'm no snooper and wouldn't have seen it except by accident. Against my name was SUP which is an abbreviation of superior and the highest they can give.

16th March 1945, 9.15pm. Preston Station

So soon again I'm writing to you, but I know you'll be lonely and at least there'll be these few lines for you. All I have to write are two words – 'Thank You', thank you my darling for another lovely holiday. So short it seems to have been – too short – and yet it's left memories which will be my companions until I come home again. And that won't be long my dear, only a couple of months or even sooner. The days will soon pass. Each one I'll cross off my calendar. One by one they'll go, faster and faster, until the days become weeks, and there's only four weeks in one month and eight weeks in two. Yes, it'll soon go darling mine. And soon, too, will come the leave now which will be the best leave of all; that leave when I'll come home and say 'well, that's that', and never go away again, never again.

17th March 1945, Saturday 3.30pm. Belfast

It's less than 24 hours since I left you and yet it seems like ages ago. I've washed and shaved now and my locker is tidied and my bag emptied, but when I landed aboard at 2 o'clock I was so tired, so begrimed, so utterly weary that I felt as if I'd been trailing across trackless wastes for days or even weeks.

It all began at Preston where there was a stampede for a train packed when it arrived. We tumbled into a corridor and were glad even of that little privilege and there we huddled for nearly seven hours, until 5 o'clock in the morning. There were three RAF kitbags piled in a heap near one of the carriage doors and on these I laid for a time, but it seemed as if they were packed with old boots and crowbars after I'd been sprawled on them for half an hour, and in the end I stood propped against a wall and tried to sleep like a horse. It didn't come off. I'm no horse! Then, at last, out into the cold dawn we stumbled, boarded the boat, raced below, bagged two lifebelts each and using one as a pillow and one as a miniature sort of mattress, laid ourselves full-length on the forms near one of the bulkheads and slept and slept. I slept from 5 until 8, awakened, had my sandwiches and the orange and weren't they good – and slept again until 10 o'clock, when at last we sailed. Whereupon I slept some more and climbed out on to the upper deck only in time to see the hotel where once we spent a night, and two cars on the coast road where once we had such a lovely day. Then, when at last we were ashore again, the train crawled as only trains in this country can crawl and it was 2 o'clock before I climbed the gang plank.

That made a total of 18 hours. Do you wonder, in spite of all that sleep, that I'm still a bit tired? Now I feel a bit settled again. Volunteers are being invited from the ship's company to transfer to the Army. And if there are no volunteers it'll probably be a case of You, You and You. No man over 35 will be accepted.

18th March 1945, Sunday 1.30pm. Belfast

We've been allowed to see our service documents today. Our chief is very disconsolate because there are so many 'moderates' and only four 'superiors'. But not one of the lads is a bit envious about my distinction, and a bit of a distinction it is, I suppose. Everywhere I've been I've been given a VG; I'm not a bit conceited about it, that's not one of my faults, but it may all help when the last day comes and special demobilisation privileges are lashed out.

19th March 1945, Monday 12 noon

We'll be off in a couple of hours. There are rumours that we're going no great distance this time, that within a day or two we may be able to post letters. There's a sense of imminent change in the air. Everything seems strangely unsettled. As I'm writing now the lower deck has been cleared of all men who went on leave and they're being told about the Army transfer plans. Many of the lads will have to go – that's certain. Some will go voluntarily, the rest will be drafted. I'm not affected for I'm over 35, but there's a fine old panic below decks, I can tell you, everybody's in a flat spin. They curse the Navy all day and every day.

20th March 1945, Tuesday 2.20pm

How these young men can sleep. I thought I was good at it but I'm only an amateur. After nearly an hour in my bunk, which is long enough, even after a morning watch, I've climbed out of the darkness of the mess up into my little caboose, where I'm writing now. It was too cold to stay below any longer. They've decided now that the mess-decks have been too hot and last night all heat was switched off in them. That was one extreme to another, a little RN habit. Now they've put thermometers in every deck. Ours was registering 60 when I left a few minutes ago. That's not too cold I suppose. Yet it's not too warm either. I know it was warmer out in the sunshine on the upper deck, where I went for half an hour after dinner and loved every minute of it, until a rain squall drove me in.

21st March 1945, Wednesday 2.30pm

Home never seems far away. About an hour ago, just before I fell asleep, the edition of 'Merry Go Round' I heard on the evening I left you was repeated. It seems funnier than ever, for that other time I was a bit sad, as I always am when I've to say goodbye. Now I'm beginning to settle into the old routine again and the days are galloping away even if it still seems almost incredible that it was only a week ago that I went with you to see the Players. Yes, I'm settling down now. I only wish the sea would settle too. It lashed itself up into a rare old fury again last night. I couldn't sleep before the middle, for the 4 hours during it everything in the office was in a state of chaos. I know nothing that can tire you as 4 hours such as those can. Fortunately it was not busy until about 2 o'clock and in those two hours I wedged myself in a corner and read the first 50 pages of James Lonsdale Hudson's book *And Yet I Like America*. It's most interesting, written in the form of a diary, each day complete in itself, almost as I write to you, except of course, that he's wandering about the States and has lots of material and I'm marooned in a little ship and can only write about all the commonplace little things which make our days and nights.

They're beginning to listen to the news now. There wasn't a whisper in the mess when they cut into the dance band to announce the American's latest advance to the Rhine last night. They're all lining up for the kill. No, it won't be long. Everything's moving to the end.

22nd March 1945, Thursday 2pm

Four days out already. In another week we may be in for a couple of days rest. We may, with a bit of luck, be in for Easter. I hope we are. But wherever it may be I'll put in a call, for just to hear your voice again would be all I ask. Only six days since I left you. Only a week since I had my long day in the garden and didn't I love every minute of it? It seems much longer and that's strange, for actually the days are beginning to fly again.

23rd March 1945, Friday 4.15pm

I've slept nearly two and a half hours this afternoon. It's the longest continuous sleep I've had for a day – or a night – or two. Every evening she begins to roll and pitch just after sunset and for the rest of the night spins in circles. Nobody seems to know what causes it, it just happens. And as a result, and with the mess-deck still cold, even I only seem to be able to sleep in snatches. But after having to rise at 4 o'clock in the morning, I was so tired again that I nearly went to sleep standing up. Now, this afternoon, the temperature's risen to 65 and so I tumbled into my bunk soon after dinner and knew nothing more until 3.15. The mess was still in darkness. So off I pottered to the bread locker on my own, found that nearly all the bread had patches of green mould on it, returned to our own cupboard, where we'd still three or four dry

116

loaves left, cut one into thin slices and toasted the lot for our lads before the other messes had risen from sleep.

Messages are coming in now, I'll finish later.

24th March 1945, Saturday 2.45pm

Do you know what I'm chewing as I write in the little caboose this afternoon? Ship's biscuits plastered with butter. It's the first time I've had them since we went to Russia over a year ago. 'Yes' said I, talking as an old sea-dog to those of the lads who've joined the ship since, 'We had them 11 out of the 14 days. It WAS a war in those days.' Were they impressed? Not a bit. We'll have to live on them now for a day or two – on them and little else – for the bread stores have ended and after the cooks had baked last night it was found that the flour had been infected too and all their bread had to be destroyed. If it hadn't been detected there might have been a dysentery epidemic. Now, I suppose, the gulls will have one instead. Although I think they can eat anything, even our famous steak and kidney puddings. Gosh, but these biscuits are hard; my old teeth won't bite through them. I've to let them soak in my mouth.

What about the news? They flashed the announcement of Montgomery's offensive just as I was going to sleep. Is it the beginning of the end? It may only be a matter of weeks now.

25th March 1945, Sunday 1.30pm

Oh, those biscuits! A year ago I could make something of them. Now I'm afraid my old teeth just won't chew them. I'll bring one home as a little relic, offer it to the dog and see what she does with it. Although I think I know what she'll do. And it won't be a bit polite. Show her the stain at the bottom of this page. Let her lick that. That's the chocolate off my fingers. Yes I'm having to raid the stores as I know you'd want me to, for the biscuits are not only so like concrete that they give you indigestion – not even in hot tea can you soften the brutes – but constipation is another of their legacies and so I'm not eating them at all, and without my beloved bread and butter I'm darned hungry at times.

26th March 1945, Monday 2pm

It's only a few days now before we'll be back in harbour. Aren't I glad too, for no bread can be baked, so I'm told, until the ovens have been made immune from infection and that can't be done until we reach base. Those biscuits! I had another go at them at breakfast but the old teeth – the few I've left – simply couldn't bite them.

She's rolling a bit this afternoon – I can't keep this pad still – but it's not too bad and the sun is shining all the time and it's still as quiet as ever. The radio's back in action and we know that the news is still good. The end can't be far off now. There seems to be a general impression that we shall all be separating pretty soon now. Jock seems to think that once they pay off, we old men will be sent to complete our time to home shore bases. What I'd better apply for – if you could apply for anything in this regiment, but you can't – is a job in Tom's office. Now that for a month or two would be a bit of all right.

27th March 1945, Tuesday 5pm*

Before the end of this week we should be in for two days. And we'll be able to do with them too. Not that, after all, we'll have to wait until then before we have a bit of bread, for they've been able to bake again after putting an emergency oven into commission and rationed to one slice a meal, excluding dinner, at least we'll not be without entirely. I've just had my first slice for four days, thick with butter and fresh from the galley. Except on that first Russian convoy I've never been as long without bread. The things we do for England.

One of the lads has just given me half his slice of bread. 'You can't eat the biscuits and I can' he says. Aren't they a decent lot of guys? I'll miss them when I have to leave them and it seems about certain that we'll have to part soon. You can say nothing for the war except that in it you make the best friends you ever make anywhere. Those who've stayed behind have missed that.

* *This was the start of a remarkable run of success for 21st Escort Group. U-965 was sunk by* Conn, Deane *and* Rupert *between Cape Wrath and the Butte of Lewis on 27 March. Later that day,* Byron, Fitzroy *and* Redmill *found U-722 between Eriskay and Skye and a combined attack by the three frigates sent the submarine to the bottom. The group continued the hunt along the 100-mile-long narrow channel, searching every cove and inlet. This perseverance paid dividends on 30 March when* Rupert *made contact with U-1021 less than 10 miles from Enard Bay, in an inshore position.* Conn *and* Deane *joined* Rupert *to destroy U-1021. There were no survivors from any of the three U-boats.*

29th March 1945, Thursday 3pm

Now all our little plans have been upset. We're to have two days rest, but not at base, but at a little outpost where it's improbable that I'll be able to call you and where they may not even sell birthday cards. And it won't be for a day or two yet either. It will be no great hardship for two days, which merely means one night ashore and a bit extra to eat are a brief interlude and nothing else. But if it means that your birthday will pass by in silence I shall be sorry.

30th March 1945, Good Friday 3pm

And what a strange Good Friday it is too. Nine out of every 10 men in this ship couldn't, I bet, tell you it was Good Friday at all. No fish, no hot cross buns, no service, nothing to suggest that it's a day different to any other. Where will I be next Good Friday, I wonder? Back home with you I hope. Remember our last one together. We went with little Judy for a walk in the Green Drive after I'd been given the afternoon off, sheltered under the trees when a thunderstorm came on and in the end raced out of the rain to the club house, where Jim Steer lashed us up tea and toast in the new dining hall. We'll have lots of half days like that again.

I'm writing again in the little caboose. It's become almost a routine two afternoons out of three – the third I'm on watch. I sleep, huddled under my hammock, out of the cold, for about two hours after dinner, awaken about 2.45, creep out of the darkened mess while the rest of them sleep on and come into this quiet room. It's almost as if I've been with you for half an hour each day again. Twice there have been brief but violent storms since I wrote to you yesterday. And what storms they were too. I was out on the upper deck this morning when the squalls began to blow, stood for a few minutes while the spray lashed my face, and retreated only when the waves began to leap up over the bulwarks. Gosh, that freshens you up. **P.S.** They're laying bets in the mess that the war will be over in a fortnight. Well, that could happen.

31st March 1945, Saturday 2pm

Nothing official yet, but we may be in tomorrow. If only because it will be a rest from these endless watches we'll all be glad of it. It promises to be little else for it's just the back of beyond where we'll be going, a territory of bare hills chiefly inhabited by sheep, with one canteen in it and very little else. Still, I'll go ashore if only for a birthday card, if only the rain, which has been falling for hours, ceases. Meanwhile the seas are high again and we're being buffeted about something horrible. Only a few minutes ago a metal stamp flew off a ledge in the office and missed my bean by inches.

1st April 1945, Easter Sunday, 4am

Good morning. Notice the time? We're still on watches even during the rest. Now we're wondering why they call it a rest. For a little recompense we were shown a film last night, *The Sullivans*, and it was one of the best films I've seen for ages. And today some time we may be able to go ashore. And later the mail, (which has come by air) should be delivered. That's what we're waiting for.

2nd April 1945, Monday 11.40pm

There were only 12 letters for the whole ship's company this afternoon. When that plane lands – if it ever lands at all while we're here and, gazing at the landscape, you could scarcely blame it if it didn't – there'll be bags and bags for me. But the chances seem to be now that we'll have gone before it ever arrives and, out for another 10 or 12 days, that'll mean that I'll have been a month without hearing from you. Still what a batch there'll be when we do reach base again. How I'll read them, every precious word, and all the papers too. And then I will have a rest – a real rest – for a whole week. And during it I'll go over to see Jack and take them the parcel which still reposes in my locker for I never had a chance to post it. And I'll talk to you – just for three minutes – if we don't make it six. It will come soon. All I hope is that my serial in two parts reached you in time for your birthday for it was the only present I could send you, not even a card. But you'll know that all the time on Wednesday I'll be thinking of you, that my first words when I wake will be 'Happy birthday dearest'.

Now Harry, the Rejected Lover has disgraced himself. He dearly wanted me to go ashore with him this afternoon. I couldn't if I'd wanted to and I didn't want to a bit. For half a gale was blowing and there were rain squalls every few minutes and the land looked bleak and bare. Apparently there's little ashore except a wet canteen – a very wet canteen. And that's where Harry went. He came back aboard under his own power, but only just. Now I've been below and tucked him in and taken possession of his wallet which he'd left in his overcoat pocket for anybody to lift.

Won't he be penitent in the morning?

3rd April 1945, Tuesday 1.00pm. Belfast

We're off again for 10 or 12 or 14 days, the estimates vary. We've been out now for nearly 24 hours. The new sheet on the calendar, the sheet for April, is in view. There's on it a path curving past a wooded hillside in Somerset. One of the lads has just wandered in, seen this path, and said 'Why, a couple of years ago I camped round that corner.' He's seen another sheet showing a village street in Hampshire. In the foreground is an old inn. In it his uncle was born. And behind the inn, in the shadow of a church spire which soars up in the background, is the house there his mother once lived. The world's small isn't it?

Poor Harry. Isn't he penitent? 'Never,' says he 'will I go ashore without you again'. And I don't think he will either. He's so ashamed of himself.

No mail has come yet, but there's a buzz that a few bags may be delivered at sea in a day or two. If only that's true. How I'm missing those letters of yours, wondering what's happening, wanting to know all you are doing, all the news about our home and the garden and everything. It seems such a long time and yet it's not three weeks since I left you. But then, whenever I'm away from you, for however long or short a time, everything seems incomplete.

4th April 1945, 9.00am. Your Birthday

I've just finished my cooks again, washed and scrubbed the deck, and now I'm in the little caboose all on my own. Up here last night I'd a lovely supper after coming off the last dog. Harry and I borrowed an old tin jug, heated water in it over the radiator (an operation which took about half an hour) toasted two slices of bread each, made a jug of coffee and boiled our last two eggs. And we boiled them for 3 minutes too, just as I like them. The pity was that just as the feast was ending the old ship gave a sudden lurch and the jug with about half a pint of coffee in it tumbled to the deck, flooded everything and left us with a bit of a shambles which took us about half an hour to clean up. Still, it was worth it.

Now I've been on the morning, up since 4 o'clock, and the bunk seems inviting but I suppose I'll have to wait until this afternoon, for naps in the forenoon are forbidden. Half an hour with my book seems indicated. Then down I'll go below for my stand-easy cuppa. Soon afterwards it will be time for rum. You know what my toast will be today – 'Happy Birthday'.

5th April 1945, 5.00pm. My Day

Yes sweetheart, it was your day yesterday and it's mine today, for a ship came out from base today with our mail, all of it, four bags of it. And there were seven letters from you and two packets of newspapers, two letters and another packet of papers from Mother and Pop and a letter from Mamie. Ten letters and three packets. It was a record for the mess, probably a record for the ship. But then nobody has a wife like mine. One of the lads just said over tea (he always professes to be a bit of a cynic) 'Seven letters from his wife. There must be something in this love business after all.'

It was noon when the mail was delivered. People would realise all that letters mean to us if they could only have been there. Everything stops for these letters. The two tables were left in a litter, abandoned by the cooks. Men squatted everywhere, smoking like chimneys, bent over this precious mail of theirs. For once the mess, which is generally as noisy as a world's fair, was so quiet that it was incredible. I crept out, the pocket of the old blue jacket bulging, climbed to the office, tucked myself in a corner, arranged my little batch in order of the date stamps and read them slowly one after the other. They gave me the happiest hour I've had since I sailed.

All I hope is that by now the two instalments of the serial have arrived to reassure you, to give you all the news, to persuade you that there's no cause for concern. It's almost merely a case of passing the time now. Last night it was so lovely and calm that, muffled in my overcoat, I was out on the upper deck until twilight came and then when I went below there was coffee waiting for me. And they pay me for this – 4/6 a day! Yet we have been distinguishing ourselves although exactly how I'm not permitted to tell you yet. One day soon it will be in the papers, so we've been told today, and we've been told to expect photographers to meet us when we berth at last. It would be a change for me to give an interview instead of asking for one. Yes, you'll read all about it one day. And this time the name of this little ship will be in the headlines or ought to be. I can say nothing more than that.*

*Three days later EG21 attracted even more press attention when it added to its tally of three U-boat sinkings from 27 to 30 March. Fitzroy and Byron sank U-1001 off the south of Ireland on 8 April, bringing the total number of U-boat sinkings to four in 12 days.

6th April 1945, Friday 2.00pm

I'm loving those papers you sent darling. I open a packet, arrange everything in order of the date and read them one by one. The Diary (how long ago it seems since I wrote it), the leaders, the letters, everything. What a grand number of the Daily Express that was too, the one with the article by William Bankeley on 'The Mystery of Adolf Hitler'. I've cut out the map of Germany on the front page. All the mess consult it after every news bulletin. At last we know how far they've gone and how fast they're going. Before, all those place names, names of falling cities and towns, meant nothing. Now we know exactly where we are and I think at last we're near the end.

We're approaching the end of this particular little assignment too. And about time. We've been reckoning it up. When we reach base this time we'll have spent 7 of the last 8 weeks at sea. That's pretty hot for a small ship, a bit too hot.

7th April 1945, Saturday 7.30pm. Belfast

I heard the broadcast of the Chelsea-Millwall Southern Cup Final, a bit of the first half as I had my tea, the second half in snatches as I ran in and out of my little cubby-hole in the W/T office between messages. At least I heard both goals. Then, as soon as the first dog ended, I went below, posted myself near the mess-deck loudspeaker and wrote the results in shorthand for the stoker's pontoon. Poor old Blackpool!* They're not what they were. And poor old Stripey too. I've had Hamilton Academicals and they didn't play at all. I was thinking seriously of asking for my bob back until I learned that in these circumstances a team is credited with three goals.

At last I've finished all the papers. How I enjoyed them, including the article from the Radio Times on 'Mulberry', which half the mess has read by now. So we were 'part of a great team who laboured to bring about a great end'. Well, I suppose we did. Yes, we're proud to have been in it; at least I know I am.

* Lost 1–4 to Oldham.

8th April 1945, Sunday 3.00pm

Wasn't I tired after the middle this morning? It was one of the busiest watches I've ever had. I was at it so fast that during the whole of the four hours I hadn't a chance to go down to the galley for a jug of cocoa. Then, after less than three hours sleep, I'd to be up to go on the forenoon at 8 o'clock and after the usual Sunday morning breakfast of bacon and eggs, was in the office again until noon.

You go from one extreme to another in these watches, there's no happy medium. I was able to write another of my back-home-from-sea letters, and to finish one of the two tales in my new Maigret book. Now I've the first tonight and the prospect of all night in my bunk. There's no confirmation of the buzz that the leave is to be extended, but definitely leave is to be granted, it will be the usual 7 days and there are to be all sorts of high jinks. There's talk about a brass band on the quay as we sail into harbour. Talk about 'See the Conquering Heroes Come'. And we're supposed to be so modest in the Navy. Actually nobody knows what will happen except that a lot of ale will probably flow. All I know is that the other day a depth charge attack slew a shoal of fish again, a lot of eels this time, and that we're to have fish and chips for supper. Which is vastly preferable to cheese and pickles, the traditional Sunday ration. I only hope we don't make a 'rill mill of ills'. Give me cod any old time.

10th April 1945, Tuesday 5.30am

Notice the time and the day. As I wrote that last word on Sunday afternoon I heard the Captain's loud-speaker calling me to the bridge. We'd gone into action – 'Action Stations' were piped immediately afterwards – and I was required to act as a sort of chronicler of events. Since then I've had the sort of exciting hours which are not supposed to be good for old men rising 42, but which seem to suit me fine. There was no danger, no heroics, it was the other fellow who was for it and who eventually had it, but from 4 o'clock on Sunday afternoon until midnight and again from 8 o'clock yesterday morning to 6 o'clock at night, with only a couple of quarter-hours snatched for meals in the galley, the rest came up to the bridge, sandwiches and oodles of cups of tea, ordered for me by the lads, I was the Captain's shadow, recording in shorthand every order he gave and every incident which followed, timing everything on a stop-watch and now and again, when the rest of the bridge staff were engaged, repeating his commands down the voice pipe to the chart house and engine room. Talk about being in the front row of the stalls at a premiere. I was there this time making news instead of writing it. And was I excited? You bet I was.

Muffled in a great duffle coat, the brown hood peaked over my head, I was perched high in the fore-bridge. The wind lashed your face, the sun burned down hour after hour, and when the order was 'Full Speed Ahead' as it often was, the wind seemed to become a howling gale and the bow wave rose in a great white cloud of spray which fell on us as if a thin rain was in the air. And there we crouched, darting in and out, as busy and as hostile as a gad-fly on a summer's afternoon. And was it grand? I loved every second of it. It was the real thing at last.

And when eventually it was all over it had delayed our return to base admittedly, but it made it almost certain that if our brass band was indicated before, a couple should be commissioned now. You should see me now. The gang were amazed when at last I went below to the mess-deck again. The wind – and there's music for you, never mind brass bands, the music of a wind wailing past the bridge of a ship cutting the water with every knot in her engines – and the sun too – had lashed and burned my face nearly brick red. It still tingles and I feel fine. Nothing like it have I felt for ages. And I ought to be tired, for although I had to be excused all watches during the fireworks, I was typing my report for the Captain until nearly midnight on Sunday, and pleased he was with it too, and was hammering away at the keys again from 6 o'clock until 11 last night, page after page, it would have made 3 or 4 columns in the old days. And now too, I'm on the morning watch which is no picnic at the best of times. But it's been worth it. What I'll have to tell you when I get home this time, if it's not in the papers before.*

P.S. Keep all this under your hat. They may not want the story to become public yet. But I think it will be told ultimately. Look out for it.

* *On 8 April HMS* Byron *and* Fitzroy *were engaged in the detection and destruction of U-1001. Byron's involvement started when she was ordered to join the hunt for a contact about 50 miles south-west of the Fastnet Rock.*

An ASDIC contact was reported at a depth of 420 feet and the target engaged with Hedgehog. An explosion occurred 16 seconds after the pattern of 24 mortar projectiles hit the water – judged to be at about 380 feet. (Unlike depth charges, which often exploded harmlessly, Hedgehog projectiles did not detonate unless they scored a direct hit, and only one or two hits were needed to sink a U-boat.) Within a minute a large bubble and a significant oil slick appeared. Byron *continued the attack with depth charges causing 'articles of German origin' to rise to the surface, accompanied by the sound of escaping air. All the 46-strong crew of U-1001 were lost, including her commander, Kapitleutnant Ernst-Ulrich Blaudow.*

Following the events of 27-30 March, this latest success meant 21st Escort Group had sunk four U-boats in twelve days – a spectacular success which made headlines in the national press when the group returned to Belfast.

12th April 1945, Thursday 11.15am. Belfast

It was just lovely hearing your voice again yesterday afternoon – just lovely. It makes all the difference once I talk to you. It gives me strength, courage, such a great happiness that I can't put it in words. Then there were your two lovely letters too. And when I came back on board last night another two and a packet of newspapers.

No there were no bands after all, but we came in flying the skull and cross-bones and, within a few minutes, Press and news-reel cameramen were aboard the group leader's ship. We've made the news this time. You should either see it or read about it, or both in a week or two. In the meantime, signs of the new times are revealing themselves. We came back last night to the news that three of the younger telegraphists and Arthur, the youngest of the three coders, will not sail with us again, are to be drafted to barracks as soon as this leave ends. One of the telegraphists is Frank who had an appendicitis operation a few months ago, has never been fit for the Navy and who will never last long in the Army, if it's the Army they're to go to, and I suppose it is.

13th April 1945, Friday 1.00pm. Belfast

I think I'm going to be given the weekend after all. Isn't it grand? I saw my friend, the correspondence officer, a few minutes ago and he said that if I wrote out a formal request it would almost certainly be granted, presumably, in some sort of recognition of the extra work I've done this week.

Another grand night out last night. I ambled along to the Christian Science Reading and Rest Room, which had several times been recommended to me as a home-from-home. And it was too. They have a reception room, and as soon as I walked in two charming old dames met me and asked 'Now, do you want to write or to read?' And before I could answer one of them said 'You'd like a nice quiet little nap wouldn't you?' I wonder how she knew? For that's just what I did want. So off I was escorted to a great drawing room scattered with big easy chairs. I simply sank into the depths of one of these and knew nothing more until an hour later when Frank, who'd been to a private doctor for the poor lad felt so ill and looked it too, was also conducted into this quiet little sanctuary. Actually he'd called at the first surgeon's he saw and after a complete examination (and out of hours too and all for 7/6) he was told that there were all the symptoms of a duodenal ulcer. That little bit of news which I communicated to the sick bay attendant has shaken that gentleman up quite a lot. Now something may be done. At least Frank was immediately excused PT this morning. Now I suppose he'll see one of our own doctors and they can be pretty good. **P.S.** Isn't it sad about Mr. Roosevelt's death? He's been one of our best friends from the word go.

15th April 1945, Sunday 12 noon. Fairway.

As I write now in one of the big armchairs in the drawing room, the sun pouring through the windows, little Lisbeth is perched on the arm, crushed against my left shoulder, asking 'Who is it you're writing to, Cliff?' She always calls me Cliff and her Irish accent is by now almost ineradicable. Meanwhile the doctor is upstairs examining little John. It's her second visit accompanied each time by a wee Scottie and one of those brown Irish terriers, since I came. It's nothing serious. When I arrived, met at the station by Jack at 3.15 yesterday afternoon, he was suffering with a septic thumb contracted when he was playing among all the debris which has accumulated since they dismantled the Nissen huts on the other side of the road. I think he's probably scratched himself on some rusted barbed wire. Anyway he was a bit feverish before tea, went to sleep while Jack and I were up at the Club, calling on our way back for a couple of blacks,* and by the time we came back for tea had gone to bed without a murmur. Gladys called the doctor, who I'm afraid is a bit of an old fuss-pot and she began to talk about chicken pox simply, I think because there happens to be a bit of an epidemic in the town. Well, ever since the poor chap has sickied up everything he's had either to eat or drink and now the doctor has said that she wants Dr Robb of Downpatrick to see him. His thumb, she says, will certainly have to be lanced. I still think that all that's wrong is a chill on the stomach, for he's all the symptoms and no sign of a rash whatever, the septic thumb is probably just a coincidence. Gladys is not a bit inclined to panic nowadays and all that seems to be concerning John is that I'm here and he can't go out with me. He's so pathetic, lying on a great big bed which seems to engulf him, his face a bit hot and flushed on the pillow.

Last night after tea Lisbeth came with Jack and I on her tricycle which she rides like a speedway ace, to Jack's famous plot which he's wanted me to see every time I've been here. It's nice, and it's as neat and spick and span as you'd expect it to be, enclosed in a little palisade of criss-cross wire – a sort of wire netting – with every row straight as a ruler, not a weed visible, and with peas and early potatoes already sprouting. I didn't realise until I walked in an adjoining nursery afterwards and saw all the spring flowers and the fresh green of the trees and the cloud shadows passing over the Mourne mountains, and the fresh air blowing, all that you miss when you're at sea for weeks. How lovely our garden must be now.

* Guinness

16th April 1945, Monday 3.00pm. Belfast

Here I am back again on the old crate, hammering at the keys, racing against those 48 hours which amongst the happiest I've ever had in the last year and a half, except when I've been on leave with you. It was a lovely weekend. The sun shone all day yesterday in spite of a wind which out on the course was nearly a gale. I was following Jack for nearly 3 hours in one of his Sunday matches. Every week he plays two of the members, giving them their full handicap, which this time averaged about a stroke a hole, and allowing their best ball to count. It's a bit of a task, but he managed it again, won 2 and 1 after being two down for half the afternoon.

As soon as he'd finished I left him at the club and as it was exactly 5.30 and I so wanted you to know what a grand time I was having, I walked into a public kiosk and put in a call to you. This time I'd my own 1/8 set out all in order, although I expected that I'd have to return in an hour or two after the call had been booked. And what happened? All the lines must have been clear. I heard them call Blackpool less than three minutes after I'd asked for the number and I heard Blackpool ringing St. Annes. But there was no reply. They must have rung for nearly five minutes. By the time they'd given it up it was nearly a quarter to six, and I'd to shoot off for tea. Wasn't it a pity? They would be able to book a call direct at a time of the day when you'd probably be out, particularly if it was such a lovely day in St. Annes as it was in Newcastle. Still, it's just one of those things.

17th April 1945, Tuesday 1.00pm. Belfast

The new coder arrived yesterday afternoon. He's a Scot, about 30 I should think, from Dundee, who after 2 years at a shore station in the Mediterranean was given 5 weeks leave and after only a fortnight was recalled and given this draft. Another example of the Navy's celebrated system. As it is he's come five days at least before we can possibly go out. Isn't it a shame? As you know everybody was so kind to me when I came aboard my first ship that as soon as I met him I made him a cup of tea, cut him some bread and butter introduced him to all the lads, showed him the office and put him wise to all he'd need to know. Then, when he'd dumped all his gear, the two of us went ashore, called at the milk bar for a couple of strawberry shakes and afterwards we went to the pictures and saw Dick Powell in *It Happened Tomorrow*.

Well, after that little lot, we set off to the canteen. Mrs Nield wasn't on the rota but I introduced Bill – Bill Cummings is his name – to the rest of the staff and we were soon tucking into eggs, sausage and beans. Already he's settling down. It makes all the difference if somebody takes you under his wing, as young Harry took me, for a day or two.

P.S. The ship's dance is at the end of the week. I shall not be there in spite of the fact that on the list of volunteers invited to entertain the guests during the intervals, some comedian has written my name and opposite put 'Jitterbug Exhibition'. They will have their little joke.

18th April 1945, Wednesday 1.00pm. Belfast

Your letters are coming as regular as clockwork this time. They give me such happiness. There was another yesterday, in it the news that the serial and the little present had arrived. What a pity that you should have chosen that particular book for my birthday. Never mind, we can both read your copy now. I've read it once already a few months ago, as you know, but some day in the future I'll read it again, and it will awaken such a lot of memories, few of them sad, except with the sadness which shadows nearly everything, even if I scarcely realise it, when I'm away from you. All you can do I suppose is to cancel the order. At least it will leave you with another half-guinea in the bank. And there's no need whatever, now that you have all those bills to pay and so little to pay them with, to buy anything else at all. Send a card on May 4th, and with that I'll be content. For I'll know that day, as I know every day, that I've all your love and I ask for nothing else. When it's all over, then it'll be different. Then we'll buy each other something super. Mine's a gold wristlet watch. What's yours? Think it over. You won't have such a long time to wait now.

19th April 1945, Thursday 1.00pm. Belfast

Just visited the office, which I've scarcely seen during this leave and crossed off 7 days on the calendar. How fast they've gone. A few minutes ago I saw today's Daily Express and read in it that Berlin was so menaced that even the Germans were admitting that it might be entered today, and saw another report that the Japs were resigning themselves to inevitable defeat. The end is near, very near.

Gosh but isn't it hot in this uniform. We can't change into our little white fronts until May 1st and now, in spite of the heat, we're still wearing those thick blue jerseys. There are times when I think I'll burst into flames.

20th April 1945, Friday 1.00pm. Belfast

This is a sad day for three lads on this ship – Cyril, the Yorkshire boy from Hull; Frank, the young telegraphist who is nearly always under the weather; and Arthur, the junior coder. All three say goodbye in a couple of hours. You hate saying goodbye to the fellows you've lived with for months and with whom you've shared everything. Somehow you form an attachment for them which is beyond words, which you can't express on paper or to them except in a casual sort of 'Well – cheerio. Look after yourself.'

Arthur, who's been on the ship ever since she was commissioned, has not such a lot of regrets, for the barracks are close to his home and Cyril, too, is taking it with a smile, for they'll probably be given home-from-sea leave and his father, who's in the Merchant Navy, is home from some distant station for the first time in three years. But poor Frank's disconsolate. He doesn't know yet, but the sick-bay attendant has confided in me that he'll be taking a letter from one of the base medical officers which will probably ensure that he'll never be sent overseas or even on a ship again. My bet is that before long he'll be out altogether, as he should have been a long time ago. But he knows nothing about that, and today it wouldn't make such a lot of difference to him if he did know. When I left him a few minutes ago he was all by himself in a corner and trying to pretend that he hadn't been weeping – his eyes were all red and swollen. They pretend to be such Jolly Jacks, but they're still very young.

21st April 1945, Saturday 1pm

We'll be leaving in a couple of hours and the mail will be collected before 2 o'clock. So it's 'Goodbye' just for a week or two, I'll not be far away in miles and I'll be near you all the time in everything that matters. Always I know I'm saying 'This will be the last time'. What will happen next I don't know but it'll probably be a land base and there, at least, there'll be none of these goodbye letters to write.

Wasn't it a surprise last night? I decided that for once I could afford a call, gave the number from the box in the cafe at 5 o'clock, was told to return at 5.20 and then, after one wrong number there was such a delay that instead of 3/11 it cost only 1/8. Now if only I'd had all the necessary silver and copper I could have made it 6 minutes instead of 3. Still I talked to you, heard all the news. I was actually in the middle of a plate of plaice and chips when the bell rang and by the time everything had been disentangled and I'd spoken to you, everything, I expected, would be cold. But do you know what the waitress had done? She'd taken the plate away into the kitchen and, instead of bringing it back, appeared as soon as she saw me at the table again with a new portion of fish, new chips and a fresh pot of tea – and a full plate of bread and butter.

It was cold and there were so many rain clouds in the sky that we decided against the walk we'd promised ourselves and as Harry wasn't due at the dance until 8.15, the three of us – Bill was the third – went yet again to the flicks and this time saw a good film too, *Three Men in White*, one of the Dr Kildare pictures, no masterpiece but with a certain charm about it and a lot of simple comedy. Afterwards Harry beat it at speed to the dance to meet Barbara – yes, he's still meeting her, even if a lovely engagement ring has persuaded him that he's out of the hunt.

The ship was almost deserted when we returned – nearly everybody was at the dance, so we'd each a hot shower in private and after reading one or two of your papers I was asleep before 11 o'clock, which was about 3 hours earlier than the rest of the crew who, I'm told, came rolling home about 2 o'clock in various stages of inebriation, but never disturbed me at all.

22nd April 1945, Sunday 3pm

Here beginneth another serial. Instalment 1 is being written where I'll probably write a few others and at the time of day too – in the peace and privacy of the little caboose, half an hour before tea, after a bit of the old shut-eye in my bunk. We've been out only 24 hours and yet already everything – this old salt included – is settling into the familiar routine. Yet there's a difference this time. You notice it when the news bulletins come on the wireless. Everybody listens to them. Today Russian shells are falling on Berlin's Unter den Linden. A link-up with the Western Armies is predicted at any hour. You can hear them telling each other 'now it won't be long' and 'this'll be the last patrol' and asking each other 'then what?' They've said it before and they've been wrong but this time there's a sort of a sense of finality about everything. Yes, this is the end of a chapter I think.

And yet for one of us it's only the beginning. Poor old Bill – he's not so old as all that, only 23, although he looks nearer 30 (those foreign shore stations take it out of them) – poor old Bill began to go a bit green about the gills when we'd been out an hour or two for she was soon up to her old tricks. He said nothing, but once they begin to refuse cigarettes, you know the old familiar symptoms are beginning. Yet I don't think he was sick and when, before I went early to bed, I climbed up to the office to see how he was making out on his first watch, he looked little the worse for wear. And when I went on as his relief at midnight he was still with us. 'But' he said 'doesn't she roll'. He don't know nothing yet.

23rd April 1945, Monday 10am

They've just announced that the mail will be collected again but as no time was given I'm writing now and popping this letter in the box as soon as I've finished it. Isn't this grand – being able to send a letter a day – sailing without tears. How long it will last I don't know, but as long as it does and a long as my stack of privilege envelopes lasts – and I've accumulated a few in the last two or three months – there'll be a letter every day for you.

Isn't the news grand? Last bulletins we heard the Russians were only two miles from the centre of Berlin and the link-up was reported to be only a matter of hours. It may be all over in Europe – all the organised resistance at least – by the time we land again. I'd the hour I'd promised myself with the last batch of papers during the dogs yesterday, and finished the lot.

Thank goodness I love books. They make all the difference, break the monotony and it could be monotonous without them. Bill is full of beans. The sea is like a mill pond and he's not suffering a bit. And he's done his first morning watch and although he's tired he's settling down fine. He's a grand fellow, as willing as they make them. The old firm of three is in order again.

24th April 1945, Tuesday 1pm

I think this is the first instalment of the serial. We're again in an anchorage but it's questionable whether the mail will be collected today. It's grand our office being where it is. You've only to walk a couple of yards and you're out in the open just below the level of the bridge. And today we've had fun too. For shortly after we'd finished scrubbing the mess a rag tag and bobtail armada came from shore with the craziest collection of craft ever assembled. The crews were the most unashamed pirates ever to sail since the days of the Jolly Roger and Captain Blood. But on board they'd boxes and boxes of stockings and chocolates and crates and crates of eggs. Harry and I went into partnership and now in Harry's locker, rolled in a couple of jerseys to protect them when she begins to roll again, are four dozen eggs. Yes, four dozen at 3/- a dozen. Packed in my case too is a pair of stockings for you. Whether you'll like them I don't know. They're supposed to be silk and I'm sure they're not, and they're not fully fashioned and I don't know what size, for it was just a case of leaning over the side and taking whatever came up. And the vampires charged 8/- a pair for them too. Still, never mind, it'll all come out of the pontoon winnings and at least they've cost no coupons. By the way, they're a brownish shade and if they're not silk, at least they're not that thick lisle stuff.

And now at the canteen this dinner time they've dished out another three oranges – that makes a dozen in three days – and with them this time a tube of silver mints off the ration. And no sooner had I packed that little lot away than a parcel arrived from the Parish Church Comfort's fund and in it a pair of gloves, a writing pad and envelopes, a tube of tooth-paste, a stick of shaving soap, even a pair of boot laces. Isn't it good of them?

25th April 1945, Wednesday 2.45pm

THIS is the beginning of the serial. No buzz about it this time. For we're out and she's 'eaving something 'orrible and so, I suspect is Bill's tum. The bandits came back in their boats last night, but this time we didn't patronise them, for all they'd to offer were half-crown boxes of chocolate for 10/- and bottles of Guinness for 1/- each or a couple of packets of cigarettes. There was a sale for the Guinness and a considerable consumption of it in dark corners afterwards, but the chocolate racket went bad on them, and eventually they departed, muttering choice oaths after one of the less scrupulous stokers had asked to examine one of the boxes, leaned over the side for it, and as soon as he had his clutches on it, walked off! He intends the loot for his beloved and he hadn't the ten shillings anyway. The same young felon and a few of his pals acquired a few bottles of Guinness in exchange for cigarette packets, all neatly enclosed in Cellophane, which, when they're opened, will be found to contain only brown paper which had been lifted from the boxes in the heads.

We've just been told that there's been a recording made about our recent little achievement and that it's to be broadcast in 'War Report' one evening soon.* That day the story will be released to the papers.

The Group was off the Black Rock light conducting a sweep along the 100 fathom line when Redmill *was hit by an acoustic torpedo that blew 60 feet off her stern. The torpedo had been launched by U-1105, nicknamed the black panther because she had been coated in a black rubberised material to reduce her ASDIC signature.* Redmill *was taken under tow by* Rupert, *while* Fitzroy *and* Byron *covered the operation.* Conn *was also available and a Sunderland flying boat of the Royal Canadian Air Force stayed on station for more than six hours.*

Despite bad weather and several parted tow lines, Redmill *was eventually passed to a tug and towed to Lisahally near Londonderry on the River Foyle. However, she was later declared a total loss. Twenty-four men had been killed in the torpedo attack, but only three bodies were recovered. These men, one of whom could not be identified, were buried in Londonderry City Cemetery.*

27th April 1945, Friday 3.00pm

Up into the office to write to you for half an hour today. Again the caboose is occupied by the radio mechanic. Again the mess is in darkness as the weary and even the not so weary sleep. And today it's so cold that I wonder how they can sleep at all. I awakened after an hour absolutely perished and then I took a peek at the thermometer it was 46. We live in the Arctic. The rest of the ship resembles the tropics. I'm nice and snug at night when I'm in my pyjamas and under the blanket and an hour in the afternoon is long enough for me. But the rest of them had scarcely any sleep at all last night and are dripping all over the premises about it today. It wasn't the cold alone that kept them awake, for again she is up to all her little capers.

28th April 1945, Saturday 1.00pm

For once I was glad of my rum an hour ago. There's no doubt that it bucks you up a lot when you're tired and jaded and I was both today after about 36 hours of being pitched about with scarcely a minute's respite. She's in one of her ugly tempers at the moment. Every other minute she reels over to starboard, lurches erect and reels to port. And when she tires of that she rears herself up in the air and when she comes down at last she shudders from bows to stern, and you shudder with her and hang on to anything within reach and if there's nothing, hope for the best. Eating a meal has become an ordeal again. You need for it as many hands as an octopus has tentacles and then a few extra.

It's fellows like Bill, on their first ship, for whom I feel sorry. The poor old lad's being tumbled all over the place, came a heck of a cropper at breakfast and splashed boiling tea all over his chest and crashed yet again at dinner time on a deck which has had such a lot of grease scattered on it from the tables in the last few days, that it's like a skating rink. I've been through an apprenticeship which Bill is having to serve and I'm sorry for him. Still, there's only about a week to go before our rest and the storm will subside sometime, and I can always tuck myself into my corner and read my book.

29th April 1945, Sunday 2.15pm

I'm wedged in a corner of the office waiting for messages to come in and hoping that many won't. For once I dislodge myself nothing is stable any more. I slide up and down the padded seat as if it's a bit of the Bowl Slide, hitting first one wall and then the other. If I climb over the back of the seat I've to wait between the rolls before making the hazardous venture and even to reach the sets where the telegraphists work is equivalent to scaling Kirkstone Pass, so steep is the angle of the tilting deck. And wherever you put books or trays or anything else, you can bet they'll come crashing to the deck in a few minutes. You develop a sort of sixth sense and learn to dodge them as they fall. And Lady Astor, after a couple of days in the wardroom of a first class destroyer, once reported to Parliament that we didn't earn our 6d a day hard-layer's money. The old faggot! I'd like to have her on here for a few hours. Parliament would be spared her babbling for a couple of years.

They were broadcasting the reported surrender and the denial on the 7 o'clock news when I climbed out of my bunk this morning, after the best night's rest I've had for a long time. They may deny it but I still think there's something in it, such a lot in it that there may be literally be the last days, that this may be for us the last time out in these waters. They stampede to the loudspeakers now every time the news comes on. Why, they've even deserted Bing and Frank Sinatra!

30th April 1945, Monday 1.15pm

Poor old Jock took the count yesterday, for the first time since he joined the ship he was so sick after tea that he'd to go to his bunk, and there he remained, after a little persuasion and a glass of a potent brew prepared by the doctor, until this morning. Bill and I shared the first two hours of the first watch for him and then, after a couple of telegraphists had completed it, Bill took one middle and I had the morning. It made all the difference. That one all night in and Jock's as perky as ever today. Yes, it's the sleep or, at least, sleep at regular intervals that we miss. And I'm missing something else as well. The bread, which for some reason is stored close to one of the boilers, has gone green on us again, and for the last 24 hours we've been on those biscuits which my old teeth simply can't chew. Still the chocolate box is up to strength, for on the ration today were three bars of Fry's Sandwich and for cigarettes there were Churchman's No. 1 and Senior Service – what I call a good week. Seven packets of cigarettes, three bars of chocolate, three boxes of matches and a cake of soap, all for 5/2d. Who wouldn't be in the Navy?

Those eggs – 26 of them still – are threatening to become an embarrassment. Some of the lads have been eating too many. I warned them. I think that's what made Jock ill yesterday. He'd been having as many as three at a time. Ours will be going bad on us yet.

1st May 1945, Tuesday 1.00pm

Still no news of when we're to go in, but if it should be Friday and I drink half the tots of rum I've been promised and eat half the mixed grills which the lads say they'll stand me at the City cafe, I'll be insensible for days afterwards. Actually I'll have neither the rum nor the mixed grills, although I probably will have a grill, but they certainly intend me to celebrate with them. They say it will be the last birthday I'll have with them and they intend to make high jinks about it.

The eggs have become a problem. I simply can't eat another for a day or two and we've still 20 left. One of these days Harry will open his locker and find a poultry farm inside. We actually fried them in fresh butter last night as there was such a lot left as a result of the bread famine. And we'd another each for breakfast today, which otherwise, as it's 'herring-in' day would have consisted of one slice of bread and butter and nothing else. But that's the lot for me for a day or two and by that time, I fear the eggs will have had their days and ceased to be eggs at all. Why, the war may be over by then. What I want is the surrender to be accepted at a time when I'm on watch and the message to be broadcast to the Fleet and for this old salt to decode it. I'd keep a carbon copy of that signal and have it photographed.

2nd May 1945, Wednesday 12 noon

What about Little 'Ole 'Itler now! The news was broadcast to us by the Captain from the bridge about 10.30 and awakened everybody except the men on watch. I was one of that small minority and knew nothing at all about it – the ship's wireless is turned off at 9.30 pipe-down and the skipper presumably heard the news on his own set in his day cabin – until about half an hour later when, after all the excitement had subsided on the mess-deck, and I'm told it caused plenty, they began to climb up to the office and to ask one by one 'Is it true?' I didn't know what they were talking about at first. Then I confirmed it for them by calling the bridge on the voice-pipe. Of course we weren't content then until we'd heard the midnight news.

Will it make any difference? At first I thought it might mean an immediate capitulation. Now I'm not so certain. This Doenitz, as we've particular reason to know, is a fighter. But he can't fight long, that's certain. It may be that it will be over as soon as if Hitler had lived, or sooner. But what I would have liked quite a lot would have been a surrender on Friday. Then it would have been a birthday – not half!

One of the seamen has just been in to tell me that our little story has been announced a few minutes ago on 'War Report' after the 9 o'clock news, it's called 'The War at Sea'. It should be released for the papers tomorrow. There'll be a full house at the loud-speaker tonight.

There's a new sheet on the calendar now. I'm just looking at it now. It's a picture of Ludlow – the bridge on market day – the Parish Church tower and the Castle rising above wooded slopes in the background – smoke curling from the chimneys of the cottages – all so quiet and serene. Every day I'll see it, at all sorts of strange hours as I come on watch. What a lovely present it was.

3rd May 1945, Thursday 1.00pm

I suppose you can't have everything. You can't have a surrender in Italy and a mass collapse everywhere else every few hours and expect the exploits of a few little ships to make news. As soon as the 9 o'clock news opened last night and it was announced that

War Report had been cancelled I knew we'd had it. It's questionable now whether the tale will ever be told. Greater events have dwarfed it and we can't complain about that. It may one day be given a line or two in the papers. All we're asking now is 'How long?' It can only be a few days now. If it should end so soon all our plans may be revised – there may be no rest period – we may go in at once or stay out indefinitely. Nobody can tell.

What news it is! Italy last night, Berlin this morning, Hamburg a few minutes ago. It's a landslide. Every inch of space near the loud-speakers is packed for every news bulletin. In the meantime the routine continues as if this were just another week. I still come into the little caboose whenever I can find it empty. When the sun's shining, which it is today I still go out on the upper deck for the fresh air which smells so good.

4th May 1945, Friday 1.00pm

Many happy returns to both of us. May it be the last birthday we ever spend apart. And with the news as good as it is, it probably will be. A queer birthday it is. It began on the stroke of time, for when I walked into the office for the middle watch at exactly midnight, I found a notice on the wall, scrawled in capitals on a big message form. 'Many Happy Returns of the Day to Old Stripey. Lang may his lum reek' I could interpret it too, a fact which surprised Jock, Bill and all the other Scots, including Jock McDonald, the young signalman who's 20 today and thinks that his youth is already ended and that he's one foot in the grave. And I'm 42 and only now and again feel it. Then when I came down from the forenoon, there was waiting for me a full cup of rum – one and one too. In it was my tot and a sipper from every guy in the mess. They said they'd be insulted if I didn't put the lot down the hatch, thinking in their innocence that I should lay down and nearly die after such a potion. They know nothing of my ancestors! I drank the lot and was so completely unaffected that they were all so disillusioned that it was almost pathetic to see them.

Isn't the news grand? I've a suspicion that a surrender has already been accepted, that we're only marking time until it's announced, as happened in Italy. I may be wrong, but the Kiel capitulation seems to confirm the theory. Now to my bunk, before taking the air out on deck, where the sun is still shining and the sea so calm. A funny sort of birthday.

6th May 1945, Sunday 1.00pm. Londonderry

What will happen to us once Germany's surrender is complete I don't know, but already, slowly but inevitably, we're being scattered. Another two signalmen have to go now, one of them the young Scot whose birthday coincided with mine and who, last night, celebrated the fact so disastrously – six double whiskies and eight pints of beer were his total consumption and he's only 20 and apparently can't be persuaded that you don't have to drink to be a Jolly Jack Tar – that when I met him he could scarcely stand and I'd to nearly cart him back on board like a sack of coals. And today he feels fine. I tell him that proves there's no justice in this world. He's one to go. Taffy Williams, who's as Welsh as his name and a darned nice guy, is another.

I can remember the time when we'd to build a double row of bunks down the centre of the mess-deck. Now we've empty ones and those extras have gone. Soon at this rate, we'll have a couple of lockers each. The parting of the ways seems near. What will happen to Jock and I, the old men, nobody seems to know.

I notice you ask in one of the letters if I could ever be persuaded to vote against the Conservatives. The question is whether I could ever be persuaded to vote for them. What I'm after when I come out is a square deal for the sort of men I've been living with for the last year and a half, ordinary simple guys who don't ask a lot and haven't always been given it, and already I've a bit of a suspicion that the post war Tories won't give it to them either. The Socialists seem all hot air and claptrap and no authority, a bit inclined to petty dictatorship – look at those two canting overlords Bevin and Morrison – and the truth is, I suppose, that if I'm anything political at all I'm a Liberal. I like the sound of the Liberal candidate too. Although my ancestors may rise in wrath from their graves, I might yet find myself voting for him, I might even become a Liberal, for at least they honestly think about the great majority instead of the privileged minority, they're constructive and not destructive as too many of the peevish, fretful Socialists seem to be, and they're not extreme; they're the sort of middle of the road men this country will need to sort out the chaos.

7th May 1945, Monday 1.30pm

Five hours ago we left on the last lap of this assignment. It may the last war patrol of all. I think it's over now, that they're only waiting to ratify the terms. They say we've been waiting for this since September 1939, since the first of the evacuee trains came into St. Annes and we blacked out the car lamps and blacked out the house and said, 'Well, it's come' and were almost glad that the suspense had ended. Already, according to the BBC, Doenitz has ordered his U-Boats back to base. He'll wait in vain for a few of them, we know that. At any time, there may be the 'Cease Fire' flash on the wireless.

8th May 1945

Well, it's come – the great day at last. I was awakened yesterday afternoon shortly after 3 o'clock by the last words of the announcement that Germany had surrendered. No, I didn't hurl myself from my bunk and begin cheering. I didn't feel like that. Nobody else did either. Everybody took it so quietly, so calmly.

And now it's VE Day. What they're doing ashore I don't know. If they're waving flags and having all sorts of high jinks – why shouldn't they? It's been no joke being a civilian in this war. For us it's just another day. Just another day – tinned herrings for breakfast, which meant that everybody had a slice of bread and butter and was glad of it, and a bit of old Flicka for dinner. Rumour has it that they'll splice the mainbrace for the King's speech tonight and that will be an extra ration of rum – and neat rum too for everybody and lime juice for those who prefer it. And the ship is even wired everywhere for Mr Churchill's speech this afternoon and definitely I'll hear that, watch or no watch. Otherwise it's Tuesday May 8th and no other particular day. But we're happy, so happy that it can't be expressed in a lot of jubilation.

All morning I've been typing out Thank You signals from the First Sea Lord, Field Marshall Montgomery and lots of big shots and, in the intervals between, typing a couple of letters too, one to the telegraphist who left us the other day and wrote me from the barracks, and the other to young Donald from the office* who, I hear, went into the Army a few months ago and came a cropper in an assault course and now has an infection of the shoulder which will mean his discharge and 2 years hospital treatment – it sounds serious to me. I'm so sorry for him and I thought a letter from his old idol (for I seem to be that) would cheer him up a bit. Now back to work again.

* Gazette office, Blackpool

9th May 1945, Wednesday 10pm

So this is VE Day plus one. I've not noticed the difference yet. When I came down from the morning watch at 8 o'clock all the butter had gone, the baked beans were in a solid cold mass on the bottom of the tray and the thick slices of liver congealing grimly in the middle of them were just nobody's business at all. Even the tea had gone cold. Still, there was a tin of Nescafe not empty yet. I boiled a small kettle of water, made some coffee and with that and a slice of dry bread and jam we made out. After yesterday, we console ourselves 'Not a lot longer now'. Since then I've helped, as I'm a cook today, to scrub out the mess and now I'm in the little caboose on my own writing to you.

The old familiar diet was on the menu yesterday – even to soya bean sausages for supper – and although the order from the King to splice the main brace was signalled, it's not yet been spliced and presumably won't be for a day or two, the assumption seeming to be that war or no war in Europe life is still real and life is still earnest in the RN. I suppose it has to be. Our present assignment, according to indications today, will last as long as, even longer than any other. There's still plenty for us to do, fastening up all the loose ends and clearing up the unholy mess. At least there's this consolation – it means the old ship will remain longer in commission and that the ultimate day of parting will be delayed.

I heard the King in the evening and Mr Churchill in the afternoon yesterday and snatches of nearly all the endless bulletins. And as I went to sleep last night a loudspeaker, a half a dozen yards away from my bunk was thundering with the cheers of the people in Piccadilly Circus.

10th May 1945, Thursday 1.15pm.

We've made news – this time I wouldn't be surprised if we haven't made history – History with a capital H. And this time I think we'll be in the papers. There should be photographs too, for even as I'm writing in the mess, official photographers are posted on a trawler at the mouth of an anchorage which was the scene of this morning's little operation, waiting to take pictures of us as we leave.*

All the middle last night was tense, waiting for the developments which have made today's little exploit, and no sooner had I gone on the forenoon today than I was called to the bridge to chronicle each incident for the captain who, I'm told, as soon as the operation began asked 'Where's my writer?' and had my name piped. It meant that Jock, who'd only just finished the morning watch, had to go on the forenoon. But I'd a seat in the front row of the stalls for a chapter in this war's aftermath which few men were privileged to see, watched it develop minute by minute, and will never forget it. She's only a little ship, this lass of ours, but she always seems to be there when the fun's on. Now, just before dinner, I've typed a report of four manuscript pages, the log's complete again and the captain who, I suspect is making a scrap book out of these notes of mine, is as happy as a dog with a couple of tails.

Yes, it's been quite a half-day. Now we're off with our prizes to another anchorage and from there, I suppose, we'll come back here again and here, according to the latest buzz, we may remain for a week or even longer.

* *After the surrender U-1009 was escorted by* Byron *to Loch Alsh to await disposal under Operation Deadlight. She was sunk by gunfire from HMS* Onslow *on 16 December. The*

Royal Navy's Operation Deadlight involved the sinking of 116 German U-boats off Northern Ireland between 27 November 1945 and 12 February 1946 and was the result of the British government's determination to destroy the German U-boat arm when hostilities had ceased. Before this could happen, Operation Pledge involved the transfer of U-boats to the naval base at Lisahally in Northern Ireland, and the anchorage in Loch Ryan in south-west Scotland.

After the German surrender, the Admiralty issued orders on 8 May for all U-boats to surrender at specified ports, chiefly Loch Eriboll in north west Scotland. To make the plan work, ships such as Byron *were directed to Loch Eriboll, arriving on 9 May. The first U-boat to surrender arrived the following day. In the next eight days, a further 17 U-boats surrendered there. Soon afterwards the U-boats were moved to Loch Alsh on the Scottish west coast where the crews were taken off, and from there the boats were moved to Lisahally. Operation Deadlight was completed on 12 February 1946, when the 116th U-boat went to the bottom, representing the destruction of almost all serviceable U-boats that had surrendered in Europe.*

14th May 1945, Monday 7.45am

Here is the little story I promised to you in an earlier letter. Here is the scene. It's the morning of May 10th, VE Day plus 2. They've been celebrating the surrender ashore – we've heard them on the wireless. Otherwise the previous two days have been little different from any others to us except that the bread has gone stale on us, is speckled with sinister green spots and we're chewing biscuits and we've spliced the main brace and been given, a day late, a double ration of rum – neat too. We've rejoiced and been glad, or as glad as we can be. It's all over. It's so good to know it that we can't realise it. It was the same, I suppose, everywhere. The tension's gone and the inevitable reaction is setting in.

We've known for a day or two that after a certain prescribed hour all U-boats have to surface, put all armaments out of commission – torpedoes, mines, everything – and sail to certain anchorages to surrender. Our old enemies have to call it a day at last, have to admit defeat, the enemies we've been chasing and killing – four in one 10 days patrol – for months. Will they obey the order? We don't know. It's of no particular interest to us – it's sufficient for us to know that we've won the long, grim merciless battle – and it's been all that.

Then the signal comes. We've to go to one of the anchorages where they're to surrender. That make us sit up! This is the day we've been waiting for. We sail for the remote isolated rendezvous, reach it in the late twilight, are disposed in position. Our little lass is given the honour, is told to wait near the mouth of the inlet as a trawler patrols outside in the open sea. Already the U-boats have begun to signal their positions according to the terms, every 8 hours. Two are approaching, should reach the inlet during the night, will wait outside for escort by the trawler until an hour before dawn before coming in – if they intend to come in. That's the question – will they come in?

The night passes. We know from our radar that one has reached the inlet mouth and is on the surface. What will he do? That again is the question. Is the battle still on? Is he obeying orders? Or is he out on a suicide gamble? We wait. Early we go to action stations. I'm called to the bridge to act as writer. At least I've a front row in the stalls. This is history, the first chapter – yes, definitely the first, in spite of the BBC's report of the surrender at another anchorage – the first chapter in the mass capitulation of a fleet which was built to rule all the seas. The sun has lifted the mist from a sea as calm as a mill-pond, but the horizon is still hidden in haze. It's against this grey curtain that we see him – a long, black shape, low in the water, with a squat hump in the middle. Through the glasses you can see that she's flying a dark flag – it may be a blue flag – the flag of surrender. Near her the trawler is fussing, self-important, perky as a little terrier gambolling at the heels of a sullen quarry which refuses to play.

Far away, three miles astern, is another of those long black shapes – the second of them. In all the vast expanse of waters there's nothing else. Only the black smoke from the trawler's stack climbs into the clear morning sky. There is no other movement anywhere. And everything is so quiet – so quiet you can hear the gentle wash of the ripples against our bow. This is zero hour in the last act. The scene is framed in the great hills, range upon range of them, which border the inlet, hills russet-brown in bracken near the water's edge, fading into purple in the distance. There's a whitewashed cottage – a shepherd's cottage, standing beneath a bluff of rock on the far shore. As I watch through the glasses I see a man come out, a sheep dog prancing near him, and walk off and away up the hills without a backward glance. I see then, for the first time, that the cottage chimney is smoking. They've just had breakfast. It's just another day for them. They do say – some of the lads who've been ashore since – that when they met one of these shepherds and told him that the war was over and we'd won, he said 'Aye. I did hear tell that they'd beat that old perisher Napoleon'. But that's probably only a fable.

Now for it. It's 8 o'clock. They're at action stations everywhere. All guns are trained on the inlet mouth. The boarding party, armed with Sten guns and revolvers – and if the U-boat crew only knew it, half of them with revolvers could only hit a haystack in a passage if the haystack was very big and the passage very narrow – climb into the motor boat, squat there, cradled above the waters, waiting to be lowered. It would be just too bad for them if the U-boat suddenly bared her fangs. We've to take that chance. Slowly everything begins to move. 'Bring her in' is signalled to the trawler. Within a minute the long black shape is approaching. You can see the bow wave, crested with foam, which she lifts even in this quiet sea. She passes the mouth of the inlet, comes nearer and nearer, the trawler shuffling after her, but outside the line of fire – if we have to fire. Nearer she comes. You can see the length of her now, the lean ugliness of her, the rust stained brown on her black hull. You can see, too, a figure on the conning tower bridge. He wears a white jersey. There's a black peaked cap pulled low over his eyes. He's the first German I've seen, although I've been hunting them for months, for nearly six years. He seems to crouch on his perch. I train the glasses on him. As the U-boat comes nearer and nearer, on a course less than 200 yards inshore from our station, I see his face. It's not a face – it's a mask, expressionless, remote. That face will never betray his intentions.

Now the U-boat is almost level with us and reducing speed. 'Stop' we signal. She obeys. 'Lower Motor Boat'. Down she goes. The stutter of her engines breaks the silence. At that second, almost as if it's all been rehearsed, the hatch of the U-boat opens and two of the crew climb out, walk half a dozen yards forwards, wheel smartly and stand at the stand-easy position to face us. They wear brown overalls, are young – I can see that with the glasses – can see they've the faces of robots, blank, emotionless.

I notice the flag then. It is blue. It is the surrender flag. We've got him – the first of the pack. The motor boat moves towards him in a wide half-circle, passes behind his stern, sweeps back, brushes alongside the low black hull. The two figures on the deck come abruptly to life, run aft, catch the mooring ropes. I see one of them stoop to help one of the boarders to the deck. It's over rapidly then.* Each armed man races to his station. Up the ladder to the conning tower and the bridge the officer in command climbs fast. He reaches the bridge. For a split second I can see the two men face each other alone – the U-boat captain, the man in the white jersey, and the enemy who has come to take possession of his ship. Crisply, the Englishman salutes. The German acknowledges the salute with one of his own, which is a model of exactitude. It's all so strictly correct. But the guns are still trained, the gun's crews still at their stations. You never know with these Huns, you never know.

All we do know is that somewhere below decks the boarders are combing the ship and that the U-boat captain and the officer of the guard have gone with them, for the bridge is empty, the upper deck is empty and everything's gone so quiet again, so quiet that again you hear the ripple of the tiny waves against our sides, and have time to notice that across on the other shore somebody has hung some washing on a line in the garden of the whitewashed cottage. It seems to last a long time but it's probably only a few minutes. Then up they climb to the bridge again and down the mast flutters the frayed blue flag, and up it the White Ensign, curling in a sudden gust of wind, fresh, clean, defiant. That's No. 1 U-boat for Britain. It's soon over after that. Still the guns are manned, but you know they'll not fire now.

The trawler is ordered ahead. She fusses into position, begins to steam down the water to the head of the inlet. After her churns the U-boat. After the U-boat we steam, down to the other waiting ships, bringing home the bacon. We've taken her out since – and another with her – to a base where they're assembling flotillas of surrendered craft and have come back again and soon we'll be out with another couple. They're all so compliant, so obliging, so courteous – the old Hun at his old games, arrogant in victory, servile in defeat. At the present rate of progress they'll soon be waiting in queues to come in. Definitely, in spite of the fact that there's not a pub within miles, no golden sands, no balloons, bands or baths, nothing but hills of heather and loneliness, this has become the most fashionable watering place for U-boats this spring. It's one of the most amazing stories in history.

P.S. As we were taking the first of our prizes in, a certain famous ship signalled to us as she passed 'Glad you've got them at last just where you want them. You've put in plenty of sea time to deserve it.'

P.P.S. Yes, these Germans are so compliant. They've only one concern. The first question ours asked was 'You won't give us up to the Russians please. Those Bolsheviks – they no good.' These Russians have got the daylights scared out of them.

P.P.P.S. Yes, ours was the first. The BBC gave the time of their reported first surrender at 11 o'clock. We were aboard at 8.15.

* The boarding party's mission was not without incident. Buck Taylor, leader of the party, takes up the story: 'We were under way and I was on the conning tower with a couple of the Boarding Party and the U-boat commander. Les Kingsley came up from below. We all had Lanchesters (a posh version of the Sten sub machine-gun) and when Les came up on top he placed his Lanchester on the deck in an upright position, butt down. For no apparent reason a round went off, shot into the sky, missing the U-boat commander's sleeve by a matter of what must have been 2–3 inches. He remained completely unmoved'.

Alan Hope's comment on the incident is fittingly droll: 'It would seem that whoever fired the first shot in the Battle of the Atlantic, Les Kingsley fired the last.'

After the surrender, U-1009 was escorted by Byron *to Loch Alsh to await disposal under Operation Deadlight. She was sunk by gunfire from the destroyer HMS* Onslow *on 16 December.*

When Cliff writes 'three miles astern, is another of those long black shapes – the second of them' he is probably referring to U-1305, the second boat to surrender. Another notable event that day was the surrender of U-1105, the black panther that hit Byron's *sister ship* Redmill *with an acoustic torpedo, killing 24 men on 27 April.*

15th May 1945, Tuesday 11am

According to Saturday's Daily Express, which drifted aboard yesterday, the first newspaper I'd seen for nearly a fortnight, Groups 1–11 inclusive may be released on June 16th and if that's correct, and if it's correct too that these groups contain only 200,000 men, they should reach Group 33 sooner than I'd begun to expect.

16th May 1945, Wednesday 10am

Lots of information in the last few hours about interim demobilisation; probably in anticipation of the Commons debate. The Admiralty already seem to think that there's nothing like presenting their case in advance and the sum and substance of that case appears to be that their commitments are still so great that releases at first will be fewer than in the Army and RAF but that ultimately, once various obligations are discharged – and not all of them in the Far East – we'll come out in a great heap. It all means that I may be in longer than we'd hoped and expected, but at least it's vastly improbable that I'll go out on active service again.

17th May 1945, Thursday 1pm

Another visitor today.* He came in as quietly as ever. And again I'd a seat in the orchestra stalls. Now we're on our way escorting him to his last sanctuary. It's becoming almost a custom these days, but somehow it's not lost the first fresh excitement. All the time you're saying to yourself, 'This is the end of a fleet that was to cut Britain's lifelines and starve her into surrender, and I'm seeing it'. It's a privilege and the familiarity has not seemed to make it anything else. The pity is that it's delaying our leave, for we have apparently come to be regarded not only as U-boat Killers No.1, but as U-boat Collectors No.1 too. The price we have to pay is a delayed leave.

Meanwhile everybody's dripping from forward to aft and all the way back again at the strict peace-time routine and discipline which is being introduced. Not only are lanyards still a compulsory fashion ashore – when we go ashore, and it's a fortnight since I trod any land – but in future at sea and in harbour we've to wear our No. 3s. The signal officer asked me the other day, when it was only a buzz and not grim reality, what I thought about it. I'm afraid I was rude and told him that in my opinion it was a lot of ruddy nonsense and that in the W/T office half the staff would probably burst into flames in the heat which the sets throw off. All of which seemed to disconcert him no end.

This was probably U-255, which was escorted to Loch Alsh by Byron *and later sunk as an aircraft target by rockets fired by a Bristol Beaufort of 254 Squadron on 13 December.*

19th May 1945, Saturday 1.00am*

We're at anchor again and a few of us are out of our bunks. No longer are all the doors bolted and barred. You can walk out now and take a breath of air whenever the atmosphere in the office becomes a little too sultry. The ships are no longer in darkness. Below, as I stand on the torpedo deck, I could see the glare of the lamp over the quartermaster's desk. Across the water the hills were dim shadows, but the little whitewashed cottages, tucked in the shallow folds, were visible in the moonlight. There was a golden glow in one window. In all the others the lights had gone out long ago. But all the ship's lamps were winking at each other across the bay, and each lamp was mirrored in the still water. And high over the hills the star which I'd not seen for weeks shone all on its own.

It shouldn't be long now for leave for the customers are becoming fewer. U-boat Collectors Incorporated that's us. And we're to get medals too. I'll qualify for the 1939–1945 star and probably for the Atlantic Star, and there's a Russian Convoy decoration promised us by Old Joe.

During 19 May many U-boats were escorted to Eriboll and then taken in convoy to Loch Ryan.

20th May 1945, Sunday 10.45am

Only a few minutes ago I leaned over the side and talked to Harry, who is one of the men who boarded one of the 15 which sailed in to call it a day last evening. One of our little lassie's two was berthed alongside us. Every minute or two you can feel her bump against our side. As I talked to Harry on the submarine's bridge two Nazi officers were close to him, listening to every word we said and probably, for nearly all of them can speak English, understanding all we said. It was of no interest to them anyway. We talked, according to the non-fraternisation orders, as if they were not there at all, either invisible or so far beneath our notice that their presence could be completely ignored. That's what they hate – this contemptuous, casual indifference. Last night this lot all came on deck and snapped off a brisk Nazi salute. Nobody took the least notice of it. They might have been holding up their hands to ask if they could leave the room.

I cut the film last night to watch them come in. It was worth it. I can see a film any time. I'll never see this again. It was a lovely evening, the sun shining and a fresh wind rippling the waters of the loch. For half an hour I watched the open sea beyond the entrance. Then I saw the smoke of the escort vessels, our own escorts – last night we were not one of them – move into position and a few minutes later the familiar squat shape of the conning towers and, a little later still, the cream surge of the bow waves churned up by the submarines. It was incredible to see it – one after the other, each flying the White Ensign, they sailed past into the loch, a whole flotilla of them, nearer and nearer in a perfect unbroken line, wheeled each to its own anchorage and came back to rest for the night. You could see them scattered about the little bay, black shapes, lifting and falling in the little waves as I came off the first watch at midnight. That was the end of a Fleet. All we have to do is to deliver them to the authorities.*

* Most of the U-boats were moored at Loch Ryan before being destroyed.

22nd May 1945, Tuesday 2.45pm

We're on the final lap now. Again we're a sort of Mary, but this time there are 15 lambs following us. They're still as meek as ever – on the surface. Yesterday morning, when I was on 4 to 8 watch and had found the galley closed and was almost panting for a drink, I walked on deck just as dawn was breaking, hailed Harry, who I knew was on the bridge of our U-boat, and asked him what he could do about it. 'Come back in quarter of an hour' he said. When I returned he'd a pewter pot of hot tea prepared and so close was the submarine berthed alongside us that he was able to hand it over the rails to me, and with it a packet of ship's biscuits – and not the sort of biscuits we have to endure either, but sweet biscuits, crisp and fresh from a sealed tin. The world's turned upside down. We never imagined a week or two ago that we'd be drinking tea brewed in a U-boat galley and eating biscuits made for a U-boat's crew. It all seems crazy, but it's happening.

I can tell you now that we've been at Loch Eriboll, a small isolated loch on the north-west coast of Scotland, not far from the Isle of Skye. Three quarters of the U-boats to surrender have sailed in there. And it's been our group, selected, so we're told, because of our achievements in the last round of the U-boat war, which was chosen to meet them. From all parts of the Atlantic they've come, from Norway and, to escape the Russians whom they fear unashamedly, from the Baltic. Our grand total is about 30. And they've all packed in without a crack out of one of them. Now we're escorting the last 15 to another reception base. What will happen to them we neither know nor care.

2nd June 1945, Saturday 1.40pm

There's a buzz that we shall be leaving the base tomorrow or Monday for the last time and sailing either to Glasgow, Liverpool or Newcastle for a refit which will last so long that it will probably mean three weeks to each watch. The other watch will naturally have the first leave. What's the refit for? The general impression is that it's for the East and, according to our Signals Officer, if it should be (and if no drafts to barracks come for either Jock or I in the next three or four weeks), we may both go, in spite of our age. I'd be out no earlier or no later wherever I go and I'd prefer to go with this little lass wherever it may be – and with all the grand friends aboard her – than anywhere else at all. And, even if we go, we'd probably only be on the Durban – Colombo convoy run, and that's a snip of an assignment.

What a journey it was, thank goodness it's the last time I'll have to make it. I'd the compartment to myself to Preston, but afterwards it was a nightmare again. There wasn't a seat left when the Stranraer train came in, but after squatting near a lavatory which smelt to heaven and beyond, I climbed out in desperation at Carlisle, walked the whole length of the train again, and by a miracle found a seat. In it I snoozed to Stranraer but the boat was as packed as the train had been and again I'd to crouch in a corner on my bag for nearly three hours this time, until at last the old tub sailed at 9 o'clock when, although it seemed calm enough, she rolled sufficiently to drive all the soldiery and the airmen to the heads not all of them, alas, got there in time – and as they didn't return I commandeered one of the seats they'd left and snoozed some more.

P.S. Harry has just brought me from the local newspaper office two photographs. One of the first U-boat to surrender and another close-up of the captain calling it a day.

4th June 1945, Monday 1.00pm. Belfast

We're still sitting on our tails waiting for something to happen and nothing has happened yet. There's to be a refit, but where and when is still one of those problems without an answer. Now Glasgow and Newcastle seem to be first and second in the betting, and it's to be Friday before we sail. I've been thinking that if we go to one of the big cities, I'll take out a short term subscription at either Boots or Smiths. It would cost only half a crown and would be worth it. There's little left in the ship's library and now that our chief is soon to be demobilised he's lost interest and is not restocking it. He's asked me to take the job on, but I'm not. I've sufficient on when we're at sea.

5th June 1945, Tuesday 1.00pm. Belfast

Latest buzz is that there's a strike at the docks where there's to be a refit and that until it's settled there can be no move at all. It may or not be true. Yesterday in preparation for the long leave they issued us with a dozen boxes of matches. Today they dished out four weeks supply of goodies – 11 Mars Bars and a packet of toffees. And tomorrow there'll be 28 packets of cigarettes for us too.

Poor old Harry is down in the doldrums. Months ago he put in for a special course for a higher grade. Nothing happened and he'd almost forgotten about it. Then last night a signal came that he'd been accepted. Now he's to go to Petersfield for 6 weeks and will probably miss nearly all his leave, and may even lose the ship too, although he's put in a special request to be redrafted back to it. It will probably be granted, but if it shouldn't and he loses us all he'll be heartbroken.

6th June 1945, Wednesday 2.30pm. Belfast

There's a shaft of sunshine on my page as I write. I'm sitting in the open door of the wheel-house and in front, across an open field I can see the skeleton of a ship which is being built inside a web of scaffolding, and can hear the whine of electric drills and the beat of rivetter's hammers. Only a few minutes ago I was down in the quiet and pitch black mess-deck sleeping after a bath. It's our D-Day Anniversary celebration. We've been given a half-day holiday but there's no shore leave unless you go to a football match in which the ship's team is playing, and as we've seen our ship's teams in action before, there's more attendance in the bunks than on the sidelines.
P.S. Harry's not gone yet but he took all his WRENS out for a farewell celebration last night.

7th June 1945, Thursday 2.30pm

Harry's just packed his gear. He'll be off within the next hour. Transport will be here for him at 3 o'clock. As a special concession he's to be allowed to go home until

Sunday. He'll have about a day and a half in Bristol instead of 21 days. And there's always the chance that he'll not come back to the ship. He's so miserable about it. And so am I too. I can't forget that he was the first guy to befriend me on this ship, to show me all the ropes, to take me under his wing, young as he was. He's often been under mine since.

Now the restless, unhappy Harry has parked himself near me on the form and is writing a few last words to his Barbara. Yes, he's still faithful to her, although she's another's.

9th June 1945, Saturday 10am

We're at sea, ordered away from port at the shortest notice, and we're not going to a refit port, but to a station off Rosyth for exercises with the Fleet Air Arm which may last a week or a month or, for all I know, the duration. The general impression is that we've been drafted back again to the Home Fleet. If that's true it probably means no long leave, or even no leave at all for a long time. But at least it means that I won't be going East and I'm glad about that.

It was sad saying goodbye to Belfast. We've been there nearly a year and everybody's been so kind to us. Unfortunately I couldn't see Mrs Nield, for I couldn't leave the ship until 6 o'clock and after I'd been to the theatre to a new play *To Dream Again*, the canteen had no hot suppers left and we came out. Mrs N wasn't on duty anyway. So we went to a cafe and had fish and chips, walked all the way back to the docks and said 'Well, that's the end of it.'

10th June 1945, Sunday 12.30pm

We're still on our way. Not until 5 o'clock are we due to arrive. Then we'll probably know what is to happen to us. Not even the captain is certain. He admitted that on the broadcast last night, when he told us that this assignment will probably take us into the Portsmouth area for an indefinite period after minor renovations at Rosyth.

Afterwards we were given the official news about the medals too. My two will be worth having, for the 1939–45 star can be worn only by men who've been a minimum of six months at sea, and to qualify for the Atlantic Star, you've to have spent an additional 6 months in the Atlantic. Then, if our pre-D-Day convoys make us eligible for the France and Germany Star, as we're told that they may, that will entitle us to wear a silver rosette on the 1939–45 award. I'll look like a blinking rainbow, particularly if Joe tips up his medal for the Russian convoys too.

Then there's news about demobilisation which is pretty encouraging. For, contrary to expectations, they expect to be releasing groups up to No. 16 after the middle of August. That's half-way to mine. At this rate I'll never go out East, for I'd be called back almost before I could arrive.

11th June 1945, Monday 1.30pm. Dunfermline

We're off to Norway. At least the skipper says so, and he should know. Just for a week, calling at Christiansund, Stavangar and Oslo, delivering stores and taking out Naval and private personnel. We should sail on Sunday, remaining here at Rosyth. I suppose I ought to be excited about it – a free tour of the Norwegian fiords. But at present I'm inoculated against all excursions and alarums, for every day now there's something fresh and then it seldom happens.

What's going to happen after this Norway excursion – nobody knows that yet. We may go again or there may be a minor refit, but it's more or less certain that unless there's a major refit with a prospect of the East at the end of it the crew will be reduced by about 50% and according to the guys who pretend to know, our staff will become such a skeleton that only one of our little staff of three will be retained. The betting is that this old man, as the oldest of the three, will be the one. I wouldn't mind. At least there'd be a bit of space, although it would seem strange to be one in about half a dozen in a mess-deck built for 16 and inhabited nearly all the time I've been aboard by 20.

13th June 1945, Wednesday 11pm. Dunfermline

I loved my first night out. Dunfermline is one of the sort of town we love – ancient and modern – neat and dapper narrow shopping streets in the new districts and wandering cobbled byways in the old town. We'd a tea of smoked haddock and chips, bread and butter and cakes in a trim little cafe, all for 1/9, and then we saw a grand 3 hour programme at one of the cinemas (1/6 the best seats, which is a bit of a change from Belfast) including the new thriller *The Man in Half Moon Street*. Afterwards we walked in one of the loveliest parks I've ever seen, the Carnegie Park, presented to Dunfermline, where he was born, by Andrew Carnegie. There are acres of it, spacious lawns, woods which are bird sanctuaries, flowers everywhere, summer-houses, wooded avenues and from the hill where it's built a great sweeping view of the Firth of Forth with the Forth bridge in the background dwarfing the ships of the Home Fleet in their anchorage. All the time the sun shone. It was still mild, and in those gardens, so quiet except for the song of the birds, even at 9.30.

16th June 1945, Thursday 2.30pm

We're at sea again – off about 100 miles into the Atlantic on a little mission which will probably take until tomorrow night. It's an unexpected order and again our plans have been upset. Our sailing to Norway has been postponed until Wednesday, if we ever go – and I'm beginning to question whether we will – and definitely Oslo is out, the one city I wanted to visit, for we've been transferred to the northern regions and are to call now at Trondheim, Stavanger and Bergen, which compared with the capital, or so we're told, incline a little towards the primitive. At this rate we'll finish up at the Pole!

20th June 1945, Wednesday 7pm

We're nearly 10 hours out and should reach Stavanger by noon tomorrow. There we're to berth until the following morning, then off to Bergen and Trondheim, back to Stavanger and en route for home, where we're due next Tuesday.

The passengers are all on board, including 2 German civilians who, segregated from all the rest, take their exercise alone and sleep in some desolate fastness far away from this mess-deck. Guests of our mess are 6 Norwegian sailors. Nearly all are wounded. One of them, who's sleeping now in my old bunk, which will be proud to have him, has his back encased in plaster of paris. Another has a silver plate in his shoulder. Not one of them has been home since Norway fell in 1940 – gosh, are they excited. And yet they're so quiet and unassuming and modest – lanky, blond giants, every one of them.

21st June 1945, Thursday 2.30pm. Stavanger

So this is Norway. It's almost 20° hotter today, and has been since 7 o'clock, than I've ever known it anywhere in England. Here, where I am, under a still awning, you are shaded from the sun and can feel a little breeze off the water. Everywhere else, on the decks and on the open quays and in the little streets which climb between rising terraces of houses, up and up, until the red shingled roofs are lost in the green of the trees on the forest line, the heat is rising and shimmering. I'm on the starboard side. Berthed on the opposite quay are oilers, drifters, and a few timber ships, all loading from wooden warehouses painted in reds and greens and pale primrose. I can see lines of men filing endlessly from the warehouses to the ships. They all wear grey-green uniforms. They are all German. All the menial labours are being done by them in this port. Half the crew are swimming off the side of the ship, gambolling in the water like a pack of young porpoises, making no end of a hullabaloo every time, from the upper deck, a hose pipe is turned on them.

And all the time on the port side, the harbour side where our bows seem to be almost in the town square, so close are the buildings, the kiosks and shops, Germans are toiling up and down between decks, unloading the 300 bags of mail and a few of the dozens of tons of provisions we're to land there. They're working just like men who have forgotten how to live, sweat streaming unheeded through the dust on their faces, silent, not even sullen, sort of negative. One of them spoke to me when I was below a few minutes ago. He was only about 18 or 19 and his big, thick-lensed glasses gave him the appearance of a brooding owl. 'Please' he said 'will you giff me a drink'. So I gave him a sip of water. 'I sank you' he said solemnly, after he'd gulped it down in one – and went back to his hard labour. No, they're not being ill treated, but they're being made to work. That's fair, I know, but today I'm glad I'm no German.

It's a glorious view down the narrow bay. On the far bank, beyond the terraced houses, are the woods, fronted by one lone white warehouse. Across the still water from bank to bank, yachts are sailing, some of them passing beneath the great rusted hulls of merchantmen out at anchor. Beyond are the hills, not vast forbidding ranges such as somehow I expected, but green and gentle in their slopes, climbing one above the other until the last of them is lost in the heat haze. And clustered in all the valleys you can see villages, all the cottages red-roofed and dwarfed by the distance to the size of dolls' houses. In the foreground on the far bank are the shipyards, the chimney-stacks, the cranes, the factories, the modern housing estates and perched on one hill, a great brick tower, probably a memorial. It's a country at peace again and, except for the silent men in the grey-green uniforms, it might never have known war.

27th June 1945, Wednesday 11am. Dunfermline

Off I went ashore with Bill, booked a bedroom at a seaman's hostel just outside the docks – for 1/6d you can reserve a bedroom of your own – took the bus to Dunfermline and had a lovely tea of smoked haddock, tea, bread and butter and Scotch scones. It's a grand hostel, the best I've been in. There are writing rooms, a billiard room, a restaurant and about 100 bedrooms. And everywhere the windows are wide and spacious, the furniture modern. The Seaman's Missionary Society have built it and a great job they've made of it too. Behind it are rising fields. When I opened my window last night a herd of cows was so close that I could hear them cropping the grass as I closed my eyes and went into a sleep which at last refreshed me.

2nd July 1945, Monday 1.30pm. Dunfermline

This threatens to be an expensive week. Not only am I having everything washed in the laundry, including my blanket, but I'll have to buy a new pair of serge trousers, for my present No. 3s are all patched and stained, and a new pair of overalls too, for they're compulsory wear in barracks.

7th July 1945. Dunfermline

I'm just fresh from a bath, and not a bucket bath either, and not a spray, which I always think such an over-rated institution, but one of those long baths where you can squat and soak. And haven't I soaked? This hostel has everything. And the baths are free. You've merely to leave your cap as a deposit for the bathroom key, and as even sailors don't bathe in their caps that's not unreasonable.

This should be the last night in my cabin – but will it? For today, when I saw the coxswain, who's back early from leave and ought to know, he said it was news to him that the draft was leaving tomorrow, and as the first lieutenant has arranged a hockey match for the afternoon it certainly makes you think. Talk about disorganisation. Still, my kitbag's packed and my old Gladstone bag too. I've simply not lashed my hammock. At least I could leave at the shortest notice. I've learned that we're all going to barracks, and that from there we'll all be sent either to Petersfield or Collingwood.

8th July 1945, Sunday 1.00pm. Dunfermline

Don't be too disappointed, but it won't be as early as Wednesday that I'll be home after all. As I suspected, we're not going today, and according to the first lieutenant it may not even be tomorrow either. I asked him today if a different date had been fixed and he said 'It won't be for a day or two yet'. That, of course, in the Navy may mean anything. Still I've not had such a bad day today. This morning I decided that as I was leaving the ship, it was a suitable occasion to ask for all the arrears of my salary as secretary of the Canteen Committee. After all, it wasn't unreasonable to ask for it, for they offered me 10/- a month, and as there's credit balance of about £100 and only a couple of months ago they spent £90 on a ship's dance, I knew I wouldn't bankrupt the business. So I asked to see the first lieutenant, and in his cabin said 'What about it?' and he paid up like a lamb. £6 for the year I've been secretary, and into the bargain expressed his regrets that I was leaving the ship, but said that it was unavoidable, that our branch was no longer required in her complement. Which is true enough. I wonder, in fact, if we are required now. Reports from Collingwood where we're to go are that the place is packed with unwanted men, that as recently as last Thursday, they sent away on accommodation leave all men over 38, and when that didn't create sufficient vacancies, reduced the age limit to 34. That shows how things are going.

Poor Jock is almost crippled, I never knew it but when he left the ship to go on leave, he fell off the gang-plank, which is always a death trap if you're not careful, and hurt his knee so badly that he's attending the doctor all the time he's at home. He could have had an extension, but preferred not to risk missing the draft. Now, unless he exercises it, the knee swells and stiffens immediately. He intends asking for an X-ray as soon as he reaches the signals school. It will probably mean a bit of extra leave, for it looks to me like a cartilage operation, and as an old footballer he agrees. He's an interesting bit of news too. The man who was engaged to replace him was a costing clerk to a building firm before the war. Now the Ministry of Labour are directing him back to the building trade, and Jock's firm have said that they can release him only if Jock can be drafted back to the position, and have asked for Jock's release from the Navy. What will happen I don't know, but something might. The lads say I should ask the Gazette to apply for my release. I suppose I could, but I dunno, it seems a bit low to me.

9th July 1945, Monday 1.15pm. Dunfermline

Here I am in the corner, where I must have written thousands of words to you, writing for the last time. It makes me a little sad to think of that. Yet it had to end sometime, and now it is ending, I've few regrets for within a day or two I'll be with you, and that makes the closing of this chapter a lot less sad than it would have been. And I'm not losing my pals, half the mess offered to lash my hammock for me and now it's laid on my dismantled bunk, a lot less plump and bloated than ever it looks whenever I've lashed it for myself. All but three of us go tomorrow. We should be in barracks at Peter Oboe on Wednesday afternoon, at Collingwood or Petersfield by Thursday, and off on leave on Friday.

13th August 1945, Monday 2.40pm. Euston

I'm in a big cosy arm chair in the YMCA rest room at Euston. Everybody else has his head down, as every good man should have at this time of the day on Sunday. But I'm writing to you before anything else to say 'Thank You' for the happiest leave of all, I'm writing too because I'm so lonely. We had such fun, every minute, as we always have when we're together. Now we're parted again, and if it wasn't for the memories of those last three weeks, I'd be so sad that I'd never be able to tell you about it. As it is I'll be content to live on those memories until I come home again, and that won't be long either, and all the time now I'm telling myself that these separations will end altogether very soon now.

14th August 1945, Tuesday. Mess KD103 HMS Collingwood, Hants

I've lost one Dave and found another. Dave the second, whom I met at Waterloo – we had to unlash our hammocks in a pitch black mess and didn't crawl into our bunks until midnight, weary, worn and sad – found a draft to Colombo waiting for him, and after the routine of medical and dental inspections, has left already on 21 days leave. We may never meet again until after the war, unless I'm still here when he returns. Before we said goodbye he insisted on presenting me with a 20 packet of Churchman's out of his draft issue – and that I can tell you, is a gift beyond price in a camp where I'd to stand in a queue for 10 Woodbines at dinner time. I almost envied him, until I met David the first a few minutes ago and heard that, according to one of his friends who's stationed there, Colombo is anybody's who wants it, and nobody who's been there ever does.

You remember Dave? David Could, who was at our Christmas party at Lowton (HMS *Caballa*) and played the piano and is one of the nicest fellows I've ever met in this outfit. I was feeling so lonely when I met him too, for Tom seems to have disappeared, and Frank leaves for Colombo on Friday, and Jock is away on three weeks 'prepare for foreign service' leave and I'd just lost Dave. He's been at a shore station in West Africa ever since we left *Caballa*, and positively envies my days on the good old *Byron*, the little I've been able to tell him about them.

Did I tell you earlier that I hope I won't be here when Dave returns, I think that is true. Not that it's a not a good camp as camps go it is. The food is still 100% in front of anything I had on *Byron*, and our mess is big and spacious, my bunk close to an open window and so near the door, that when I awakened this morning I could see the flower beds and a lawn just beyond the threshold. Yes it's good enough, but if this first day's a fair example of all that's to come, it'll be so monotonous that the days will crawl. They've nothing new to teach us, but there are classes all through the day where we simply gaze at instruction books which we learned by heart in training and try not to sleep. And that goes on day after day I'm told.

Still, I've one consolation, while I'm here I'm near to you, and if I remain on the draft list for eight weeks I come off it and qualify immediately for accommodation leave. And if I should get a draft in the meantime, there's almost certain to be leave attached to it – although it's now certain that poor old Frank has to go on Friday without any leave at all, although he had 21 days prepare for foreign leave a few weeks ago. It's all a lottery I suppose. Your name might be broadcast any minute on the loudspeakers and then you've had it for better or worse, although the general impression seems to be that once there's been VJ Day few men in groups below 40 will go East. If only they adopt the policy introduced by the RAF and begin releasing men according to their category, coders may be amongst the first out.

15th August, VJ Day. Portsmouth

Well, it's come at last. Now I know it's true and it's all over. Now it's happened we can at least take a little pride, for each of us has done what little we could to bring this day – not a lot I know – but all we could, and with that we'll be content. All I regret is that I'm not with you and that we can't celebrate quietly together, for it's such a great day, not only the end of a war which seems to have lasted so long, but the beginning of a time when we shall all come home again.

A bit of a celebration seems indicated, for it's not only VJ Day, it's Tom's 21st birthday – and whatever happens we can dive into the great iced birthday cake he brought with him, when unexpectedly he arrived off a fortnight's accommodation leave last night. Yes, we'll make a bit of a day of it. It won't be the day it would have been if only we'd been together, and in any case as happened on VE Day, I can work up no great excitement, but feel instead strangely quiet and subdued, and inclined only to say 'Thank You' and leave it at that.

16th August 1945, Thursday 12 noon. Portsmouth

They're just queuing up for accommodation leave again. Tom is among them. He'll probably be off again tomorrow. I'm not eligible because I'm on the draft list, and shall have to remain on it for 8 weeks unless I'm sent off in the meantime. Don't I envy those other guys? Still, I'm settling down. A few minutes ago I was excused from class to visit the dental clinic where, when I'd explained the circumstances, they stamped my card as 'Dentally Fit' and so gave me the all clear for accommodation leave if ever I have the chance of it.

Soon now I'm off to dinner and then, after putting my head down – for we've been given another half day to celebrate VJ – I'm going ashore with David, probably to Fareham, the nearest town. I went to Portsmouth last night with Tom and Frank and saw all the high jinks – and there were plenty – so many that we cut the pictures to watch them. After all you can see a film any night, but there's only one VJ day in a lifetime.

18th August 1945, Saturday. Fareham

David, the last of the old gang, went off on accommodation leave a couple of hours ago and the hut where we sleep is almost empty, not that it won't fill up again soon. But already I've had the chance to choose my own quarters, I've gone down into the lower bunk, remained near the door where there's plenty of space, and acquired a locker for myself. And I've got a job – not the sort of job I'd have chosen for myself admittedly, working in the baggage store where all the hammocks are stored for men on leave. It's another big loaf but it's preferable to those infernal classrooms, and I have a few privileges, among them an exemption from divisions and from the perpetual wearing of No. 3s, which in this hot weather are murderous. A new set of overalls which I bought before I left *Byron* are a lot cooler.

I'm on duty today, and from midnight to 1 o'clock will have to patrol one of the signal school blocks, equipped with a tin helmet and a truncheon as a fire patrol – a black and white truncheon which looks like something from a Punch and Judy show. Later this afternoon I'll have a little nap to prepare for this little ordeal. Then I'll be up in time for 7 o'clock Communion in the morning – there's a celebration every day at that time. Then afterwards I'll potter off to Fareham on my own and go to the evening thanksgiving service.

I'd a grand night with David the First in Portsmouth on Thursday, while the VJ celebrations were still on – we celebrated with a smashing tea of crab salad – and another with Frank last night, definitely his last night ashore, for he sails on Monday. We went to Fareham, a nice modern little town, about a mile from camp, and there I lashed him up to tea at a Mission to Seamen's canteen, and afterwards to the pictures where we saw Charles Laughton in *The Suspect*, a murder film. Poor Frank, he was a bit sad. He'd proposed to his girl by letter a couple of days before, and before we had tea he sent a prepaid telegram asking her to say Yes or No. Now he's had his answer. The wire raced the letter and the poor lass has telegraphed to ask him exactly what he means!

19th August 1945, Sunday. Fareham

Names for the draft are being piped every few minutes, but not yet is mine among them. I'm beginning to think it may never be. It's the young ones they seem to be selecting now, or the specialists. If it means, as it may, a few months in this camp I'll not complain. Already I'm beginning to feel at home. I'm sleeping tight in my bunk and although there's scarcely a chap left in the hut who was there when I arrived 6 days ago they come and go all the time – they always seem such a decent lot in residence.

Yesterday I wrote a letter to the lads on *Byron* and, after supper, went to the cinema show in the camp – it's been free during VJ Week and is only 3d any other week. There I saw Judy Garland in *Little Nelly Kelly*, quite a nice little show. Then, after I'd patrolled from midnight until 1 o'clock, armed with my truncheon and tin hat, and acquired as a companion one of the dozens of cats which stalk this establishment, arose at 6 o'clock not a bit tired, and went to a communion service in the camp chapel.

21st August 1945, Tuesday. Fareham

I expected a letter, and instead there was a lovely parcel and a letter inside it. Only a few minutes ago I collected it from the mail office. I was so excited when I recognised the writing on the label that I began to tear the string off before I reached the canteen – actually in the middle of the parade ground. And what a grand parcel it was too, thank you. I'd actually only 3 cigarettes to last me until morning when it came, for we're rationed to 10 a day and too often they're Woodbines. Your 30 will be a luxury, but they're too expensive for you and too scarce for you to go hunting them. Once I can buy a tin of Navy tobacco on Saturday, I'll begin to roll my own, for I've discovered my machine in the old kit-bag and several packets of papers. Once I go into action I'll be making them cheaper than ever. So don't go spending your precious pennies on them regularly.

So VJ Day was a bit of an anti-climax for you too? Strange isn't it? And yet perhaps not so strange. It's the inevitable reaction after all those years of war, I suppose, and yet the truth is that unless we're together everything seems to lose a little of its colour and is inclined to go a bit flat. But not for long shall we be separated. It's absolutely official that all Coders up to Group 18 have to be out by September 13th. Only another 16 groups to go.

23rd August 1945, Thursday. Fareham

We were so packed in the hut last night that, contrary to regulations, two men had to sleep on the deck and one on a table. No wonder another 300 left on accommodation leave this afternoon. How I hate watching them go. I thought I was doing well with 23 days and another 6, why I'm not in it. There's not a chap in the hut who's not had 40 or 50 days in the last 60 or 70. 'Only six' they say, as if it was only a short week-end, when I tell them to prepare for foreign leave service. The average for that leave alone is 3 weeks. Yet I should worry, it's not for long. And if a draft should come there's almost certain to be a long leave for that. If only I could be home for the 9th, already I'm wondering what I can buy for our 20th anniversary.

24th August 1945, Friday. Fareham

Fancy the RN getting ahead in the demobilisation stakes. They must be forgetting Nelson. Why, if Group 26 is out by the end of the year, and even if they don't give priority release to coders, I should be home by May at the latest and probably even sooner. That's about 8 months I know, but they'll soon pass. I saw Jock's hammock today, marked August 30th, so he'll be back next Thursday and I'll have a companion in exile for he's on prepare for foreign leave too. Dave's not back for another 12 or 13 days yet, but he's definitely on draft and may not be here long.

25th August 1945, Saturday. Fareham

Hundreds have left on week-end leave. All the queues for anything and everything have gone. Three men had again to sleep on the deck last night. One of them arrived, all sad and forlorn, at midnight and, as I slept, dossed down at the side of my bed. The result was that, not knowing he was there, I tumbled out at 4 o'clock this morning for my 2 hours in the Divisional Office, and trod right into the middle of his tum which effectively wakened him up and gave me no end of a start.

I've been thinking that if I'm not sent on draft, and after I've taken all the accommodation leave to which I'll be entitled, I might take one of these short week-ends and have it with you in London. We could book a few weeks in advance for the Strand Palace and a theatre, have all Sunday together, and I shouldn't have to leave until early Monday morning.

28th August 1945, Tuesday. Fareham

According to the latest rumour, this may be one of my last weeks here, draft or no draft. The story is that the overcrowding has become so serious that all the coders, telegraphists and signalmen are to be transferred to a new camp within the next few weeks. The camp is an establishment at Belmont Park near Havant, a town about 20 miles down the line nearer London. What sort of a camp it is nobody seems to know, but if it's as clean as this one, and the food as good, we'll be lucky. Yet it will be such a change not to be in such a dense herd, everywhere packed, queues for everything, even for easy chairs in the canteen lounge. Anyway it'll be alright with me whatever happens. I've become quite a philosopher nowadays.

30th August 1945, Thursday. Fareham

Back in the canteen again for a quiet hour. How lovely it is to have a bit of peace, to be out of the way of the swarm of men herded everywhere, queuing and milling wherever I go. The position's become so desperate that they accepted 500 for accommodation leave today, dozens of them for the fourth time. There's not one in 50 who's been in the camp as long as a week at a time. Soon I'll be qualifying for a medal as one of the oldest inhabitants. Not that this leave isn't necessary because it definitely is. Six of the men in our hut – and I was one of them – slept in the canteen last night as fire patrols, and gave up our beds to new arrivals. Yet I'm told that there were still 4 sleeping on the deck. Gosh it's grim. At meal times you've to sit in such a huddle that you can scarcely lift the food to your mouth, and if you're late you just stand.

Still it's a fairly easy day in the store, and tonight as I'm not at all tired, I'm queuing complete with book, for *Arsenic and Old Lace* which the lads say is the best film we've had here for weeks. It'll mean having supper in the canteen, but they always serve a good one here and I've come equipped in advance with my fork.

Then, by the time I come out, Jock will have arrived back and we'll have a lot to tell each other I bet, and be able to console each other too, for he also is one of the minority who've to watch the rest going off on leave time after time. Nobody seems able to understand why men in our age groups have been selected for a prospective foreign service draft in a camp packed with young coders in the 50s and 60s Groups. They've done it nevertheless, and we've to just put up with it. But if the Government should announce that no men in groups lower than ours – and they've reached 29 already – are to go out East, you won't see us for dust.

31st August 1945, Friday. London

It's been a case of Hello and well, Goodbye, to Jock. I met him last night soon after he'd arrived and, as there was no bed for him, he slept on the deck close to my bunk, giving us the chance to continue our long chinwag in whispers until long after we should have been asleep. And now, so soon, I've said goodbye to him. For awaiting him last night was a draft to Colombo, the draft to which Dave and Bill have been assigned. As the available date is Wednesday of next week and you've to be in camp a minimum of

48 hours in advance, they've been able to give him only a long week-end until Monday midnight. He'll not reach his home in Glasgow until tomorrow morning, and will have to leave again on Sunday night.

Poor old Jock, he's very fed up about it. And it seems a bit strange, I must admit, sending to Colombo a bloke who's had 18 months at sea, is 38 years old and in Group 36, at a time when there are young coders capering off on accommodation leave every week, many of whom have never been out of the country. Still, as I told him, he's at least had 21 days leave in addition to his in-from-sea leave and I've had only six, and in any case, whatever happens to him, whether he goes East or stays in this country, the date of his release won't be delayed. That, at any rate, is how I look at it and I know, dear, that you agree. When you come out – that's all that matters.

1st September 1945, Saturday. Fareham

Half the personnel of this camp has left on weekend or accommodation leave. Now at last there's a bit of living space. And aren't those of us who are left glad? It's our duty weekend this time but there'll be no watches for us until tomorrow. It makes a grand break. Well, dear, this ends the third week. Only another five to go, unless I'm given a draft, and then unless I'm mighty unlucky, I'll see you sooner than ever. How I want to see you too. Never, I think, have I missed you as I am missing you in this camp. Bless you, darling, another of your letters came last night just before I went out to Fareham. I took it out with me and read it for the second time over a cup of tea in the Mission to Seamen canteen and for a third time over a fish pie supper after I'd seen *They Were Sisters*, one of the best films I have ever seen I think and one you'd love. How sorry I am that we didn't see it when I was on my last leave and it was on at the Palace. Don't miss it if it returns to the district. It shows what a good and natural film we can make if we set our stall out – why, the Americans can't touch us.

Of course, I understand that you can't write every day – there's literally not sufficient to write about. I write only because I've such a lot of free time and, to be frank, love writing such a lot. All I'm afraid of is that sometimes these letters of mine must be a bit boring, for all the tittle-tattle of this camp can't, I know, can't be as interesting as all that. It's just that I love to devote just one half-hour of every day entirely to you. I know you understand. Well, another eight days and it'll be our 20th anniversary. And still I'm searching for a present for you – I toured the few shops in Fareham in vain last night. I think it'll have to be a library subscription again and I'm glad in the circumstances that you've decided to remain at Boots, for long before this subscription expires I'll be back to choose your books for you.

Yes, I think we'll make it that – I'll send the £1 nearer the date – and then on my next leave we'll hunt and hunt and find a lovely present for each other. What do you think about that?

2nd September 1945, Sunday 5.45pm. Fareham

I've just returned from the strangest Sunday watch I've ever had. For four hours from 12.30 to 4.30 I've been one of a patrol of 6, each of us solemnly arrayed in gaiters, a belt and an NP armlet, parading in the gutters of the main street in Fareham, hunting for delinquent Jacks who walk the streets with their caps on the backs of their heads, with their Burberry collars turned up or who in any way are guilty of disturbing the peace. It was all very well in theory but as all these hardened sinners invariably go to Portsmouth anyway, finding Fareham too respectable and sedate for their revolting exploits, we saw only two all the afternoon whose caps were out of perfect alignment and they put them straight quicker than that when they saw us approaching. It's all to be done in slow motion too.

You don't walk the gutters – you crawl in them. And for four hours non-stop, except for a precious five minutes when we sidled furtively into an alley, two by two, and smoked half a cigarette each. Talk about a pleasant Sunday afternoon. It's reputed to be the most hated assignment of all. As soon as we heard today that our hut had to supply today's patrol we drew lots for the order in which we should go out. Thank goodness I draw the first watch. What about the poor guys who drew the last – eight o'clock to midnight? They won't be back until about one o'clock in the morning for Fareham's a mile from the camp and our hut is another half-mile from the main gate and transport, if it's supplied – and it often isn't – is irregular.

No further news about Jock. Whether his draft has been given an extension I don't know, but if it hasn't I'm going out to Fareham tomorrow to meet him at the canteen. He's not due back until midnight, but has to travel tonight and will reach London early in the morning. We'll have at least one evening tomorrow.

4th September 1945, Tuesday. Fareham

Now they're nearly all back. Dave and Jock are in my hut – Dave sleeping on the bunk above me, and Jock just opposite, and both waiting for the Colombo draft to leave, which may be tomorrow or next month or never. Bill, the other *Byron* coder, who's on prepare for foreign leave, is also in camp but exactly where we don't know yet. And Tom returns tonight, although unless there's a draft waiting for him, he'll probably be off on accommodation leave before the end of the week, for there's still lashings of that left. It's nearly like old times.

I met Jock in Fareham last night, we went to see Laurence Olivier's *Henry V*. There were only 1/- seats left when we arrived and we'd to sit so close to the screen – only three rows back – that there were times when I thought we were in the cast. But I loved every minute of the two hours it lasted. The colouring was perfect, the language so wonderful that you listen to it entranced, and Henry's speech before Agincourt – 'we happy few, we band of brothers' – I'll never forget.

What a letter from the Ministry of Pensions. There's still magic in the mention of the Press. Now I hope that everything will be cleared up. I'm so glad too, for it was a bit worrying, in spite of the £50 windfall from the office, to think of you being reduced to a 12/6 pittance.

A quiet night tonight with my book. Again I searched Fareham for a present, but nothing could I find except inferior handbags at excessive prices and lots of other trash. It'll have to be the £1 for the library after all. Already I've the registered envelope and the £1 note. After all it's a present that will last all the year, and on my next leave, which should be in five weeks if not sooner, we'll find something really posh. We don't celebrate a 20th anniversary every day.

I forgot to tell you about our cats and kittens. Authority decreed the other day that they should be properly mustered. So a great cat and kitten hunt began and as they were rounded up, each was given a string collar and a label bearing the number of the hut or store to which it has been allotted. Our hut has a little tortoiseshell kitten. All over the camp now you can see them prowling, big labels attached to their necks, and on a few labels the two letters 'UA' which is the Navy's abbreviation for ratings under the age for rum issue!

5th September 1945, Friday 3pm. Fareham, on the hammock with Blackie

I've been to the dentist's, had eight X-ray photographs taken and developed while I waited, and at the end of all that had my gums painted with a purple solution which has coated my tongue and with a taste like ten hangovers, and so coloured my lips that I must look positively grim. I couldn't eat dinner, for everything was tainted with this foul bromide. And now I've to go to the galley every hour for a hot mouth wash of salt water and am excused all duties. Tomorrow I've to go to the clinic again at 8.30. I nearly lost all my bottom teeth when the dentist, after examining the X-ray photographs and confessing that they told him nothing, said 'I think I'll take all these teeth out'. Horrors. 'But, sir' said the nurse, 'This man will be out soon.' 'What's that?' said the surgeon, 'Yes, Group 34, I suppose he will.' So I was reprieved, but it's not certain that the reprieve will be indefinite. It all depends on the result of the purple horror and the mouthwash treatment.

What's happened is that a few days ago one of my bottom teeth began to ache a little, it was nothing much. But yesterday all my cheek was swollen and as today the inflammation was still there and it seemed to be spreading down towards my throat, I decided it would be wise to go to the clinic.

23rd September 1945. Preston Refreshment Room

This is probably the last time that I'll have to write to you at the end of a leave. Next time there will, I hope, be no note to write, no goodbyes to say and I won't be going away again. We'll not have to count the days, even the hours as every time I looked at the clock and counted them today. Next time I'll come home and not go away again.

24th September 1945, Monday. Mess 12, HMS *Eastway*, Palmers Dock, Hebburn, Newcastle-on-Tyne.

I feel such an awful fraud, as I intend telling you on the telephone when I go ashore tonight. We said our goodbyes last night and you were so loving and so brave. There was £1 note you hid in my cigarette case. Then when I opened my bag an hour ago, I found the packet of sweets, and in one of the pockets your little note. And now I've probably to go on leave again, I hope it won't seem too much of an anti-climax. I never dreamed the day would come when I'd feel almost apologetic about accepting a leave, but it's happened this time.

25th September 1945, Tuesday. Newcastle-on-Tyne

The cake is lovely. Nearly half of it is gone already, and I've only had one slice. I opened the tin when we had our cup of tea at stand easy in the coding office where I'm writing now – an office which was painted while I was on leave and is now as clean and fresh as I never thought it ever would be again. They all walked in one by one, had a slice each, said it was fine and wished us 'many happy returns'.

It was a grand night ashore last night with John. I've known him for less than a week, but neither of us liked saying goodbye. He's sending me a scrap of Atlantic Star ribbon sufficient for the bar, as soon as he can unearth it from all his possessions. And he's left me too, half a bottle of Brylcreem for the old mop, and a coat hanger, if I can find space in corner to hang it and that seems improbable. The yeoman of signals is one of the youngest yeomen in the RN, only 21. He has ambitions, wants to learn shorthand, has sent home for the books which arrived today, and I've promised to teach him. That will pass a few empty hours and there'll be plenty of them. That will be the chief trial I think – the endless loafing, the packed ship.

26th September 1945, Wednesday

Already on this ship they've learned that I can type. I've had one commission from the signals officer and was typing for a couple of hours during the dogs last night on a machine which should have been pensioned off years ago, for every time you hit a key it threatens to disintegrate. Still it keeps me in practice and I'm told that it actually belongs to our office and will be transferred back to us as soon as the ship's in commission.

The coders in this ship have to hoist the Ensign in the morning and lower it at sunset every day we're in harbour. I did it for the first time this morning and didn't tangle the halliards, but some day you bet I will.

2nd October 1945, Tuesday. Newcastle-on-Tyne, after leave

Nearly all morning and again this afternoon I've been on telephone watch, which means that every few minutes – half a dozen times since I began this letter – the telephone rings with a call for one of the 23 officers and I've to go hunting for them all over the ship, which I'm told was featured in an article in the *Newcastle Chronicle* on Saturday as the 'ugly duckling of the Royal Navy'. I must find a copy of that the first time I go ashore again and send it to you. When will I go ashore again? I don't know. Tonight I've an appointment with the young yeoman for his first shorthand lesson up in his own little private caboose.

P.S. A letter from Harry. He's trying to find a scrap of ribbon for me, but as he says, it's all to be signed for, so I may be unlucky again. We shall have to depend on Tom for it.

3rd October 1945, Wednesday 2.00pm. Newcastle-on-Tyne

Isn't it grand about the demobilisation speed-up? And for once it's official too. If on average Group 31 are to be out by the end of the year, coders in a higher group will probably be released by that time. Definitely it won't be six months now, and it may be a lot less. There seems to be a general impression now that we shall be in the fleet which is being mobilised to bring back men and materials from the East, that we shall go out and as soon as all our accommodation has been packed to the last inch, shall sail home again. So we shouldn't be away too long wherever we're sent. If I go at all – and now, in view of this new development, I might not.

Already at this base, men are being divided into sections according to their groups. Section II is reserved for men in groups 25–35 and I'm in that. What section II's destiny is to be nobody seems to know, but the yeoman seems to think it improbable that it will be the East in view of the fact that as men for demobilisation are often sent to dispersal units weeks before they are finally dismissed, there might not be time for Section II to go out and come back again, however fast their passage, before their groups are required for the long demobilisation preliminaries. I don't know, it's all a bit chaotic.

I'm going tonight with the other coder, chiefly to visit the *Newcastle Chronicle* office for a few cuttings of the Eastway article – I'll enclose one with this letter if I'm lucky. Then while I'm there I'm trying to fix up a tour of the building for a few lads in the ship who've been so interested in what I've told them about newspapers that they'll never be content until they've been in a newspaper office and seen the wheels going round.

4th October 1945, Thursday. Newcastle-on-Tyne

We've moved our berth again today, about a couple of hundred yards further from Hebburn, which is a quite a voyage for this old tub. Address your letters in future to Hebburn Quay, Hebburn, Newcastle, although actually the old address would still find me. All the difference it's made is that we're off the telephone and now I've to walk over to the quay every hour to see if any messages have been sent to us instead of waiting at the telephone to take them as they come.

6th October 1945, Friday. Newcastle-on-Tyne

Everybody, we hear, has to have a medical examination before we sail, and as there are still rumours that all the lower age groups are to be sent back to barracks instead of to the East, my particular fate is still uncertain.

It's so quiet in the ship now that half of them have gone. I've been left in more or less sole control of the Signals Distributing Office and will be on duty both tonight and all Sunday. 'Keep your eye on things Lofty,' said the yeoman before he left and added, which is funny when you think he's only 21 himself; 'These young ones let everything slide when I'm away'. Of course, like Tom he's not an HO (that means Hostilities Only) and can't afford to take chances. It means that every hour I'll have to potter down to the quay for telephone messages, collect and log and distribute every signal that comes to the ship – and there are plenty – and ensure that the Ensign I hoisted for Colours every morning at 9 o'clock and lowered every evening at sunset, whilst the bo'sun's mate plays a hideous tune on his whistle. Now I must be off to the telephone again, for I mustn't let the yeoman down.

7th October 1945, Sunday. Newcastle-on-Tyne.

Well what do you think of the news? It wasn't entirely unexpected and yet, like everything else in this outfit, it came like a bolt from the blue. I'll tell you exactly what happened. I awakened this morning to find four strangers wandering around the mess. Two had come from Petersfield and two from Collingwood – all crash drafts – and reached Newcastle at four in the morning after all night on the train and announcing that they'd been drafted as reliefs. There was a coder, a signalman, and two telegraphists. As soon as I told him my name, the coder said 'I'm your relief, that's definite, your name's on my draft note.'

The other three had also the men they were to replace nominated. In my case it was not unexpected, for apparently the latest decree in barracks is that all men in Group 39 and below are exempt from foreign service. But reliefs for the other three seem to make no sense, for the men at present on board are all in their 40s and the men sent as their reliefs are in each case only two or three groups higher. It's all a bit of a thunderbolt. After all those excursions and alarums I'm not to go after all. And to be frank, although a few months in either Petersfield or Collingwood are not too attractive in prospect I think I can admit now that I was scarcely jubilant at the grim time I'm afraid everybody will have in this old crate once she reaches the hot belts. Frankly she's not adapted to the tropics and never will be; the mess decks are already as airless as ovens and packed to the last square inch.

8th October 1945, Monday. Newcastle-on-Tyne

Back from your holiday yet? I hope you've had the loveliest time. The weather here is glorious. It was grand just to walk the packed streets of Newcastle when I went ashore as orderly this morning – the sun shining and a gentle breeze blowing. I called at

Fenwick's and took back my library books. I'd only read one of them but I decided that while I'd the chance I'd better return them, for although definitely we're not going today, it's possible that we'll leave tomorrow and I didn't want a bill for 9/6 novels. I'll want all my pennies for the leave which will probably come once we reach either Petersfield or Collingwood. I hope it's Collingwood for John's there – the coder from Eastway to whom you sent the soap – and it's possible that Jock, Dave and Tom may also still be in residence, Jock almost certainly unless he left for Colombo before the last speed-up was announced. It would be grand to meet the old gang again. They're the old originals and you always seem to have the biggest attachment to them.

Take Harry – he's gone and broken all the regulations by swiping some medal ribbon for me and has made me a complete bar and sent it off. It arrived today, and it's not the Atlantic Star ribbon after all, but actually the France and Germany ribbon – red, white and blue – which probably ranks even higher, with a silver rosette in the middle for Atlantic patrols. I'll look like a dog's dinner when I get that lot up. Well at least it will show that we've done something.

P.S. In a letter from Mamie I hear that a lieutenant commander met David in Hull the other day and took him aboard the Louis, one of the American frigates based with us at Belfast, not in our group – the good old 21st – but still built where *Byron* was commissioned and her exact duplicate. She's sailing back to the States in a day or two. *Byron* will be going soon, but I won't be with her.

10th October 1945, Wednesday. Newcastle-on-Tyne.

They've all had medical inspections for foreign draft today. That's to say each man has walked into the sick bay and unless he fell down in a heap or reported a malignant disease, has been passed as fit. I've not heard of one reject among 200 of them. I'm spending every day in the office until the end now and have been exempt from all evening watches. Which means that I'm free to go ashore every night.

14th October 1945, Sunday. Mess 111, HMS *Collingwood*, Fareham, Hants

Just half an hour in the everlasting joining routine, which is being continued today and should end tomorrow with a kit muster – I'll pass with honours. If you lifted my kit-bag, assuming that you could lift it, you wouldn't be surprised either. Yes, I've everything I should have and a lot you needn't have. It was nearly lights-out – 10.30 – before they called it a day last night. At 10 o'clock they were issuing blankets to us. 'I'll only need the one.' I said. 'That' said one of the WRENS in the store 'is what you think. You take two.' Those words of wisdom. Even with three blankets on me and an extra hammock I was a bit cold, for sometime during every night I seem to uncurl myself in a bunk, which is never long enough for me, and then out of the end shoot my feet and then cold blasts hiss up the bed and I've to curl myself in a knot again. Won't my own bed be grand after all this?

Dave is still waiting for a draft, his assignment to Colombo cancelled, he is in the foreign service pool which I was in before I went to the Eastway, ineligible for all leave, loafing the days away. Poor Dave, he's fed up to the gills and in group 50 the outlook for him is decidedly bleak. Jock's away on 14 days accommodation leave, and as he's in group 36 won't be sent overseas – no man is to be sent from here under group 45, although whether that's a general principle I don't know, his draft to Colombo has been cancelled too. Tom, who never wanted to be a telegraphist anyway, has volunteered for the writer's branch and is serving two months probation in the Pay Office. He likes it too. It will mean that his demobilisation will be delayed, for the writers are far away down the field, nearly the lowest of all the non-commissioned grades, but as he's in Municipal Government Accountancy it's keeping him in training and will probably be worth it. It's been grand meeting them all again. We never stopped talking last night – in the hut, mine is opposite 193 where they're all billeted – in the canteen, in the mess-deck, everywhere. Chief item of news was about *Byron* being at Portsmouth preparing to sail to the States for return to the US Navy.

Being in charge of a draft, even a draft of three, is no joke. It was all a mix-up from the beginning, for one of the officers has ordered transport from the ship to Newcastle station and made such a mess of it, that although it should have arrived at five o'clock it was still missing at eight. In the end I was given permission to order a taxi which cost 10/-, which will be refunded on the next day-sometime-never system. Still we reached Newcastle in time for a supper at the NAAFI and as I persuaded the RTO to put a 'Not for public use' label on one of the windows, we'd a carriage all to ourselves and slept so heavily after York that I never awakened until I heard passengers leaving the train and found it was King's Cross. The other two didn't waken even then. That was 5 o'clock in the morning. Then, after a cup of tea in a station hostel, we'd to wait until 6.30 for transport to Waterloo, where I gave one of the lads who lives in London permission to go home for a couple of hours, all against the regulations, but what the heck.

What happens next? I don't know to be honest. But I may be on leave by tomorrow, even if not necessarily for 28 days. Home seems near at last.

HOME AGAIN

GOODBYE TO THE SEA

by Cliff Greenwood, Blackpool *Gazette and Herald*, November 10th 1945

I shall be coming home soon.

They will never come below and shake me again a few minutes before the middle watch – that old familiar hissing whisper 'Ten to twelve, Lofty…Are you awake?'…

I shall never answer again 'Righto' or 'OK' for I never learned to say 'Aye, aye', and uncurl myself in the bunk, in the corner, which was always too small for me, and slide out of it to the steel deck over the table, praying that nobody has left the bread knife loafing or a couple of empty condensed milk tins, or a few crusts of stale bread, and so often they had!

The mess deck was always dark as the pit, except for the red satanic glow of the two pilot lamps on the fore and aft bulkheads.

I can hear now the sighing and rustling of 16 men sleeping restlessly as the ship lurches and tilts and creaks and talks to itself in those night watches and the hiss and gurgle of the sea washing the half inch steel plates which are the mess deck's walls. That has happened for the last time.

I shall never again go hunting in the darkness, crawling on the cold deck under the table for the socks which always came adrift from under the pillow; or lean against the table like a drunken stork as I pulled on a pair of frayed bell-bottoms. I shall never wear again the open necked shirt and the old tattered golf jacket, or strap the blue life-belt into position.

I shall not grope for the book which I always hid under my bunk and tuck it under my arm and climb through the hatch to the narrow gangway which I have walked a thousand times with the eight wash basins on the port side and the three open showers on the starboard side which were considered adequate to ensure the cleanliness of, if not the godliness, of 140 men.

I shall not pass again the artificer's workshop and the silent lathes, the galley where the night cocoa was always simmering and bubbling in a huge cauldron, the wardroom pantry and, facing a stairway, the chaste grey curtains which screen and preserve the sanctity of the wardroom – that little Ritz with the panelled walls and the opulent chrome and leather chairs, the cool cabins and the closed showers, where they serve gin and whisky at about Boer War prices and God (according to the wardroom inhabitants) is in his Heaven and all's right with the world.

For the last time I have climbed the stairway, and on its first landing opened the door, painted silver grey with a panel over it, on which in white letters on a black base are the words 'Radio Room', and passed into the harsh white brilliance of its lights and heard the muted chatter of Morse from the sets where the telegraphists sit, four hours at a time, some of them alas – nearly all of them for the first two or three days out – flanked by buckets about whose purpose I will leave you to speculate.

I have sat myself down for the last time on the bench clamped to the deck and, at the narrow desk, waited for the signals and translated the hundreds of groups of letters and figures into the King's English – something like it! – and in the quiet intervals, gone below to the galley for jugs of cocoa hot and thick and sweet as molasses.

Happy Days? Yes, they were happy days. I know that now in retrospect. Even the grim days and the grimmer nights are gilded by the sort of spurious glamour which alone makes war at sea endurable.

I can think now without any particular emotional disturbance of the night on the first of the two Russian convoys when the bell began to toll for 'Action Stations' and, above its sinister pealing, the Skipper announced in a voice empty of all expression, that a front line destroyer close to our position in the screen had been torpedoed and was at standstill in the Arctic seas which were death to men and doom to a ship adrift.

There was no panic, no stampede. Into the W/T office – the 'Radio Room' as the American builders of the ship had called it – the telegraphists and the coders packed.

As soon as I opened the door I heard the voice in the R/T loud-speaker high in the starboard bulkhead, the voice, clear and firm above the crackling atmosphere of the young telegraphist, whose name I will never know, whose grave is in those Northern waters where so many of his companions sleep with him…

MEN OF THE LITTLE SHIP

Blackpool *Gazette and Herald*, November 24th 1945

We seldom went to the NAAFI which seemed so darned impersonal and always closed too early. At the NAFFI canteen onboard there were luxuries – fresh eggs, boiled ham, sauces, biscuits – plain, digestive, or any other sort.

It was the NAAFI or nothing aboard – and we were glad of it. But ashore we always visited the voluntary canteens, searched always for those three letters 'WVS.' and knew everything would be fine there.

There was the church canteen in Belfast, where whenever you ordered a poached egg on toast you invariably found one egg on top of the toast and another hiding coyly beneath it.

And the little eating house close to the prison in Londonderry, where two years ago they were still serving a couple of eggs, a cutlet, a sausage, fried tomatoes, chips and plates of bread and butter – fresh country butter – for half a crown.

And the WVS buffet on Newcastle station which opened its doors during the first week of the war and has never, night and day, closed them since.

Blessed are the matrons and the maidens of the voluntary canteens. No medals for them – but our everlasting gratitude, our big 'Thank you'.

I shall miss all that. I shall miss the lads, too, the gang in the little ship.

I have said 'Goodbye' to a few of them already, for they have sailed away to deliver the ship back to the States, where some of them saw her built in a Boston shipyard in 23 days. They have gone, but I shall not forget them.

They were no unworldly innocents. Too many of them drank too many pints when they were ashore. Their love affairs were so complex and tangled that they would have given Ann Temple a headache. Their language was at times unseemly – what a polite word for it – punctuated every few words by oaths florid and violent.

But at heart they were good – kind, generous, loyal – as good men as I have ever met or will ever meet again. I shall miss them such a lot, I know.

But – again I have to write it – soon I shall be going home and if the day is to come, and probably will, when I shall begin to ask 'Where are they now?' and to think 'There were never such guys as those' and know the bitter-sweet nostalgia for things that can never come again – with all that I shall know content.

For I am going home soon. There's magic in those words.

She who has been so brave and patient will be lonely no longer. We shall do everything together again. We shall prune the apple trees and, if it is not too late, cut the lawns, and when we see the cherry tree, its branches bare and gnarled, we shall know that when it flowers again and is hidden under a mantle of white, I shall be there to see it next time.

We shall take Judy walks – and now probably she will condescend to go with us when we are together again.

We shall sit by the fireside – where are those slippers? – and I will read all that J.B. Priestley and Gerald Bullett and Monica Dickens and Ernest Raymond and John Dickson Carr and all the others have been writing whilst I have been away and listen to Tommy Handley in 'ITMA' and 'Saturday Night Theatre' and, with all the lights off and shadows creeping up the walls, 'Appointment with Fear'.

And I will go to bed – a bed which is not too small for me – and know that nobody will come hissing, 'Lofty! Lofty! It's 10 to four. Time to get up!' and that I shall not have to begin crawling about on a cold steel deck hunting for those socks.

For I am coming home soon. Is that good?

I'll say it is.

APPENDICES

APPENDIX A

PEOPLE

This list includes people mentioned in the letters, members of the crew found in lists and letters provided by Alan Hope, and members of the Byron Association. It has not been possible to find surnames for some of them.

Barker, Denis

Briggs, Stan – engine room artificer

Burfield J.B. – lieutenant commander, MVO, DSC, captain of *Byron* from 1944

Chatt, Tom – communications rating

Cummings, Bill – coder from Dundee

Cunningham, John

Fletcher, Peter – telegraphist

Gleadhall, Tom – leading seaman, radar

Goff, Tom – telegraphist S

Hammond, Jack

Hampson, Jimmy

Hargreaves, Denis

Hemmings, George – telegraphist

Hobson, Alec

Hope, Alan – petty officer, radio mechanic

Johnson, Cyril – from Hull

King, Ken – from Bristol

Kingsley, Les – petty officer

McDonald, Jock – signalman

Milne, Alec – from Glasgow

Morgan, Jimmy – telegraphist P/JX 580651

Murdoch, Ginger – telegraphist

Nield, Mrs – WVS canteen volunteer Belfast

Noble, Percy – chief engine room artificer

Repard, Dave (JDL) – first lieutenant

Seeley, Denis

Smith, Dick – leading seaman

Southcombe KGL – lieutenant commander, first captain of HMS *Byron* until 1944.

Taylor, Ted (AE) – from Nottingham

Whithouse, John – able seaman

Williams, Taffy

Young, Frank – telegraphist

Barbara – WREN

Fizz – telegraphist

Arthur, coder

Mrs Nield – from Belfast

Mrs Ritchie – from Belfast

Tiny – telegraphist

ANIMALS

Boston, Rita and Sparks – three of many ship's cats

Blackie – one of many ship's dogs

APPENDIX B

BOOKS READ

Cliff said 'Thank goodness I love books. They make all the difference, break the monotony and it could be monotonous without them'. There was plenty of time for reading on board ship and during the over-land journeys to different bases. The on-board library was a good source of reading matter, enlivened by books sent from home and obtained from Boots the Chemist Lending Library. Boots ran the Booklovers Library from 1899 to 1966, the subscription was 2s 6d during the war years. WH Smith also provided a library service, and libraries in towns could be used, provided the stay was sufficiently long. Penguin paperbacks made a huge difference, small and light and cheap, ideal for posting, and relatively free from paper rationing with many titles available. From all these sources Cliff made sure that he was always within reach of a good read and managed to read all of the following books, providing comments in many cases (shown in brackets).

February 1944

Wilkie Collins *The Woman in White*

March 1944

Jon Galsworthy *The Patrician*

Flying Officer X *The Best People in the World*

Peter Cheyney *Dangerous Curves*

Winifred Holtby *South Riding*

April 1944

Lloyd Douglas *Disputed Passage* (It's a good book, all about doctors in America.)

Anna Paterson *Take These Hands*

Phillip Gibbs *The Streets of Adventure*

A.D.M. Hutchinson *If Winter Comes* (I enjoyed it, over-written in parts and a little complex in its construction.)

Franz Werfel *The Pure in Heart*

Earl Stanley Gardner *The Case of the Counterfeit Spy* (A new author to me, but quite good.)

Mark Gifford's Body (That book from Boots was decidedly queer. It was one of those futuristic experiments that darted about in time and space until you were nearly dizzy.)

Michael Harrison *What are we waiting for?*

Sinclair Lewis *Arrowsmith* (A new edition of a book which will be on the B shelves at Boots.)

Naomi Jacobs *Under New Management*

Barnaby Ross (Ellery Queen) *The Tragedy of X* (A mystery about a man murdered in a crowded street-car, and it was the conductor who done it after all, and there were sufficient red herrings to fill a crate of tins.)

June 1944

Anthony Berkley *The Poisoned Chocolate Case*

July 1944

John Marquand *So Little Time* (Wasn't it good, he has a peculiar style, but his people live.)

Agatha Christie *The Mysterious Affair at Styles* (It'll be good to meet old man Poirot again.)

Great Novels of Today (I've snaffled that great tome *Great Novels of Today*, the one which contains John Galsworthy's *The Apple Tree* and has about 1,000 pages in it and a dozen great stories. It's about the best book on the ship, I can tell you.)

Joseph Conrad *The End of the Tether* (Grand sea story. However, did I come to miss Conrad before I came in the Navy?)

R.H. Mottram *The Spanish Farm*

John Steinbeck *Of Mice and Men*

Halliday Sutherland *A Time to keep* (What a good book this is, a lot of random reflections, it's charming and so entertaining.)

August 1944

Phyllis Bottome *The Mortal Storm* (It promises to be one of the best books I've read for ages.)

September 1944

Monica Dickens *The Fancy* (A first class book.)

Margaret Iles *Season Ticket* (It's good as *The Fancy*, which was very good.)

November 1944

Godfrey Winn *Home from Sea* (It's nearly everything in it that's happened to me and it's full of all the slang phrases that creep into your vocabulary without your realising it.)

A.S.M. Hutchinson *The Soft Spot* (Quite good too, even if the style is a bit tortuous. The pity is that with a lot of our library books you find that a page here and there is missing. I know we're short of paper at the heads but, darn it, there's a limit.)

Gilbert Frankau *Three Englishmen* (One of his earlier and better books which I snapped out of the new library batch.)

December 1944

John Galsworthy *The Forsyte Saga*

Hugh Walpole *The Dark Forest*

Richard Llewellyn *None but the Lonely Heart* (Tough but quite classy, although not at all the sort of book you'd expect the author of *How Green Was My Valley* to write.)

John Dickinson Carr *Poison in Jest*

Agatha Christie *Murder at the Vicarage* (Found out at last whodunit – and very neat and ingenious it was too.)

E. Arnot Robinson *The Signpost*

January 1945

Anne Bridge *The Frontier Passage* (Thundering good.)

Elizabeth von Armin *The Jasmine Farm* (There's a chuckle in every line so far.)

February 1945

Kate O'Brien *The Last of Summer*

L.A.G. Strong *The Bay* (I may have read it, but such a long time ago that I'll read it again…excellent – a simple little story, but every character in it lives.)

Dashiell Hammett *The Thin Man* (Not so hot, too darned complicated.)

Pearl Buck *This Proud Heart* (Liking it a lot. It is not, as most of Pearl Buck's books are, about China, but has a modern American setting, a sort of family chronicle.)

March 1945

Humfrey Jordan *The Day Without Evening* (Liking it too, for it's a simple sincere story of a sea captain.)

J.L. Hodson *And Yet I Like America* (Published only a few weeks and costs 10/6. It's most interesting, written in the form of a diary, each day complete in itself, almost as I write to you, except of course, that he's wandering about the States and has lots of material and I'm marooned in a little ship and can only write about all the commonplace little things which make our days and nights.)

Jeffery Farnol *The Definite Object* (One of the best books he ever wrote and worth reading again. It's a modern setting, pre-war New York, but half the folk talk like old Jasper Shrig, and I love it. It must be twenty years since I read it last.)

Ernest Gann *Island in the Sky* (It's about the commercial air pilots who fly transport ferries for the US Army and fine it is too.)

Georges Simenon *The Patience of Maigret* (The first of the Maigret books I've read and very good it seems too. Very neat and ingenious it was too. They're worth reading.)

A.P. Herbert *The Secret Battle* (Probably the best of all the books I've read in the last fortnight, the best novel of the last war, according to Winston Churchill in the preface, ever written.)

Gladys Mitchell *Speedy Death* (Now I'm on with a blood and thunder for a change. A couple of folk have been drowned in a bath already and I'm only on page 46.)

April 1945

Warwick Deeping *One Secret Sanctuary* (Written in those days before he was famous and when he was a finer novelist, I think, than he is now. I think so at any rate. I'm loving it and it's a good length too.)

Eric Ambler *Epitaph for a Spy* (All his books are good, but this is the best I've read.)

F.L. Green *The Night of Fire* (It's class, there's no doubt about that, but it's grim and at times sordid and introspective.)

William Shiver *Berlin Diary* (A book I've wanted to read ever since it led to his expulsion from Germany when, as one of the American newspaper corps, he wrote it. It's all about Hitler's preparations for war. It should be interesting to read it now that Berlin is encircled and Hitler is doomed.)

May 1945

J.B. Priestley *Blackout in Gultey* (I've read it before, but it's worth reading again, as all his books are.)

Ethel Lina White *The Third Eye*

Mountford Williams *The Happy Chase* (Selected merely because Heinemman's had published it – and very good it is too, a detective story which is not set at all to the usual pattern.)

June 1945

David Bolster *Roll on my Twelve*

Peter Cheyney *Sinister Errand* (A smasher.)

August 1945

Hammond Innes *Attack Alarm* (Story of an AA station during the Battle of Britain. The first two chapters have real punch.)

J.B. Priestley *Benighted*

September 1945

Gladys Mitchell *When I Last Died* (A new thriller I've found in my locker, a library book which somebody has probably forgotten to return. It's a good one too.)

October 1945

Jerrard Tickell *Soldier from the War Returning* (It's as good as expected – and it's a second *Rough Justice* I think.)

Emery Bonnet *High Pavement*

Helen Ashton *Yeoman's Hospital*

APPENDIX C

FILMS AND THEATRE

While in port there was an opportunity to make use of the facilities of the local town – cinemas, theatres and local amateur dramatic or ENSA events and shows. On board ship films were shown in the cramped messdeck. Cliff and his fellow crew members took every available opportunity to see films and plays.

October 1943

Citizen Kane

November 1943

White Cargo

February 1944

Under Suspicion

March 1944

Now Voyager

Shadow of a doubt

Model Wife

Berlin Correspondent

City for Conquest

Hay Fever

Green Hell

April 1944

True to Life

Captain Fury

The Sky's The Limit

Seven Miles from Alcatraz

May 1944

This Demi-Paradise

Dangerous Moonlight

The Ghost and the Guest

The Road to Zanzibar

June 1944

The Dancing Master, Laurel & Hardy

That Uncertain Feeling

Goodbye Mr Chips

In Old Oklahoma

July 1944

The Shipbuilders

Stagedoor Canteen

Mutiny on the Bounty

Claudia

Action for Slander

Night Train from Munich

August 1944

Holy Matrimony

The Purple Heart

Pennies from Heaven

My Friend Flicka

Fanny by Gaslight

Something to Sing About

Stage Door Canteen

They Walk Alone (Theatre)

September 1944

Journey into Fear, Charity Begins (Theatre)

October 1944

Husbands are a problem (Theatre)

November 1944
The Way Back
For Whom the Bell Tolls
Uncle Harry (Theatre)
Trilby (Theatre)
Dixie

December 1944
Medal for the General, The Singing Musketeers.
This is the Army, Dear Octopus

January 1945
The Woman of the Town
Storm over Lisbon
Goodnight Sweetheart
Don't Take It To Heart
We Three
The Man from Frisco
The Sea Hawk
Double Indemnity
Love Story
The Seventh Cross

February 1945
Going My Way
Western Approaches
Arms and the Woman
Goodbye Mr Chips
A Dog's Life
Seven Days Ashore

March 1945
Show Business
Greenwich Village

April 1945
The Sullivans
Song of Russia
Madonna of the Seven Seas
Action in Arabia

Is Your Honeymoon Really Necessary (Theatre)
Helen's Dilemma (Theatre)
You're a Lucky Man Mr Smith
Kismet
It Happened Tomorrow
Three Men in White.

May 1945
The Seventh Cross
Sahara
Murder in Thornton Square

June 1945
The Thin Man Comes Home
Hotel Berlin
Lady Let's Dance
The Man in Half Moon Street

July 1945
Practically Yours
Mrs Parkington
In Our Time

August 1945
The Suspect
Little Nelly Kelly
A Tree Grows in Brooklyn
Lover's Leap (Theatre)
Arsenic and Old Lace
They Were Sisters

September 1945
Nine Girls
Henry V
Wilson (Theatre)
The Enchanted Cottage

October 1945
Ten Little Nigger Boys

APPENDIX D

HMS BYRON – MOVEMENTS HISTORY
1943

14 August	Launch at Bethlehem-Hingham shipyard, Boston, USA
September	Fitting out, Bethlehem-Hingham
10 October	Commissioning ceremony
November	Trials, Casco Bay, Gulf of Mexico
14 December	To HMS *Malabar*, Bermuda for working up

1944

14 January	To Newfoundland
27 January	To Belfast – escort to Convoy HX 275 with HMS *Conn*
17 February	Scapa Flow
20 February	To Bear Island in B1 Escort Group protecting Convoy JW57 to Russia
March	North Atlantic Convoys
20 March	Leave Londonderry
2 April	To Nore Command
April	Refit in Sheerness, North Sea escorts from Harwich, Thames to Humber
May	Escorting Mulberry harbour and Pluto parts to Weymouth
6 June	In River Blackwater waiting, took no part in D Day landings, Escorts in English Channel
July	Escorts in Channel and North Sea
4 August	To Belfast, then refit
September	Belfast refit
1 October	21st Escort Group formed, Group working up
29 October	Escort Convoys JW61/RA61 to and from Kola Inlet
6 November	Captain – Lt KEG Southcombe appendicitis on return
November	Covering Escorts in North Atlantic
December	Patrols in Bristol, English Channel and Channel Islands, Plymouth
16 December	Collision with HMS *Tanatside*, damage to bow
17 December	Action to sink adrift LCM (Landing craft mechanised)

1945

2–27 January	To Glasgow for repair to bow
27 January	Trials
February	Patrols Irish Sea, North Channel and Bristol Channel
March	Patrols Bristol Channel and Minches
27 March	Group sinks U722 and U965
30 March	Group sinks U1021
April	Patrol SW Approaches, NW Ireland and Minches
8 April	Group sinks U1001
27 April	HMS *Redmill* torpedoed
1 May	Ship listed for Far East service
7 to 22 April	Loch Eriboll to take U-boat surrender
7 June	21st Escort Group disbanded, orders for Far East cancelled
11 June	To Rosyth
20–26 June	Duty transport to forces in Norway (Bergen, Stavangar, Trondheim)
July	Partial rundown commences
August	Dundee and RNAS Arbroath as torpedo target ship for FAA Barracudas
September	Target Ship
October	Target Ship
10 November	Arrive Boston (USA) for hand back to US Navy
24 November	Paying off ceremony and hand back to US Navy December Crew return to UK on LST 3522

1947

October	Ship sold for breaking up.

SOURCES OF INFORMATION

The Letters of C.G. Greenwood 1943–1945. Originals in Imperial War Museum London, Sue Seabridge

HMS *Byron* Newsletter – Summer 1992, John Whithouse and Alan Hope

HMS *Byron* Newsletter – Autumn 1992, John Whithouse and Alan Hope

HMS *Byron* Newsletter – Winter 1992, John Whithouse and Alan Hope

HMS *Byron* Newsletter – Spring 1993, John Whithouse and Alan Hope

HMS *Byron* Newsletter – Summer 1993, John Whithouse and Alan Hope

HMS *Byron* Newsletter – Autumn 1993, John Whithouse and Alan Hope

HMS *Byron* Newsletter – Winter 1993, John Whithouse and Alan Hope

HMS *Byron* Newsletter – Spring 1994, John Whithouse and Alan Hope

HMS *Byron* Newsletter – Autumn 1994, John Whithouse and Alan Hope

Recollections of HMS *Byron* and the 21st Escort Group, 1943–1945, John Whithouse and Alan Hope

HMS *Byron* – events and movements history, Alan Hope The 21st Escort Group

HMS *Byron* – BBC WW2 People's War – an archive of WW2 memories written by the public bbc.co.uk/ww2peopleswar/stories/19, BBC

Newspaper article *Gazette & Herald* 10 November 1945 *Goodbye to the Sea*, Cliff Greenwood, *Blackpool Gazette*

Newspaper article *Gazette & Herald* 24 November 1945 *Men of the little ships*, Cliff Greenwood, *Blackpool Gazette*

Letter from Leading Signaller Harry Burnell to Cliff Greenwood, 31 October 1945, Sue Seabridge

Letter from Ted Taylor to Sue Seabridge, 17 August 1984

Letter from Ted Taylor to Sue Seabridge, undated, 1984 describing events at sea

Letter from Tom Goff to Alan Hope clarifying events in Cliff's letters, 27 June 1986

Convoy XK234 Arrives – Wartime story of the missions to seamen. Useful for shore canteens and lodgings information, Missions to Seamen

A Trophy of War Geoffrey Allen & Mark Jarrold.*Guns Review* March 1992

The Grey Wolves of Eriboll David M. Hird, Whittles Publishing 2010

Blackpool: The Complete Record Roy Calley, DB Publishing 2011

Sailor's and Soldier's Free Buffet – Preston Station 1917, Lancashire Record Office Ref DDX2016/1; NRA 3510 Lancs R.O. Misc.

Churchill's Navy: The Ships, Men & Organisation 1939–1945 Brian Lavery, Conway 2006

The Allied Convoy System, 1939–1945: Its Organisation, Defence and Operation Arnold Hague, Chatham 2000

Convoys to Russia: Allied Convoys and Naval Surface Operations in Arctic Waters, 1941–1945 Bob Ruegg and Arnold Hague, World Ship Society 1992

U-boats vs Destroyer Escorts Gordon Williamson, Osprey 2007

A Seaman's Pocket Book, June 1943 Lords Commissioners of the Admiralty, Conway 2006

The Royal Navy Officer's Pocket-book, 1944 Brian Lavery, Conway 2007

History of World Sea Power Bernard Brett, Hamlyn 1985

Citizen Sailors: The Royal Navy in the Second World War Glyn Prysor, Penguin 2011

Engage the Enemy More Closely Correlli Barnett, Penguin 2000

Sky over Scapa 1939–45 Gregor Lamb, Bella Vista Publicaitons, Orkney

Web Sources

Destroyer Escort Sailors Association desausa.org

Lincstothepast

Captainclassdestroyers.com

u-boats.com

http://uboat.net/articles/84.html

http://www.secondworldwarni.org/details.aspx?id=2&pagerecordid=1472&themeid=2

INDEX